AN ENDLESS PANORAMA OF *Beauty*

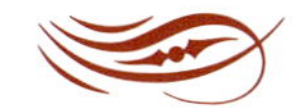

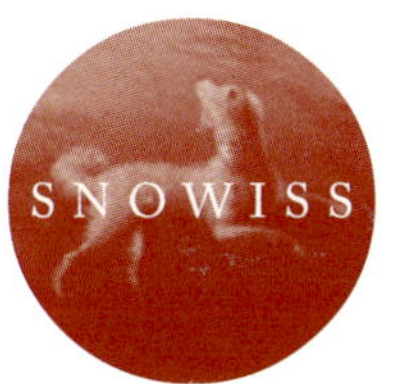

Selections from
the Jean and Alvin
Snowiss Collection
of American Art

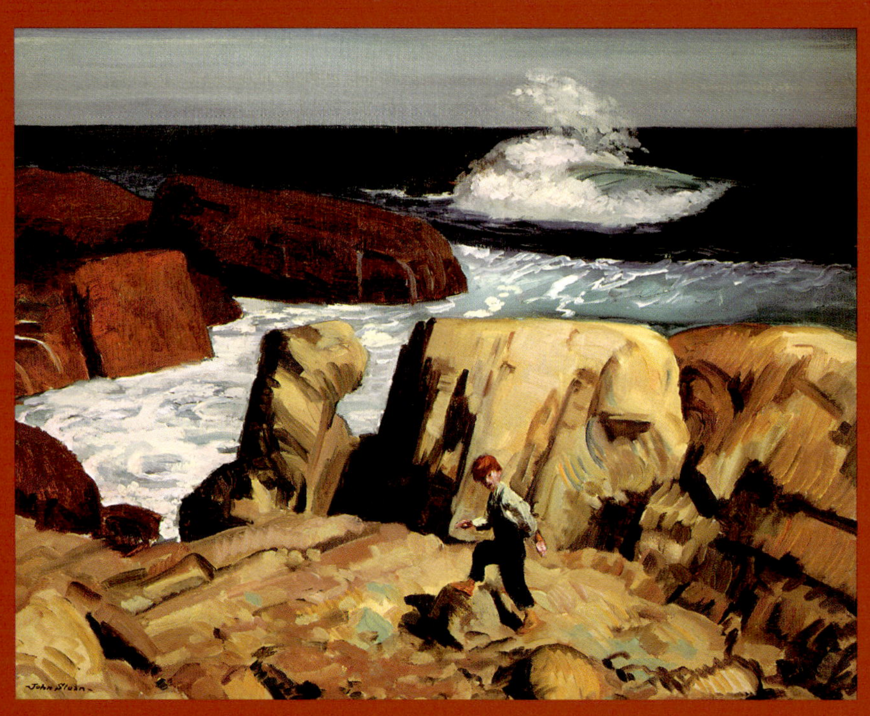

An Endless Panorama *of*

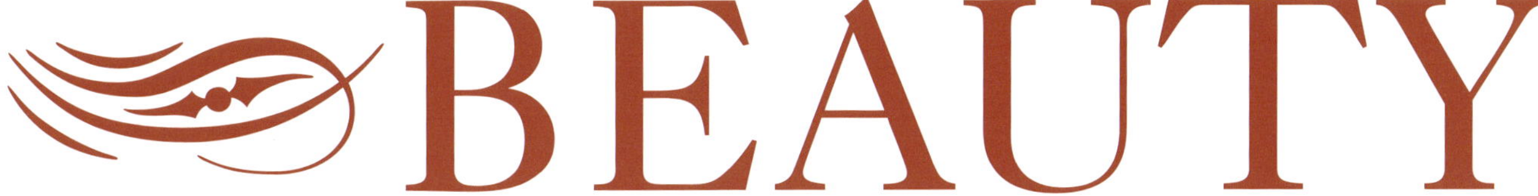

BEAUTY

Selections from the Jean and Alvin Snowiss Collection of American Art

Joyce Henri Robinson

With an essay by Leo G. Mazow and contributions by Julia Dolan

PALMER MUSEUM OF ART

The Pennsylvania State University, University Park, Pennsylvania

Distributed by The Pennsylvania State University Press

Title page:

JOHN SLOAN

Reddy on the Rocks,
1917, oil on canvas,
26 x 32 inches

Published in conjunction with the exhibition *An Endless Panorama of Beauty: Selections from the Jean and Alvin Snowiss Collection of American Art*, held at the Palmer Museum of Art, November 12, 2002 – May 16, 2003.

ISBN (Hardcover) 0-911209-55-7
(Paper) 0-911209-57-3

U.Ed. ARC 02-439
Library of Congress Control Number: 2002111940

Designed by the Penn State Department of University Publications.
Printed by Broudy Printing, Inc., Pittsburgh, PA

TABLE OF *Contents*

Director's Foreword

When Jean and Alvin Snowiss purchased their first painting—a landscape by the Philadelphia artist Robert Street—in 1976, they surely could not have envisioned the comprehensive scope that their collection would one day attain. We selected the Street for the cover of this catalogue in part because of its magnificent panoramic vista and its promise of a world of beauty and drama yet to be discovered. Perhaps, too, the diminutive couple in the foreground of the painting became visual surrogates for Jean and Alvin in our minds, gently reminding us of their acute attention to looking and their curiosity. With this exhibition, the Palmer celebrates not only the expansion of the museum's exhibition space and its concerted efforts to augment its collection of American art but also the longtime and ongoing support of the Snowisses. Needless to say, *An Endless Panorama of Beauty* would not have been possible without them, and we are delighted to have this opportunity to share works from their collection with a wide audience.

Joyce Robinson, curator, took on the monumental task of preparing the informative entries for more than fifty works of art. Her knowledge and appreciation of American art and the Snowiss collection, in particular, come through clearly. For her tireless energies we owe a tremendous debt. A large measure of appreciation also goes to Leo Mazow, curator of American art, who wrote the introductory essay that provides some context for the collection, in addition to writing several of the catalogue entries.

As Joyce Robinson indicates in her acknowledgments, this project also involved a number of talented students who helped with a myriad of details. A final word of appreciation goes to colleagues at University Publications. Larry Krezo has provided a distinctive design that complements the Snowiss collection, and Amy Crownover kept an attentive eye on production details.

We hope that this select survey of works by many important American artists will be enjoyed by students, scholars, and collectors alike.

JAN KEENE MUHLERT, *Director*

A Statement from the Collectors

Jean and I never contemplated that we would become collectors of American art in 1976 when we went to New York City for business purposes and to look for a painting to fit over the fireplace in the home we had recently purchased.

Because we were in the neighborhood, we stopped at Kennedy Galleries and there met Larry Fleischman, the director and, later, the owner. Recognizing that we were novices at purchasing art, he spent five hours over the next several days showing us American art of all kinds and explaining to us the different genres. Neither of us had any background in the visual arts in high school or college. We left the city with the purchase of an oil painting from the Hudson River School and a watercolor by Charles Burchfield, as well as many books on American painting and an intense fascination with art.

Over the years we began to educate ourselves by reading about art and seeing numerous exhibitions. In addition, a strong personal friendship developed between Barbara and Larry Fleischman and us, which led to vacations together and great learning experiences.

Before making a purchase, we would consider four criteria: 1) Of utmost importance, could we afford the painting? 2) Did we both agree that we liked and wanted it? 3) Could we agree that it would be appropriate at our home and not be put in a closet? and 4) Should we have to sell it in the future, would we not lose money? After each purchase, we experienced the thrill of hanging the picture in the right place and, as history buffs, studying in depth the artist and his contemporaries. Art history became a fascinating and time-consuming pursuit.

Our taste and our eye for art have changed over the years, which has given us a wide range of paintings from representational to nearly abstract and from Colonial portraiture to western scenes across the continent. The collection, with its broad array of many great American artists, is eclectic, which has made it more interesting for us.

Collecting American art substantially changed our lives and tastes and helped us appreciate so much more the scenes around us and our American heritage. We understand that we are mere caretakers of this art for a short period of time; however, in that time it has given us incomparable satisfaction and enjoyment.

JEAN AND ALVIN SNOWISS

PANORAMIC SENSIBILITIES

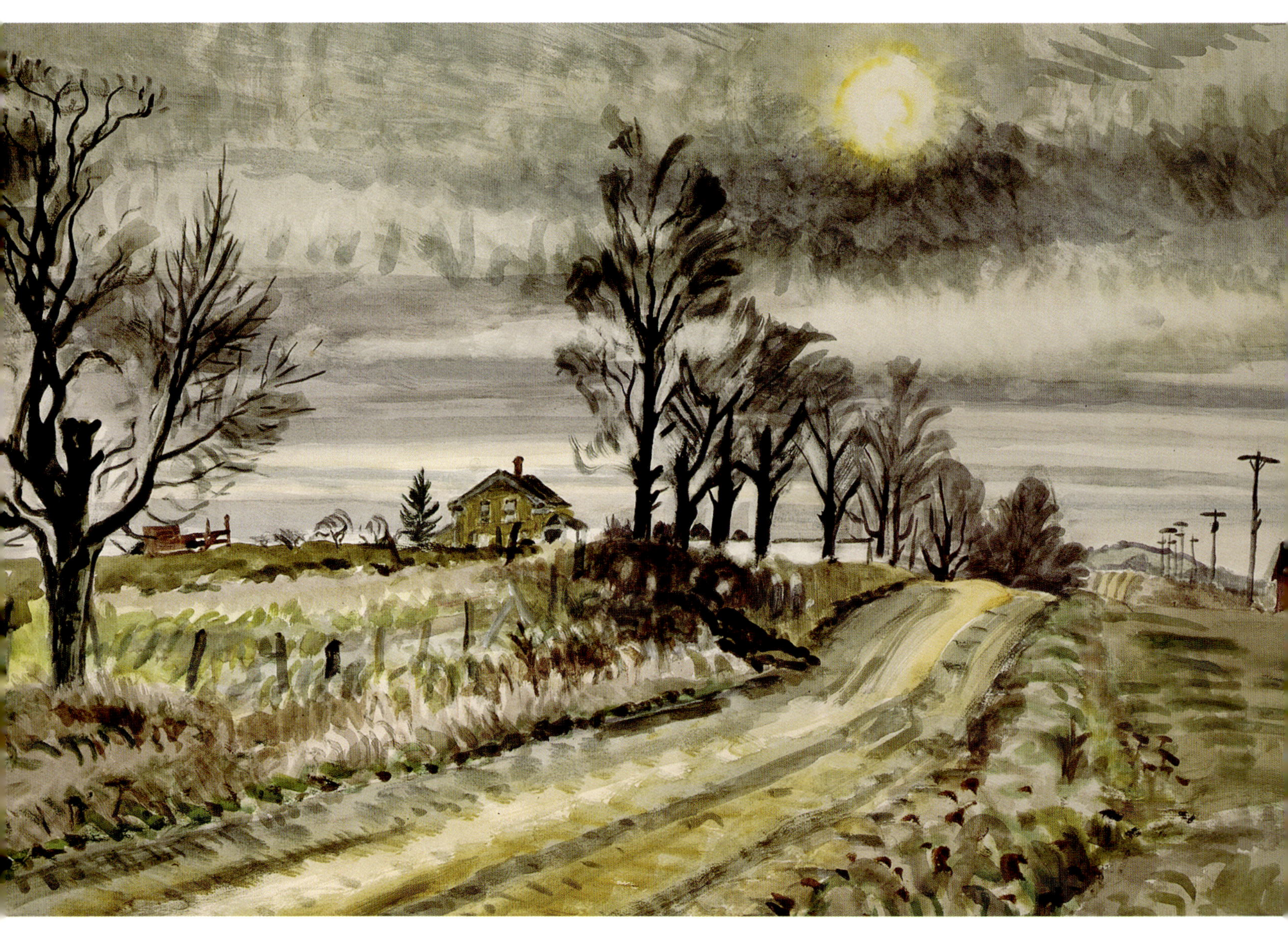

CHARLES
BURCHFIELD

Country Road in December,
1949, watercolor on
paper, 26 x 40 inches

Panoramic Sensibilities in Nineteenth- and Twentieth-Century American Painting

Leo G. Mazow,
Curator of American Art

INTRODUCTION: *Burchfield's Panorama*

This book takes its title from a diary entry by Charles Burchfield, who is represented here by two works, *A Flash of Lightning at Night*, 1916, and *Country Road in December*, 1949. Musing on nature's life cycles, the artist noted his excitement for both the "decay of vegetation in the winter" and the "resurgence of plant life in the spring." In 1952, when Burchfield wrote these lines, the critical fortunes of Abstract Expressionist painting were approaching a zenith, and he frequently recorded his disillusionment with the waning popularity of his version of modernism, a cosmically inspired American scene painting. In spite of the public's neglect, Burchfield noted, he still found in those natural transformations "an endless panorama of beauty and drama."[1] With the dark, curvilinear reverberations in *A Flash of Lightning at Night* and the softly illuminated, gently rolling landscape in *Country Road in December*, the artist certainly evokes the "beauty and drama" of the natural world.

Of particular interest, however, is his choice of the phrase "endless panorama." "Panorama" derives from Greek roots meaning "view all," and Burchfield's preceding adjective captures the word's suggestion of a seemingly infinite vista.[2] Beginning in the late eighteenth century, the painted panorama offered English, French, and German audiences elaborate views of rural and urban landscapes, often with intricately drawn battles and other historical incidents spanning the length of the surface. With imagery on long, curved panels and canvases whose very shape emphasized the bounty of vision, the horizon-exaggerating medium was usually viewed in a rotunda, where audiences would be barraged by 360 degrees of hyper-realistic imagery. Those partaking of this wildly popular form of entertainment reported the dazzling sensation of being immersed in an all-enveloping environment.[3] An understanding of the panorama and its appropriation on American shores can be particularly useful for interpreting Burchfield's paintings and many other works in the Snowiss collection.

AMERICANIZING THE PANORAMA

Panoramas first appeared in New York in 1804 and, shortly thereafter, would be found in Boston and Baltimore. In 1819, John Vanderlyn produced the elaborate *Panorama: Palace and Garden of Versailles*, which can still be seen in its entirety at the Metropolitan Museum of Art in New York. Vanderlyn's minutely detailed, enormous painting was widely toured, but neither it nor other American examples generated quite the excitement that the medium was eliciting among contemporary European audiences.[4] The panorama did enjoy a brief but significant period of popularity in America from 1846 through 1850, when John Banvard's *Panorama of the Mississippi River*—promoted as "The Largest Painting in the World"—helped galvanize support for western settlement.[5] In America, as in Europe, the panorama was often exploited for propagandistic purposes. Message and medium were distinctively intertwined. Indeed, the unbound, moving panorama matched nineteenth-century American metaphors of progress, freedom, growth, and optimism.[6]

Today, when we use the word *panorama*, we often have in mind not the medium of visual entertainment, but the sort of view it denoted and the sensation it produced. By the second decade of the nineteenth century, panorama carried secondary meanings of "continuous passing scene" and "an unbroken view of the whole surrounding region," and by the 1880s, *panoramic*, meaning "commanding a view of the whole landscape," entered the vernacular.[7] Architecture, landscape painting, and garden design were certainly influenced by the panorama, and by the Civil War the term itself had become a popular classification with which to understand each of these visual experiences. Even when the term was not used, the panoramic sensibility—the desire to encapsulate as much as possible in one's glance—was frequently invoked. This expansive mode of vision is found in the prose and poetry of some of America's most renowned writers, notably William Cullen Bryant, Ralph Waldo Emerson, and Walt Whitman.

These writers sought to put in verse the optical and imaginative potential of human vision, as well as the rewards for those who took the time to scan the bounty of nature. In his poem "Monument Mountain," for example, Bryant comments that "Thou who wouldst

Ascend our rocky mountains …
Shall feel a kindred with that loftier world
To which thou art translated, and partake
The enlargement of thy vision."[8]

Artists joined poets in grafting the panoramic vocabulary onto identifiably American subject matter. In *Descent from the Mountains*, 1833, Robert Street demonstrates the manner in which landscape painters also sought to "enlarge vision." With the tree at left holding in check the dramatically unfolding chasm, the painting pays homage to several conventions of European art and anticipates more than a half-century of Hudson River School painting. Works like *Descent from the Mountains* utilize meticulous modeling and deeply receding vistas to emphasize the grandeur of nature and the hope and historical promise of republicanism and popular Christianity.[9]

In contrast to the rough-hewn group of figures in the right foreground of the Street painting, who appear oblivious to the majestic vista, the man and woman at left are outfitted in sumptuous fabrics and elaborate headwear, suggesting that the enlightened appreciation of nature had become, by the 1830s, a genteel activity. Encouraged by ever-popular guidebooks and related tourist literature, individuals could attain a sort of "visual etiquette," armed with which they sought to appreciate such natural attractions as Niagara Falls, the White Mountains, and the Catskill and Allegheny ranges. Momentarily stopping under the tree, the male figure gestures into the distance, as if comprehending the entirety of the scene before him and instructing his female companion on the best way to appreciate the view.

Centuries prior to Street's work, certainly since the Baroque era, painters had enlisted foreground staffage figures to direct one's gaze upon a landscape. But Street's variation on the pictorial motif—placing a well-dressed, gesturing couple at lower left or right—was especially popular in early and mid-nineteenth-century America.[10] Appropriating British theories of the "picturesque," particularly as popularized by the artist and travel writer William Gilpin, American tourist literature provided strategies with which to behold the land for maximum visual stimulation.[11] Street's protagonists display a keen understanding of how to position one's view before a rolling landscape. Like actual tourists of the period, who were frequently instructed to climb to those precipices offering the most expansive view, the figures extend their gaze across the broad sweeping vista of mountains, plains, river, and foliage.

PAINTING AS PANORAMA

Art historian Alan Wallach has coined the phrase "panoptic sublime" to characterize the overwhelming sensation yielded by the sudden unfolding of such dramatic scenery. Wallach points out that excursionists went to great lengths to find precipices that, once ascended, would grant the viewer this dizzying elation.[12] The view in Street's painting is typical of the kind tourists sought for bemusement. With the rapid development of the genre of landscape painting in the nineteenth century, however, artists increasingly catered to the taste for such panoramic views, and audiences could entertain themselves visually and imagine exotic terrains without actually traveling to them. Although looking at art was not a surrogate for immersion in the landscape, American audiences could certainly experience panoramic sensations similar to those proscribed in the landscape literature and reported by tourists. Landscape paintings, that is, were a vehicle for "the enlargement of thy vision."

Samuel Colman's *River Bend*, 1863, and David Johnson's *Rogers Slide, Lake George, New York*, 1870, exemplify the broad, romantic views of nature toward which readers of tourist literature would have been predisposed. Often called "Big Slide" and "Great Slide," Rogers Slide—from which one can see all the way to Vermont—for example, is described in several guidebooks.[13] With its varying terrain of river, hills, plains, and foliage, *River Bend* addresses both picturesque and panoramic sensibilities. Providing both a compositional axis and an attention-grabbing lateral stripe, the horizon line is especially significant in the picture's creation of expansiveness. In *River Bend, Rogers Slide*, and other works in the Snowiss collection, translucent layers of light tones create an ethereal haze on the horizon, suggesting a spatial recession beyond what is actually seen on the canvas. These blurred lines function as vanishing points in the perspectival systems of many of these paintings, connoting hope and potential, as well as infinite progression to sites the beholder cannot at present see.[14]

Perhaps more than any other work in the Snowiss collection, Alfred Thompson Bricher's *Low Tide, Bradford's Cove, Grand Manan*, n.d., exploits the elongated horizon to emphasize an all-encompassing panoramic gaze. The watercolor's width is two-and-a-half times its height, thereby evoking lateral immensity in spite of its modest size. Located on the south part of Grand Manan Island, in the Bay of Fundy, New Brunswick, Bradford's Cove is periodically subject to dense fog, a phenomenon captured in this watercolor. About the time Bricher painted *Low Tide*, topographical engineers working for the U.S. Geological Survey commented on the deceptive nature and strange effects of blurred vision. One Survey member wrote the following lines about the Grand Canyon, but his remarks illuminate Bricher's view of Grand Manan: "[In] the ever-present haze ... a thousand forms, hitherto unseen or obscure, start up ... and stand forth in strength and animation."[15] *Low Tide* is one of many works from the period that demonstrate the manner in which cloaked vision, paradoxically, reveals nature.[16] What is significant here, however, is that the gauze-like middle- and background suggests an ever-expanding vista, as if the view itself is in the process of becoming, ebbing and flowing like the tide depicted.

The vogue for all-enveloping, expansive vision persisted well into the twentieth century. As paintings like Childe Hassam's *Ice on the Hudson*, 1908, demonstrate, however, the terms with which artists and audiences engaged the landscape changed dramatically in this period. As in several landscape paintings reproduced in this book, the uninterrupted horizon extends the width of the canvas, luring our gaze across its expanse. The thin stretch of sky is rendered majestic—if not ethereal—by the light painterly tones with which it is modeled. Like other well-known American landscape paintings from the decades around the turn of the century, *Ice on the Hudson* reduces the composition to a series of horizontal bands whose thin elongation exaggerates the width of the vista.

More than the above-mentioned painters, however, Hassam offsets the pastoral mood with the presence of industry and commerce, signaled by the factory and smokestacks just right of center on the far bank of the river. The rich broken brushwork, rendering the scene a tableau of converging tones, yields the sense of an easy give-and-take between these two regions—that is, between nature and civilization. Perhaps more than any other device, though, the panoramic format naturalizes the industrial interruption; Hassam's expansive mode allows viewers to move optically between these horizontal zones without much visual adjustment. In this logic, the factory becomes another abstract form, harmonizing with other irregular shapes (note the floating ice in the foreground) in an airy mosaic of atmosphere and color.

INVERTING THE PANORAMA

Several of the panoramic sensibilities discussed above are challenged, and ultimately collapsed, in Winslow Homer's watercolor, *Sea and Rocks During a Storm*, 1894. As we have seen, Street's *Descent from the Mountains* and Colman's *River Bend* presented vistas from elevated perspectives, where actual and implied viewers enjoyed the safety of dry land and seemingly firm footing. In Homer's painting, however, the viewer is brought precariously close to the frothy waters and craggy rocks in the rapidly shifting space of the foreground. In the two former works, as well as in Johnson's *Rogers Slide*, gently receding mountaintops act as orthogonals in the paintings' perspectival plans, inviting the viewer into the work and creating compositional stability in spite of the vast, dizzying depths portrayed. Homer, conversely, flattens the perspective and guides the diagonals not in the direction of a distant vanishing point but, rather, directly toward the viewer, eliminating the possibility of detached observation.

Yet Homer's painting may be considered as panoramic as any in the Snowiss collection. Many contemporaries visited the site depicted—Prout's Neck, Maine—precisely for the all-encompassing dramatic views it afforded.[17] In *Sea and Rocks*, a prolonged back-and-forth, lateral gaze is required to comprehend the work in its entirety. Further, much as the panorama sought to overwhelm and entertain audiences with 360 degrees of minutely detailed imagery, so Homer's work barrages its beholders, formally and thematically enveloping them within a total environment of rocks, ocean, and hazy mist. The close observation of nature, meticulously rendered with carefully applied washes, adds to the sense of a vast, overpowering force.

What is at stake here may well be the viewer's ability to behold and make sense of a site. Homer's vision robs us of the familiarity of place—the image might be said to depict not Prout's Neck but the unyielding elements of nature. The beholder has neither a clear view nor an assurance of a navigable route to the figures at top right, individuals whose miniature scale accentuates the incapacity of humans before nature's wrath. Late nineteenth-century audiences on both sides of the Atlantic were accustomed to depictions of waves breaking on shorelines by such artists as Bricher and Alexander Harrison.[18] These artists, however, followed the time-honored landscape conventions seen in paintings by Hudson River School artists. In their works, waters are placid and largely unthreatening, the lighting romantic and often ethereal. Perhaps most importantly, in striking contrast to Homer's watercolor, this romantic landscape tradition used several devices (foreground *repoussoir* figures and symmetrical, intelligible vistas) to facilitate the viewer's perspective. In Homer's *Sea and Rocks*, beholders approach the image more from the vantage point of an explorer than that of a picturesque traveler or leisurely tourist.

Nineteenth-century Americans made an equation between seeing and knowing, that is, between looking and possessing.[19] By the end of the century, the nation's expansionist ethos came to match neatly this logic, and art historians have coined such phrases as "imperial sublime" and "magisterial gaze" to characterize the ways in which visual containment facilitated a sense of territorial possession.[20] It is precisely this ability to see—one might say to have "visual power"—that is denied in Homer's work. The leisure to look, so celebrated by Street and romanticized by Bricher, is challenged in *Sea and Rocks*. The tables are now turned, with the painting disabling the beholder from visually taking hold of the landscape; rather, in this case, the forces of nature dominate the viewer. "We feel the awful, elemental force" of Homer's late seascapes, wrote the early twentieth-century art historian Samuel Isham. The artist's biographer, William Howe Downes, concurred: "it is natural to be carried away by the sheer strength and swiftness of the movements of these ocean symphonies."[21]

With its high horizon line, irregular rocky abutments, and deceptively calm foreground waters, *Reddy on the Rocks*, 1917, by John Sloan inverts the panoramic sensibility in a manner consistent with Homer's watercolor.[22] Instead of guiding our view across the Gloucester shore, the little boy looks back to us, introducing a psychological inwardness instead of the visual outwardness of earlier landscape painting. In several other paintings in the Snowiss collection —including Charles Demuth's *Roofs and Tree Forms*, 1919, Arthur Dove's *From Lake, Geneva*, 1938, and Stuart Davis' *Coast Town Landscape Study*, 1940—our gaze is similarly restricted. Modern architecture dominates at least half of the picture plane in each painting, with the "machine" blocking the view of the "garden," to quote the title of Leo Marx's classic study of the awkward intrusion of industry in the American pastoral.[23]

CONCLUSION: *The Value of the Vernacular*

Demuth, Dove, and Davis confine the viewer's gaze by way of compressed foreground architecture, yet their works nonetheless pay homage to the American panoramic tradition. A crucial difference between images by the latter trio and those by Hudson River School artists concerns what is encapsulated in the panoramic gaze. The complex manner in which American modernists experimented with and ultimately poeticized "enlarged vision" is also demonstrated in John Marin's painting *Sailboat and Sea, Maine*, 1938. Here, our eyes quickly move beyond the rhythmic triad of masts in the middle ground toward the immensity suggested by the horizon. Where the earlier generation created a pictorial inventory of flora and fauna, often romanticizing nature and rendering it nostalgic, twentieth-century modernists reckoned with the reality of the inhabited American landscape. Flour mills, fish markets, and anonymous façades have replaced valleys, streams, and sunsets. If there is a continuum from antebellum panoramic sensibilities to the occasionally expansive mode of modernism, it would suggest the manner in which both groups sought to locate value in the vernacular and culture in the commonplace.

Still, for all their horizontal elongation, many early American modernist pieces present views that are neither vast nor unobstructed. Modernists often intimate but do not represent "plenty;" the "more" and the "merrier" are frequently conceptual, not actual. Yet herein rests the hope of American modernism, as well as the promise of its forebears: that a world of experience lies just beneath the pictorial surface.[24] Through their paintings, the artists in the Snowiss collection suggest that in this sometimes real, sometimes imaginary place resides an "endless panorama of beauty and drama," a place to see *more*.

That insatiable appetite for *more* is as old as the republic itself. As early as 1787, Thomas Jefferson noted the "immensity of land courting the industry of the husbandman," his words only an early version of what would soon be repeated refrains equating "more" with "merrier," and "peace" with "plenty."[25] By the mid-nineteenth century, of course, industrialists and, eventually, advertisers would effectively "cash in" on the romantic longing for either a mythic nostalgia or a future utopia, where elbow-room is aplenty and vision is vast and unobstructed.[26]

That several *non*-landscape works reproduced in this book also hint at panoramic sensibilities is a testament to the unyielding longing for *more* in American culture. Consider, for example, John F. Francis's *Still Life: Peaches and Grapes*, 1860, a painting rife with allusions to such themes as *abundantia*, cornucopia, and the horn of plenty. It is not land—as in the original moving panorama—but fruit—grapes and peaches—that engulf us in this variation on voracious vision. Simultaneously appealing to our senses of touch, taste, and sight, the fruit seems to overflow from the basket, plate, and stone surface, as if on the verge of bursting forth from its fictive two-dimensional space. In the background, at upper right, a landscape is allotted only a part of the pictorial space, its abundance replaced by the all-enveloping still life in the foreground.

It is a tribute to the richness and variety of the Snowiss collection that we are able to trace a narrowly circumscribed theme in American art and culture from the early republic into the twentieth century through a representative selection of artworks. As the images in the present volume amply demonstrate, the Snowiss collection indeed supports the exploration of several other topics in American painting, from the industrial revolution to popular entertainment to the lure of foreign lands. Ultimately, the panorama and its essential meaning, "view all," symbolize a heartfelt mission to see, know, and experience one's time and place. This drive permeates the art represented here and has played a crucial role in the development of the Snowiss collection.

Endnotes begin on page 120.

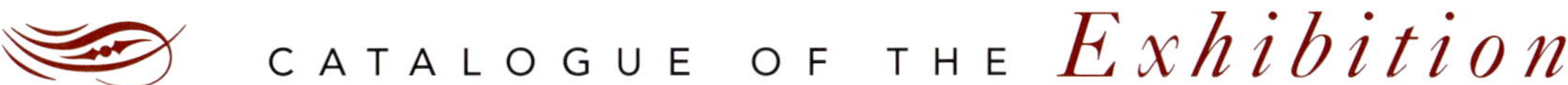

CATALOGUE OF THE *Exhibition*

Entries written by

Joyce Henri Robinson (JHR),

Leo G. Mazow (LGM),

and Julia Dolan (JD)

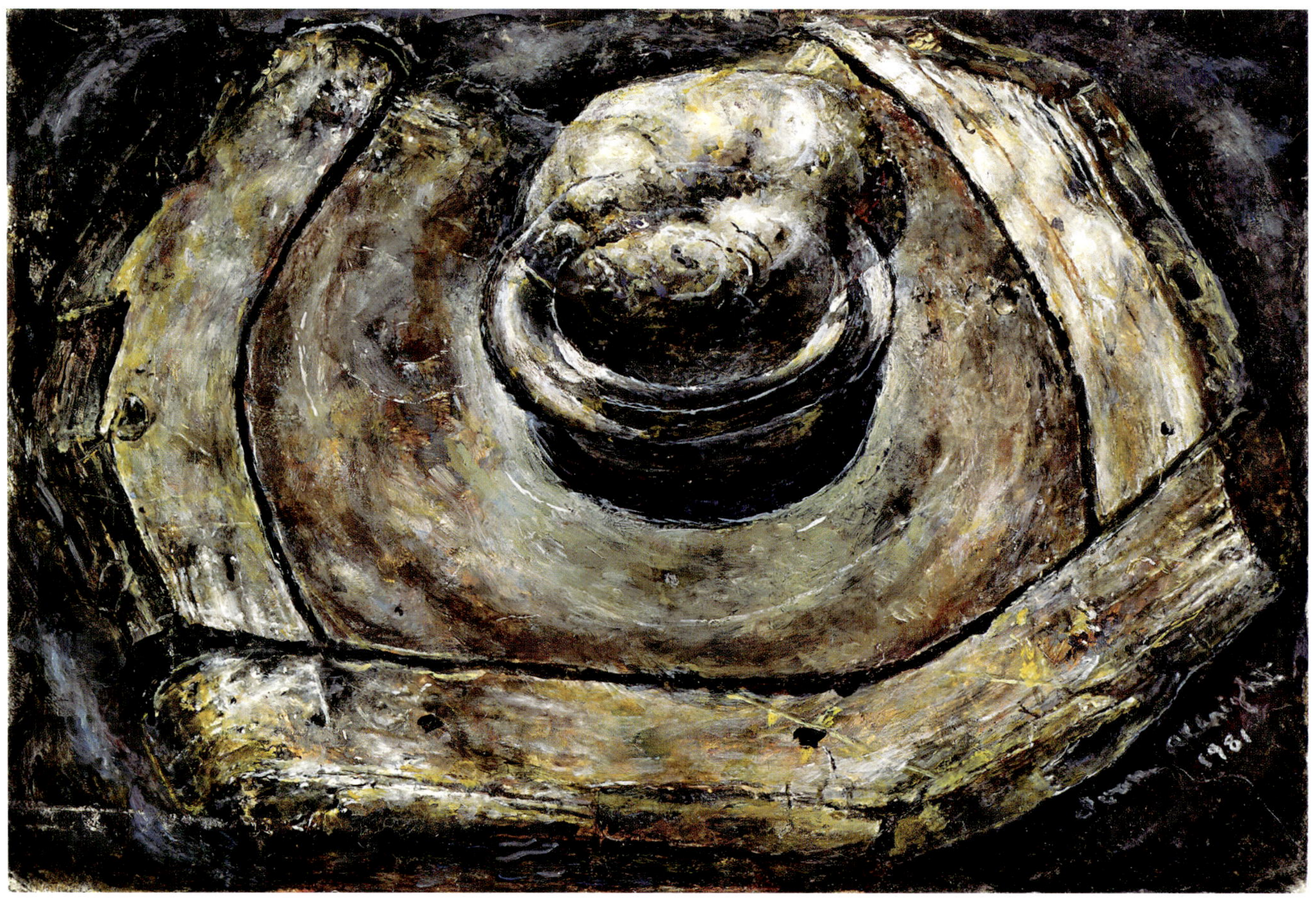

Still Life with Potato (The Lonely Potato), 1981, oil on panel, 6 1/2 x 9 1/2 inches

Ivan Albright (1897–1983)

Ivan Le Lorraine Albright, son of genre painter Adam Albright (1862–1957) and twin brother of artist Malvin Albright (1897–1983), was raised in a household that actively encouraged artistic pursuits. Although he originally eschewed his father's profession to study engineering and architecture, Albright launched his own artistic career just prior to entering the U.S. Army in 1918. Serving as an artist for the American Expeditionary Forces Medical Corps, he was required to illustrate medical sketchbooks during World War I.[1] Albright adamantly refuted suggestions throughout his life that the ominous undertones, physical decay, and emotional degeneration evident in his mature works were a direct result of his experiences during the war. Although it was his belief that natural change induced by time could be expressed through the flesh of the human being, he disagreed with the prevalent critique that his imagery was horrific.[2]

Albright's post-military education included instruction at the School of the Art Institute of Chicago, the Pennsylvania Academy of the Fine Arts, and the Art Students League of New York. The once-reluctant artist initially fashioned a career out of simple, moody portraits, but his style rapidly matured and Albright became known for his intricately detailed, psychologically poignant paintings. Although some contemporary audiences found his creations disturbing, critical success quickly earned him numerous awards.[3]

Albright remained an active artist even after his eyesight became severely compromised by cataracts during the last decade of his life. His vision was restored by surgery in 1977, and he entered into a phase of intense creativity, refocusing his efforts on self-portraiture and still life.[4] Completed just two years before his death, *Still Life with Potato (The Lonely Potato)* is an example of Albright's unique artistic vision and exemplifies the comparatively loose brushstroke that the artist favored at the end of his career. The potato sits precariously on a turntable, an electrically driven studio prop of Albright's own devising, which can be seen in its entirety through the transparent vegetable.[5] Like Albright's unnerving portraits, many of which explore the dark psychological state of his sitters, this "portrait" of a mottled potato features a solitary vegetable ready to collapse into itself, just as many of his human subjects appear to cave inward, surrendering to the pressures of the outside world.

JD

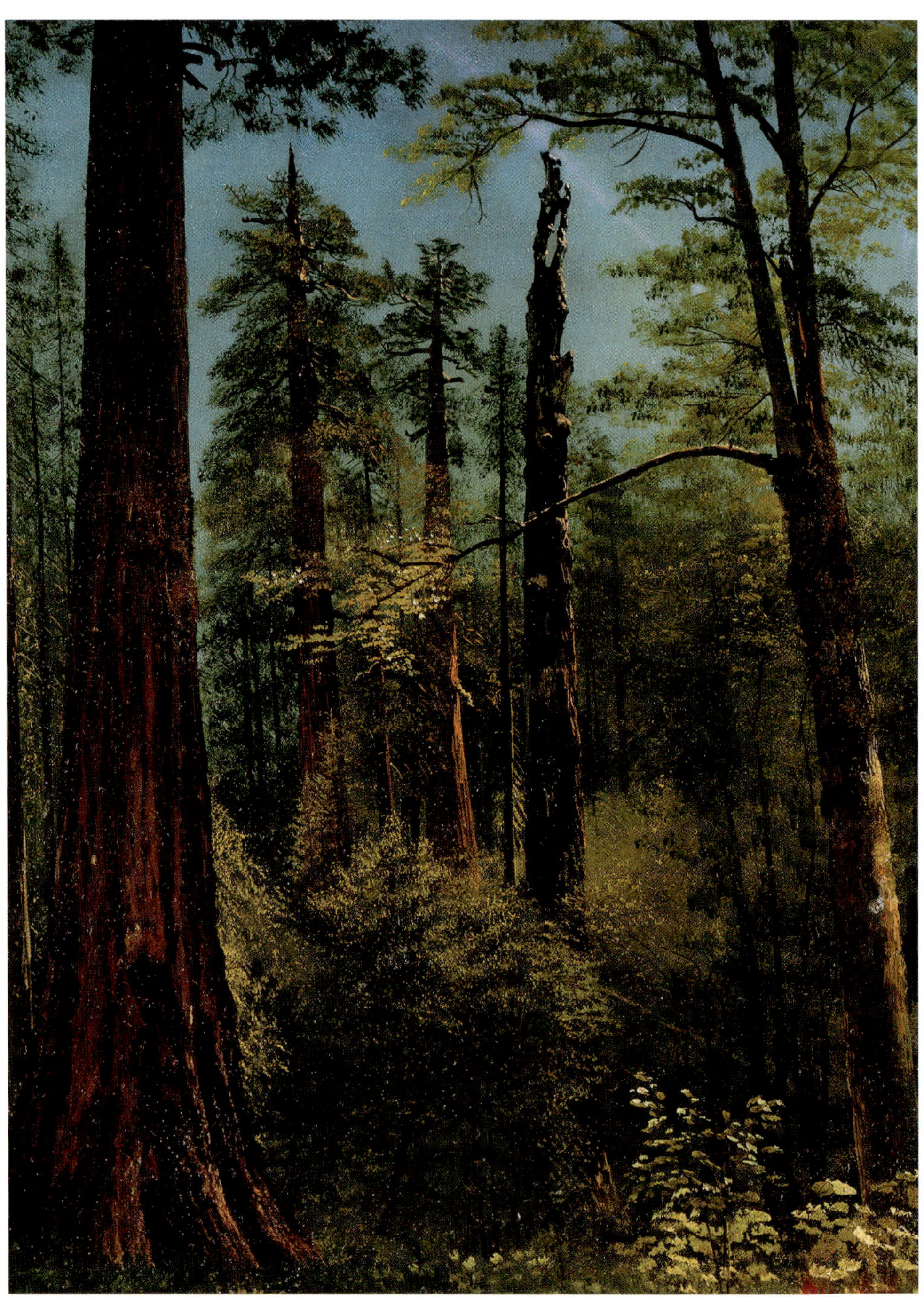

Redwoods, California,
c. 1872–1873, oil on paper,
18 1/2 x 13 1/2 inches

Albert Bierstadt (1830–1902)

Albert Bierstadt, a self-trained artist who established his own studio in New Bedford, Massachusetts, by the age of 20, was confident enough in his skills to offer monochromatic painting lessons to area residents in 1850.[1] A three-year stay in Düsseldorf, Germany, beginning in 1853 exposed him to the tradition of German landscape painting, which favored a detailed visual description of the natural world. Bierstadt also received informal critiques and mentoring from Worthington Whittredge (1820–1910) and Emanuel Leutze (1816–1868), two of the many American artists who studied in Germany during the nineteenth century.[2] Soon after his return to Massachusetts, Bierstadt fashioned paintings in exacting detail from the many landscape studies he had completed in Europe and exhibited his first canvas at the National Academy of Design in 1858.[3] The following year, Bierstadt embarked on what would prove to be the first of no fewer than eleven trips to the American West.[4] Tapping into the country's voracious curiosity for the largely unexplored terrain west of the Mississippi, he fashioned a wildly successful but fleeting career out of these excursions and the resultant landscape paintings.[5]

At the height of his career, Bierstadt commanded as much as $25,000 for a single canvas. The display of a major work was often treated as an event unto itself, with the painting swathed in theatrical drapery and an admission charge levied to gain entrance to the showplace.[6] Many of his canvases were enormous—as much as ten feet in length—causing the *New York Tribune* to muse, "'Tis mere village gossip, not worth repeating, that he has built his studio at the point where the Hudson River is the widest in order that he may have room to turn his canvases."[7] Critical to the success of such monumental works, however, were the comparatively diminutive plein air sketches that Bierstadt used as reference material when working in his New York studio.

Redwoods, California, which might more aptly be titled *Sequoias, California*, may have been completed during the artist's first trip to the Yosemite area in 1863, but the study more likely was produced ten years later during an extended stay in the same region. Writer Fitz Hugh Ludlow (1836–1870), Bierstadt's traveling companion during his first journey to Yosemite, described the elusive grandeur of the region's massive trees: "Of course our artists neither made nor expected to make anything like a realizing picture of the groves. The marvelous size does not go into gilt frames. You paint a Big Tree, and it only looks like a common tree in a cramped coffin .... What our artists did was to get a capital transcript of the Big Trees' color—a beautifully bright cinnamon-brown, which gives particular gayety to the forest, 'making sunshine in the shady place.' "[8]

Bierstadt indeed managed to capture the vibrant color of the sequoia trunks in this sketch of Yosemite's famed trees. Although, as Ludlow makes clear, the true scale of the sequoias is impossible to capture within the bounded confines of an easel painting, Bierstadt skillfully hints at their great size by contextualizing the "Big Trees" within their surrounding environment. While the sketch was meant to assist Bierstadt in his composition of larger works, the artist did not forego the painstaking detail found in his largest canvases, creating a small but thorough record of his visual experience of the majestic landscape of the American West.

JD

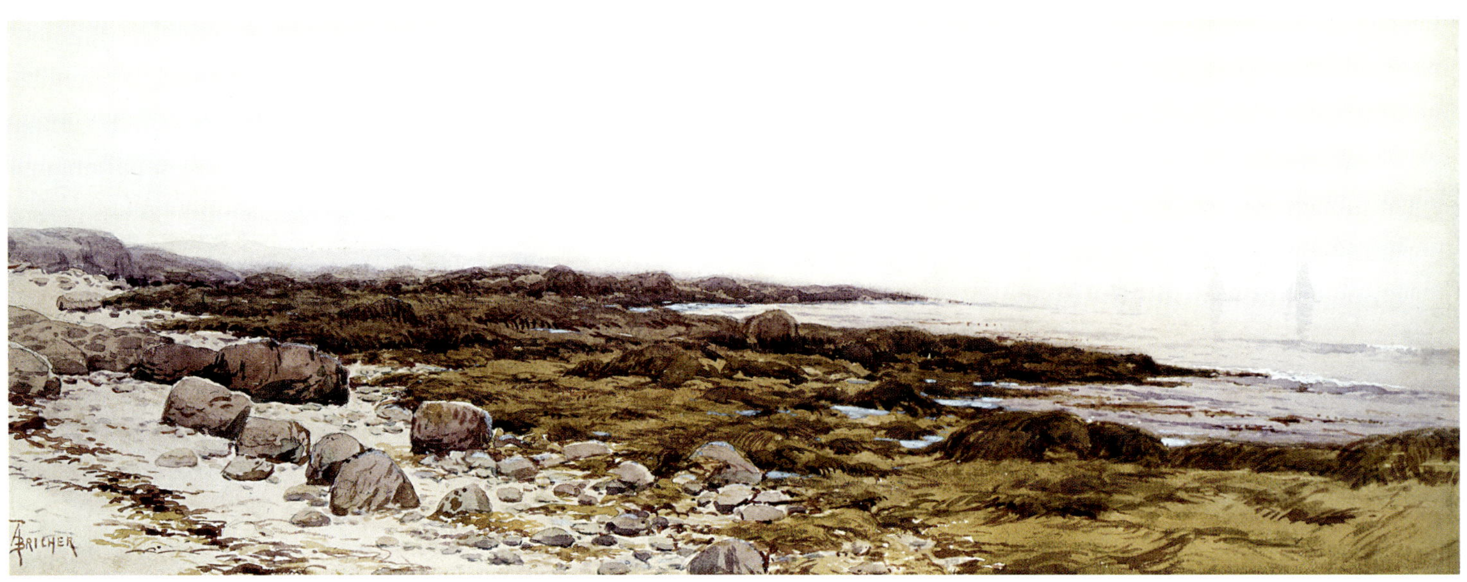

Low Tide, Bradford's Cove, Grand Manan, n.d., watercolor on paper, 10 1/2 x 26 1/2 inches

Alfred Thompson Bricher (1837–1908)

The artistic development of landscape and marine painter Alfred Thompson Bricher, recognized today for his serene paintings in both watercolor and oil, remains obscure. Little is known about his childhood, which was spent primarily in Newburyport, Massachusetts. After living in Boston and working as a clerk in a dry goods store, Bricher returned to Newburyport in 1858 and established a studio. Although his artistic instruction and contacts during this period are unclear, it is known that Bricher was acquainted with Martin Johnson Heade (1819–1904), and may also have encountered Hudson River School artist Frederic Edwin Church (1826–1900) and maritime painter Fitz Hugh Lane (1804–1865) during the early 1860s.[1]

Bricher returned to Boston in 1859 and was exhibiting his paintings at the Boston Atheneum by 1864. In addition to his successful showings in fine art institutions, Bricher's work was popularized throughout the United States by prints based on his compositions, which were disseminated by Louis Prang and Company, the popular chromolithography firm.[2] After relocating to New York City in 1868, Bricher added his name to the rosters of such professional art societies as the Art Union, the American Society of Painters in Water Colors, and the National Academy of Design, where he was elected an associate member in 1879.[3] His studio activity in New York was limited primarily to the winter season, as he gathered source material for his landscape paintings during warmer months.

Bricher's style, although mysterious in its development, was clearly influenced by the luminist aesthetic, a late manifestation of the Hudson River School of painting. Bricher sought to capture the unique grandeur of the American land and seascape while simultaneously paying close attention to the ethereal qualities of light and the subtleties of atmosphere. He frequented regions favored by Hudson River and luminist artists, including the White Mountains of New Hampshire and the Catskills in New York. Beginning in 1874, Bricher journeyed farther north to New Brunswick and the island of Grand Manan. *Low Tide, Bradford's Cove, Grand Manan* is a thoughtful consideration of just one of the many inlets found on the island. While foreground components, newly exposed by receding waters, are rendered with precise detail, background objects such as sailboats and seagulls are engulfed in haze and quietly disappear into the diffuse light of the sky. Bricher's attention to the atmospheric qualities at Bradford's Cove indicates beyond a doubt his allegiance to the tenets of the luminist aesthetic, and confirms the contemporary observation that the artist's brush was infused with "poetical power."[4]

JD

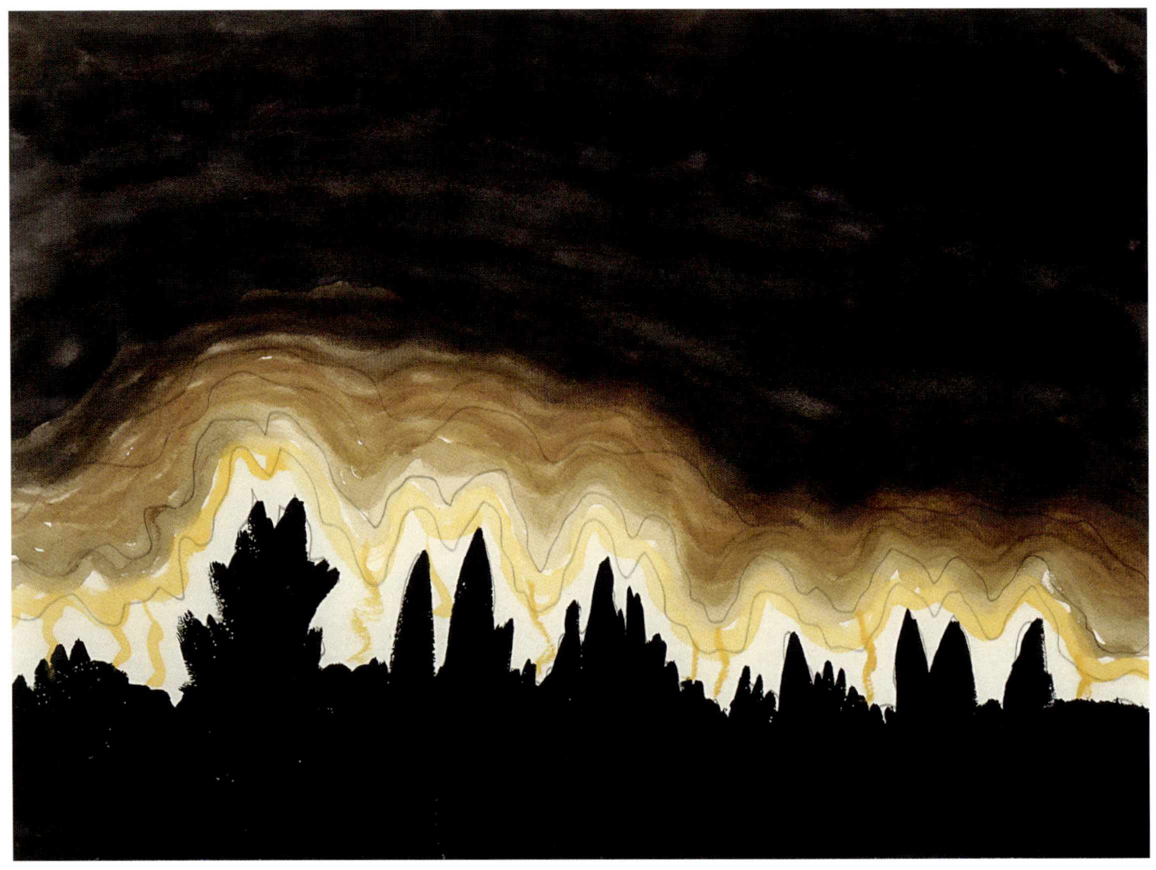

A Flash of Lightning at Night, 1916, watercolor on paper, 9 x 12 inches

Charles Burchfield (1893–1967)

As art historian John Baur was fond of noting, Charles Burchfield was "perhaps the last great figure in America's long pantheistic tradition."[1] Like his contemporary John Marin (1870–1953), Burchfield demonstrated an abiding love for nature and a strong spiritual tie to its varied manifestations throughout his life. Unlike Marin, however, who continued to maintain close contact with modernist ideas in New York virtually his entire career, Burchfield for the most part pursued his art in two relatively isolated locations—Salem, Ohio, and Gardenville, New York—quiet towns seemingly worlds away from the machinations and posturing of the New York City art scene.

A Flash of Lightning at Night was painted in 1916, the year Burchfield graduated from the Cleveland School of Art (now the Cleveland Institute of Art), where he had been a student since 1912.[2] Born in Ashtabula, Ohio, and raised in the small town of Salem, Burchfield returned to his hometown the summer after graduation and found work at a manufacturing plant. In the spring of 1915, the artist had begun producing his "all-day sketches," a result of his desire "to show in continuity the transitions of weather and of the seasons; such as the development of a thunderstorm from a calm clear day." In a journal entry from late December of that year, Burchfield included "lightning" in a list of meteorological desiderata for further exploration and commentary, along with wind, rain, storm, snow, and ice. He apparently had the opportunity to witness "flashes of lightning" on a September evening in 1916 and recorded his nearly mystical response in his journal: "Stepping out doors tonight to see the moon, flashes of lightning from the north drove the moon from my head. I saw great piles of cold moonlit thunderheads, lit up with rapid flashes from their depths, now being black, now cold white. I went to the fields & in the big wind, & ragged rush of clouds & the startled moon, & the clatter of huge raindrops, I felt I was in the dissolving of nature."[3]

Many of Burchfield's watercolors from the mid-teens reveal a similar interest in the decorative play of flattened, broad shapes against the surface of the paper. As a young artist, Burchfield often first sketched a design in pencil adding washes of color after, although he appears to have abandoned this practice by the end of the summer of 1916. Scholars have long contended that Burchfield was unaware of European modernism at this time and arrived at these vividly colored and boldly designed works virtually on his own in the barren confines of northern Ohio. William Robinson has recently demonstrated, however, that the artist was well aware of advanced stylistic practices through forward-thinking mentors at the Cleveland School of Art and through the participation of progressive artists, including William Zorach (1887–1966), in the city's art scene.[4]

Like many other advanced artists at the time, Burchfield was interested in giving visual form to sounds and music, and the wavelike undulations of color across the nighttime sky suggest a kind of shriek of the heavens in the midst of one of nature's most spectacular displays. The abstracted waves of color in *A Flash of Lightning at Night* may also relate to a series of sketches, "Conventions for Abstract Thoughts," completed by Burchfield in 1917, a group of some twenty abstract pictograms representing a range of moods from fear and "dangerous brooding" to insanity and "fascination of evil." The symbol for melancholy and meditation features a similar undulating design set against a darkened background and includes the annotation "Memory of pleasant things are gone forever."[5] While the connection to this project is far from certain, *A Flash of Lightning at Night* nonetheless reveals Burchfield's belief in the inherent expressivity of the formal elements of line and color, a concept at the very heart of modernism.

JHR

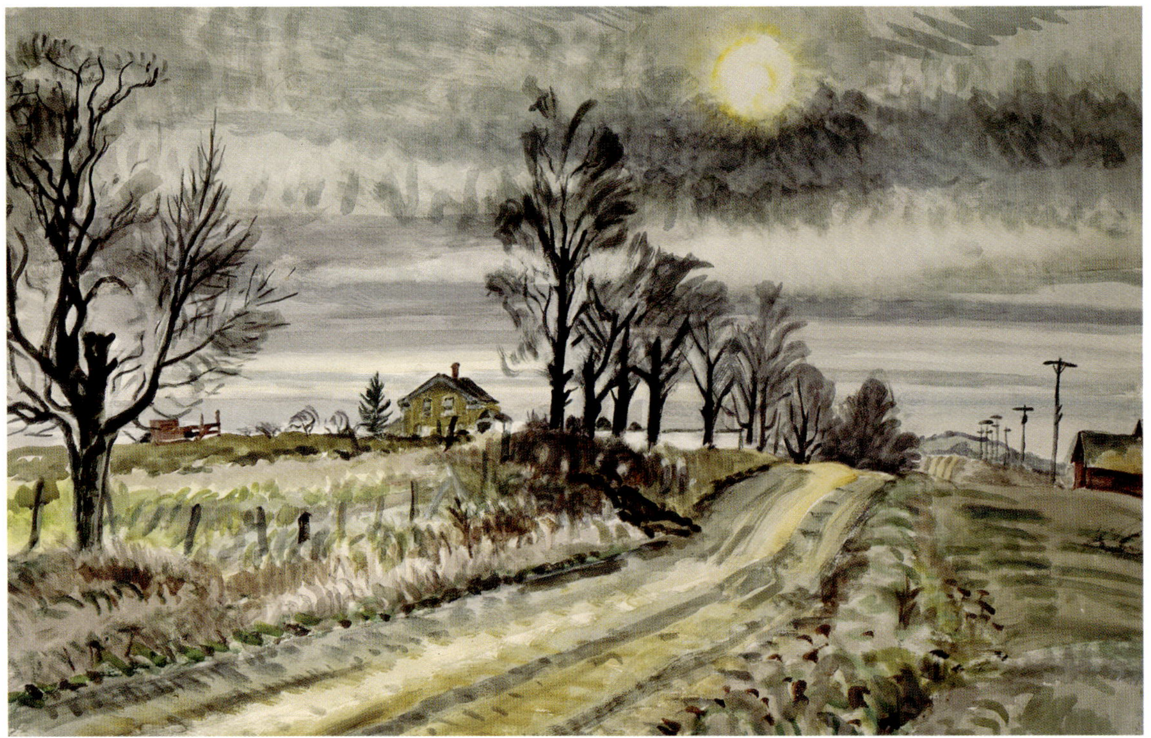

Country Road in December,
1949, watercolor on paper, 26 x 40 inches

Charles Burchfield (1893–1967)

The career of Charles Burchfield is typically divided into three stylistic periods: the early watercolors produced in Salem, Ohio, from the mid-teens until 1921; the "regionalist" depictions of the mid-western industrial scene and local landscape produced mostly in Gardenville, New York, on the outskirts of Buffalo until the early 1940s; and the late visionary pictures revealing at times ecstatic "images of God's presence in nature."[1] The prosaic realism of *Country Road in December* counters the strict delineation of the artist's mature career into mutually exclusive categories and suggests rather the consistent shifts throughout his oeuvre between naturalism and expressionism, "the twin poles of his artistic vision of nature."[2] "I must have the freedom to move up and down the scale," Burchfield commented late in his life, "uncommitted to one way of painting."[3]

Like other works of the "middle years," *Country Road in December* is quite large with an ampleness of form not typically found in the fluid washes of a more traditional watercolor technique. John Baur has characterized Burchfield's practice as "basically a system of heavy, overlapping strokes that created effects of great breadth and solidity" more often associated with oil painting than with watercolor. The inviting diagonal movement of the road into the distance lends great depth to the composition, furthering the image's "largeness of structure and design."[4]

Burchfield was keenly sensitive to nature's most transient aspects, from the change of seasons to the variations of weather throughout the day, and didn't seem to mind the inconvenience of painting outdoors in inclement or cold weather. "I love the approach of winter, the retreat of winter, the change from snow to rain and vice-versa; the decay of vegetation and the resurgence of plant life in the spring. These to me are exciting and beautiful, an endless panorama of beauty and drama …. "[5] While *Country Road in December* might not be construed as particularly dramatic, the breaking of the sun's resplendent yellow rays through the darkened cloud cover of a chilly December day suggests nature's inexorable ability to renew itself. Perhaps Burchfield was right when he declared himself a "romantic-realist," acknowledging that what he sought to portray ultimately was "the romantic side of the real world."[6]

JHR

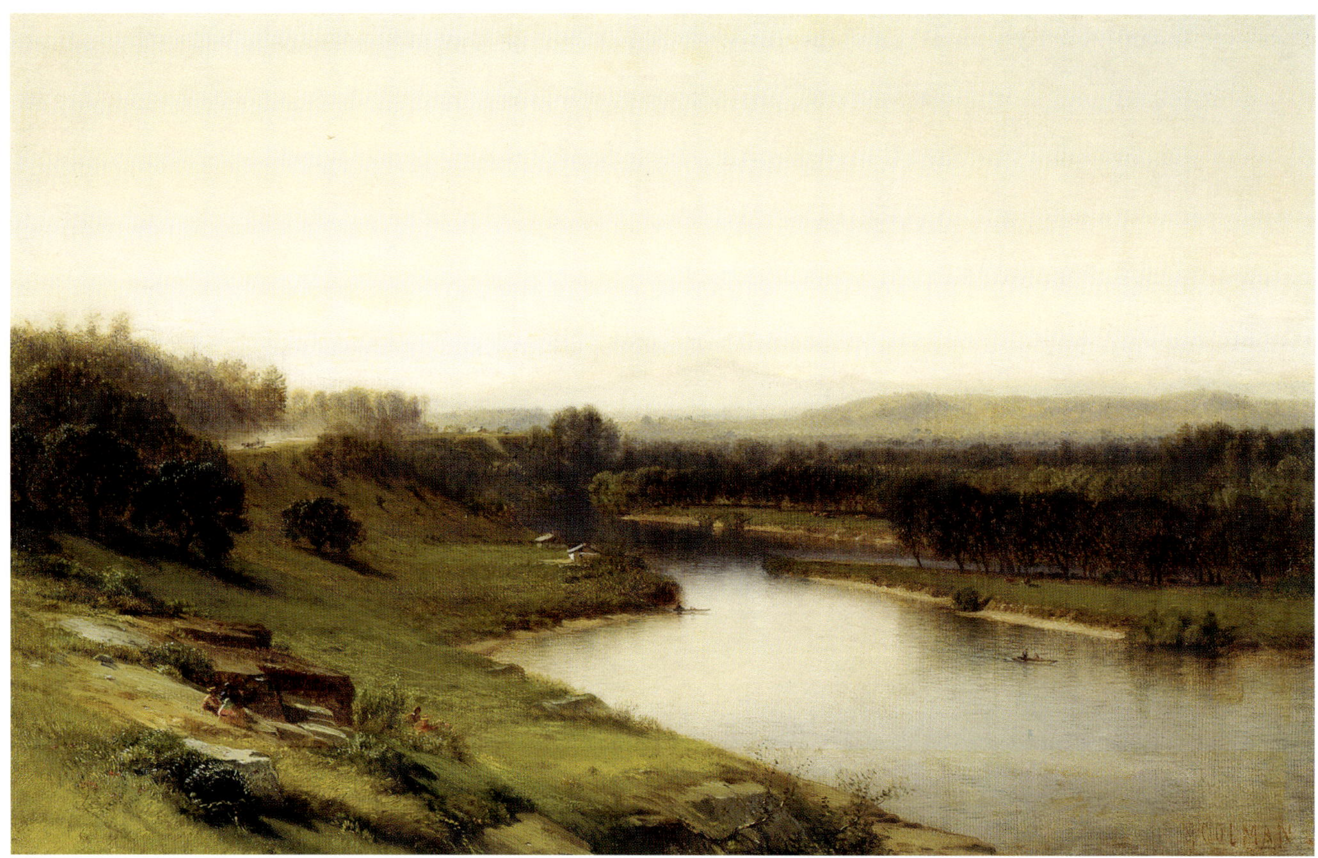

River Bend,
1863, oil on canvas,
13 7/8 x 21 1/2 inches

Samuel Colman (1832–1920)

As scholar Wayne Craven has noted, Samuel Colman was "one of the most colorful, versatile, prolific, admired and successful of American artists" in the latter half of the nineteenth century.[1] Born in Portland, Maine, but raised in New York City, Colman was the son of a much-admired bookseller and publisher whose shop on Broadway was a "unique depository of pictures, and a favorite resort of artists and littérateurs."[2] Nurtured in this artistic environment, Colman made a precocious debut at the National Academy of Design in 1851 while still in his teens. Most biographical accounts suggest that the young Colman studied with the noted Hudson River School artist Asher B. Durand (1796–1886). Although this tutelage with the famed landscape painter remains unconfirmed, Colman's early work indeed reveals a familiarity with the geographical sites, compositional formats, and detailed technique of the influential landscape school.

Like most ambitious American painters, Colman traveled to Europe in 1860, desiring no doubt to expand the thematic scope of his work. Visits to Paris, Rome, Seville, and, notably, to Morocco broadened the artist's artistic horizons, infusing a romantic strain into an oeuvre previously tied to rather parochial imagery. Upon his return to the United States in 1862, Colman was elected full academician and became actively engaged in the New York art world, producing ambitious oils thematically related to his European sojourn, as well as smaller works drawn from continued travels through the Hudson Valley.

River Bend was painted in the years just after the artist's return from his first trip abroad, its modest scale and looser technique suggesting an awareness of the French Barbizon school of painting. Scholars have also identified the influence of George Inness (1825–1894) in the delicate touch, increased sense of atmosphere, and pastoral sensibility revealed in Colman's work of the period.[3] Although the present title offers no indication of the exact locale of the setting, *River Bend* may be one of several works inspired by Colman's travels through the Genesee Valley in western New York. The artist's diploma painting for the Academy, *Landscape—Genesee Valley*, c. 1862, features a similar narrow river, as well as a bucolic landscape framed by gently rolling hills in the distance.[4] Both works confirm the sentiment of Henry Tuckerman, an early historian of American art, writing in the early 1860s: "The delicacy of this artist contrasts strongly and perhaps unprosperously with the more material attractions of our popular landscape-painters; but to the eye of refined taste, to the quiet lover of nature, there is a peculiar charm in Colman's style which, sooner or later, will be widely appreciated."[5]

JHR

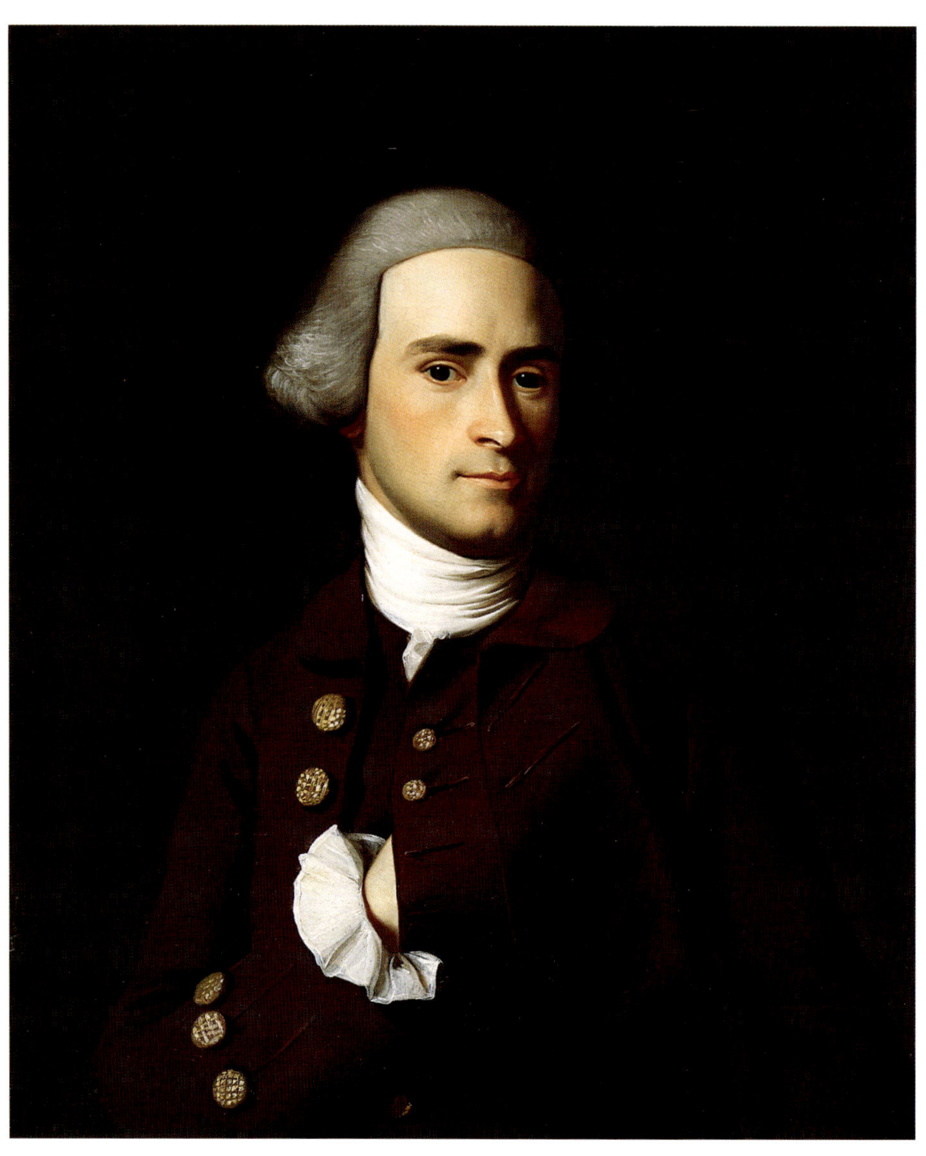

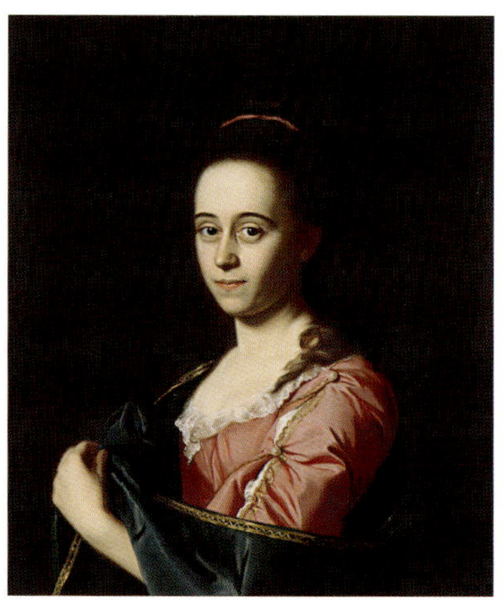

Joshua Henshaw II,
c. 1770–1774, oil on canvas,
30 1/4 x 25 1/2 inches

Portrait of Mrs. Joshua Henshaw II (Catherine Hill),
c. 1772, oil on canvas,
30 5/16 x 22 1/16 inches

Museo Thyssen-Bornemisza, Madrid.

John Singleton Copley (c. 1738–1815)

In the eighteenth and nineteenth centuries, painters and sculptors generally adhered to a hierarchy of genres, a system ranking subject matter according to its worthiness and appropriateness for pictorial representation. Academic institutions and artistic treatises placed the depiction of historical scenes at the top of the classification scheme because biblical, mythological, and nationalistic themes provided religious values, moral lessons, and educational precepts. Because it potentially offered exemplars of virtue, portraiture followed history painting in the hierarchy.

Longing to improve his art, the Boston portraitist John Singleton Copley sought the advice of two leading history painters, Sir Joshua Reynolds (1723–1792) and the American expatriate Benjamin West (1738–1820), both residing in London. Copley sent them his painting *Boy with a Squirrel (Henry Pelham)* (1765, Museum of Fine Arts, Boston) as a sort of test piece and for exhibition in spring 1766 at the Society of Artists in London. The two men passed judgment on the work's hard linearity, but joined other observers in finding ample reason to praise and encourage the artist.

Painted at least five years after *Boy with a Squirrel*, the portrait of the prosperous merchant Joshua Henshaw II (1746–1823) uses similar devices—light reflecting on the forehead, the placement of the subject in the near foreground—to endow the sitter with psychological bearing. Both works demonstrate Copley's endeavor to uplift the artistic profession on a par with that which it was accorded in Europe. The Henshaw family—several of whom sat for Copley—was only one of several hundred to give business to the painter, who, by the 1760s, had established himself as the preeminent painter in British North America. Longing to follow in West's and Reynolds' footsteps as a history painter, and growing ever disgusted with the seeming utilitarian taste for portraits, Copley commented in 1767, "was it not for preserving the resemble[n]ce of perticular [sic] persons, painting would not be known in the plac[e]."[1]

Joshua Henshaw II contains several clues to the lingering persistence of British sensibilities. In the years preceding the Revolution, colonists spent a large amount of their disposable income on British fabric, which signified prestige and success, and which, as the present portrait demonstrates, was attractive for its luxuriant sumptuousness.[2] Like several other portraits by Copley from the period, *Joshua Henshaw II* portrays the figure with his hand in his waistcoat, a gesture that would have been recognized as an archetypal English emblem of "manly boldness tempered with modesty."[3] Even the color scheme—the deep, dark red of the coat in particular—evinces painterly conventions codified in the British artistic circles to which Copley aspired. In his enormously popular *Discourses*, Reynolds had advised "that the masses of light in a picture be always of a warm mellow colour."[4]

In both *Joshua Henshaw II* and its pendant, *Portrait of Mrs. Joshua Henshaw II (Catherine Hill)* (c. 1772), Copley captures his sitters' countenances with the rich coloring and modeling of form Reynolds described. The closely observed subjects also suggest the artist's awareness of the figures' underlying emotions and almost brooding demeanors. Copley suggests their psychological intensity through their piercing gaze, the slight pivoting of the head from the torso, and their placement against the dark background, into which they appear to dissolve. Due to the dramatic contrast of light and shadow, the faces themselves contribute strongly to the sense of underlying temperament and cerebral activity.

On June 10, 1774, shortly after painting *Joshua Henshaw II*, Copley sailed for England, where, after additional travel in Italy and France, he was quickly elected into the Royal Academy. Working alongside Reynolds and West, Copley embarked on a fruitful second half of his career, in which he created several epic history paintings. In its psychological directness, hand-in-waistcoat symbolism, and academic references, the Henshaw portrait foreshadows his British work that followed. Indeed, although limited to the genre of portraiture on American shores, Copley invests Henshaw with the dramatic intrigue—one might say *monumentality*—expected of a history painting. Copley, that is, transcended the hierarchy of genres.

LGM

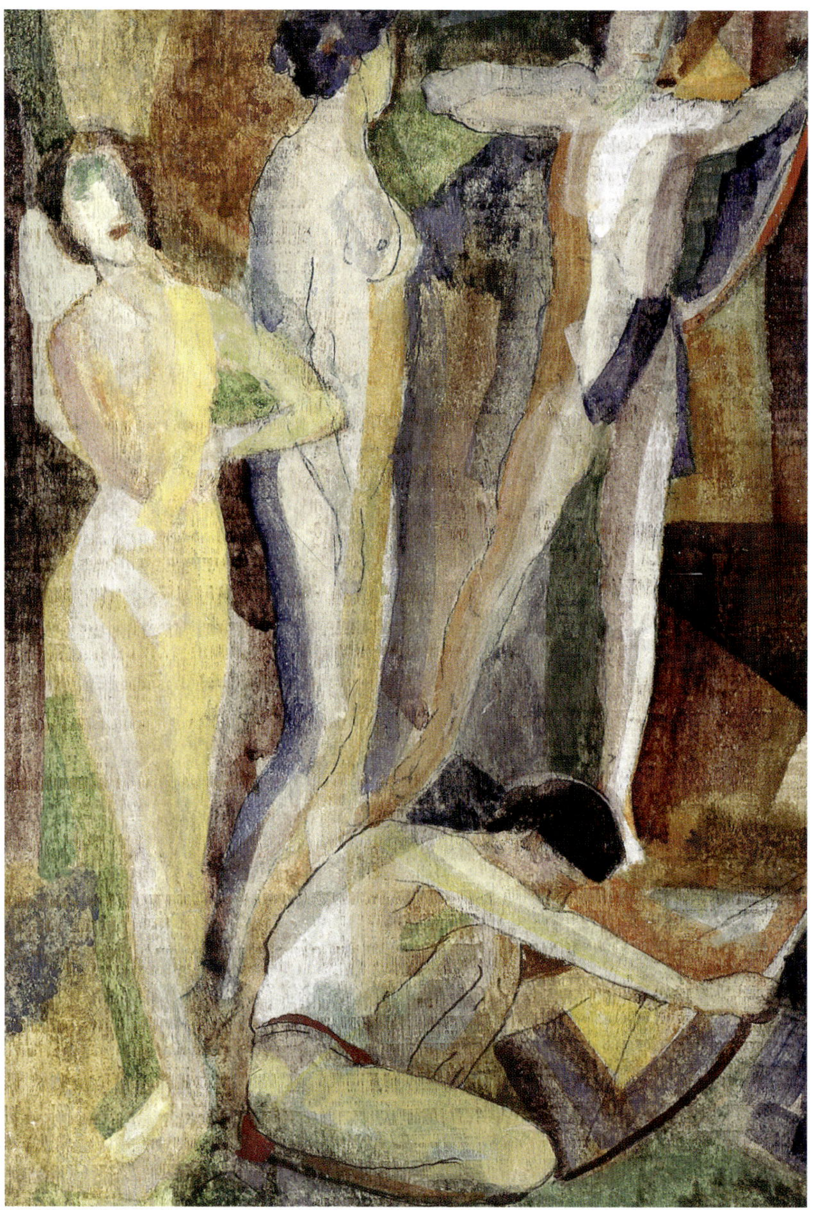

Untitled (Synchromy with Figures), c. 1916, oil on panel, 16 x 10 7/8 inches

Arthur B. Davies (1862–1928)

Arthur B. Davies is arguably one of the most enigmatic artists in the history of American art. Often characterized along with Elihu Vedder (1836–1923), Ralph Albert Blakelock (1847–1919), and Albert Pinkham Ryder (1847–1917) as an "American visionary," Davies continues to resist easy classification. Much of the puzzlement regarding the artist results from his seeming conservatism as a creator of images paired with his staunchly progressive attitude toward modernist art in both Europe and America. While much of his work is downright *retardataire*, some of his paintings, including *Untitled (Synchromy with Figures)*, reveal a curious admixture of the old and the new, the traditional and the modern—ultimately not such odd bedfellows in the mind of Davies.

The artist was born in Utica, New York, the son of English and Welsh immigrants who arrived in this country just a few years before their son's birth. Davies received his formal art training at the Art Institute of Chicago and later at the Art Students League in New York. In 1888, Davies met the art dealer William Macbeth (1851–1917), initiating a collegial and productive relationship that lasted for many years. Macbeth sent his young protégé to Europe as a purchasing agent for the gallery in 1895, and while abroad Davies had ample opportunity to immerse himself in the great art of the past. Two years later the artist returned to Europe, this time more cognizant of recent developments in contemporary European art, and was particularly taken with the work of the French muralist Pierre Puvis de Chavannes (1824–1898). Like many symbolist artists, Puvis was greatly inspired by antiquity in his choice of subject matter, and Davies soon began painting the dreamy pastoral landscapes inhabited by nymphs and unicorns for which he became best known.[1]

Davies' first teacher, a landscape painter from upstate New York by the name of Dwight Williams (1856–1932), once remarked that despite his seeming nostalgia for the antique, Davies always "manifested an intellectual and artistic independence and inclined toward radical movements."[2] The truth of this statement is evidenced by the artist's participation in the landmark exhibition of The Eight at the Macbeth Gallery in 1908. United more politically than aesthetically, the artists in the infamous show banded together to protest the rigid exhibition policies of the National Academy of Design.[3] In a few short years, as president of the Association of American Painters and Sculptors, Davies would be instrumental in the organization of the International Exhibition of Modern Art, better known as the Armory Show of 1913, which brought the most recent works of European modernism before an unsuspecting and, for the most part, unprepared American public.

In the years immediately following the Armory Show, Davies experimented with a stylized, pseudo-cubist language that was greatly influenced by the synchromist works of Stanton Macdonald-Wright (1890–1973) and Morgan Russell (1886–1953). The two American artists hit upon their new movement, Synchromism,—meaning simply "with color"—while in Europe in the early teens. Their vibrantly colorful, pulsating nonobjective paintings were first shown in New York at the Carroll Galleries in 1914, and two years later were among the most radical works exhibited at the Forum Exhibition of Modern American Painters held at New York's Anderson Galleries in 1916. The subtitle of the work in the Snowiss collection is more revealing perhaps of Davies' interest in the color abstractions of Macdonald-Wright and Russell than is the painting itself. Davies' short-lived adoption of synchromism was superficial and decorative at best and, as the emphatic presence of the figures attests, ultimately unsatisfying for an artist grounded in the traditions and mythology of the past.

JHR

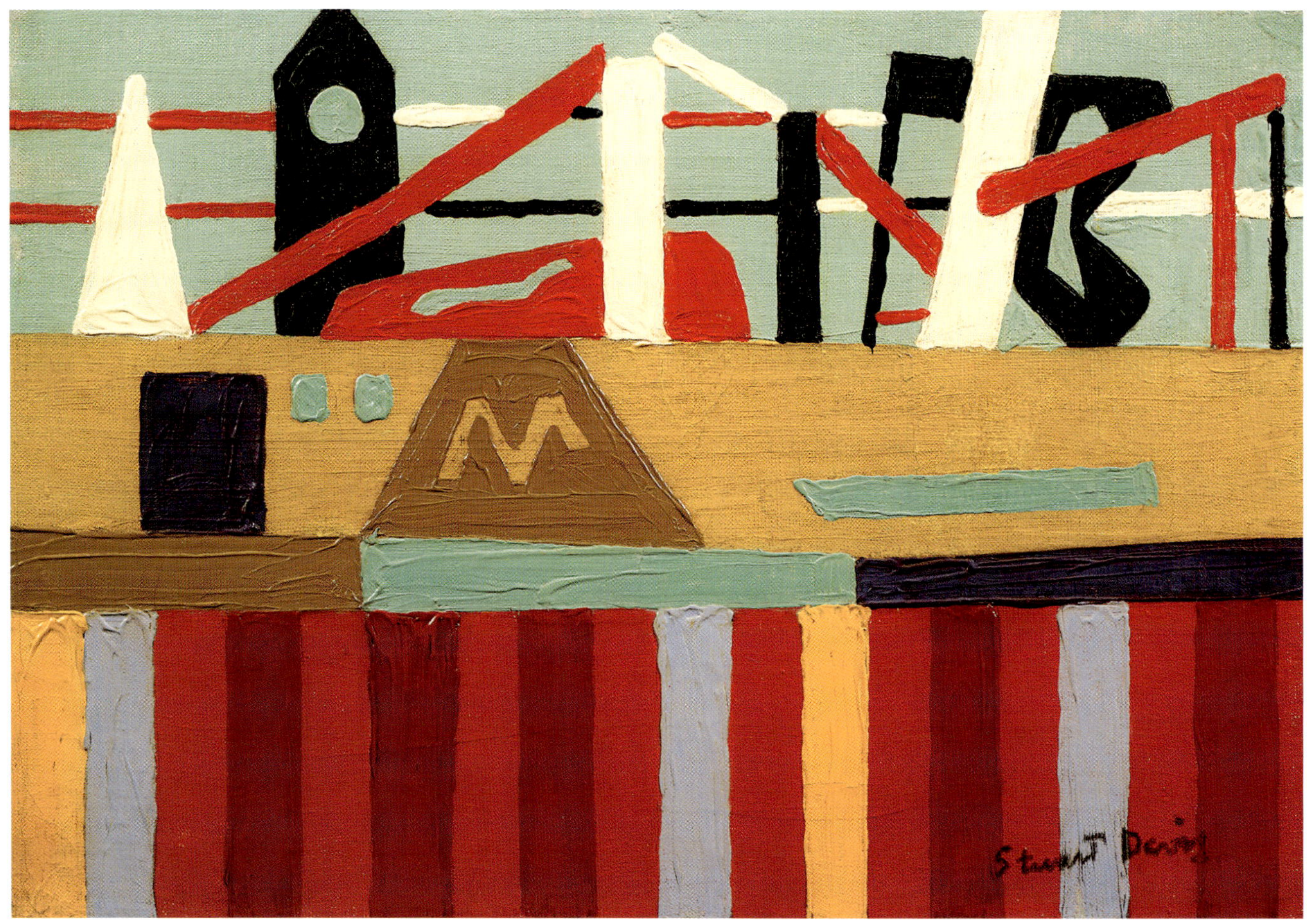

Coast Town
Landscape Study,
1940, oil on canvas,
10 x 14 inches

Facing page:
Gloucester Harbor,
1924, watercolor and crayon
on paper, 12 3/4 x 18 inches

Collection of The Butler
Institute of American Art,
Youngstown, Ohio.

Stuart Davis (1894–1964)

As the son of an art editor of a leading Philadelphia newspaper, Stuart Davis came by his career as an artist honestly and rather straightforwardly. Included on the roster of young artist-illustrators working for his father were John Sloan (1871–1951), William Glackens (1870–1938), and Everett Shinn (1876–1953), who would later join with Robert Henri (1865–1929) as members of the infamous group known as The Eight. Davis left high school after one year and in 1909 enrolled at Henri's School of Art in New York, where he embraced his mentor's realist credo. In a few short years, Davis began producing cover illustrations and cartoons for *The Masses*, a radical socialist magazine, and in 1913 exhibited several works at the groundbreaking display of modern art known as the Armory Show, along with other progressive American artists of the day. Davis spent the next several years digesting the formal innovations of European modernism on view at the infamous exhibition and by the early 1920s arrived at his idiosyncratic variant of synthetic cubism with its boldly vernacular American content.

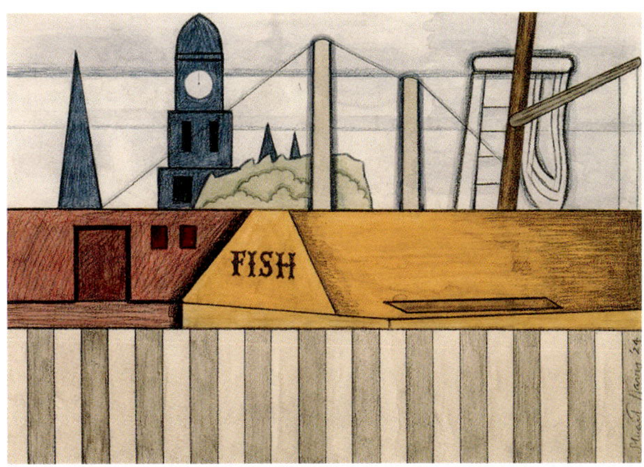

As a mature artist, Davis drew inspiration both from the energized cityscape of Manhattan and the picturesque landscapes of New England harbor towns. On the recommendation of John Sloan, Davis visited Gloucester, Massachusetts, in 1915, having spent the previous two summers in Provincetown. "That was the place I had been looking for," he would later recall. "It had the brilliant light of Provincetown, but with the important additions of topographical severity and the architectural beauties of the Gloucester schooner."[1] Davis found the streets and harbors "full of interest," as he wrote his cousin during that first visit, and he continued to summer in Gloucester almost without exception until 1934 with intermittent visits thereafter.[2]

A comparison of *Coast Town Landscape Study* with a much earlier work, *Gloucester Harbor*, a watercolor and crayon drawing from 1924, reveals that the subject of the later painting is indeed the harbor of his favorite seaside town.[3] Both images feature the same church spire and clock tower in the distance, the rigging and mast of a schooner in the middle ground, and the low roof and awning of a fish-processing factory in the immediate foreground.[4] In the 1940s, Davis frequently reworked or improvised on earlier compositions, and Gloucester imagery continues to appear in his later work long after he had ceased making regular visits to the town. *Coast Town Landscape Study* is one of at least three reprises of this specific harbor composition painted in 1940–1941, each a colorful, abstracted distillation of the original scene.[5] These works testify both to the artist's career-long reliance on concrete subject matter and to the increased appearance of decorative or invented elements in his work of the 1940s and 1950s, most evident in the abstract squiggle of the fish signage.

Clearly Davis was less interested in the quaint personality of the working harbor than in the at times discordant complexities of its peculiar equipment and vessels.[6] The boats of Gloucester, which Davis included in his list of "things which have made me want to paint" in 1943, indeed appear to have aided the artist as he composed his abstract "configurations." "The schooner is a very necessary element in coherent thinking about art," he once noted. "I do not refer to its own beauty of form, but to the fact that its masts define the often empty sky expanse. They function as a color-space coordinate between earth and sky. They make it possible for the novice landscape painter to evade the dangers of taking off into the void as soon as his eye hits the horizon. From the masts of schooners the artist eventually learns to invent his own coordinates when for some unavoidable reason, they are not present."[7]

JHR

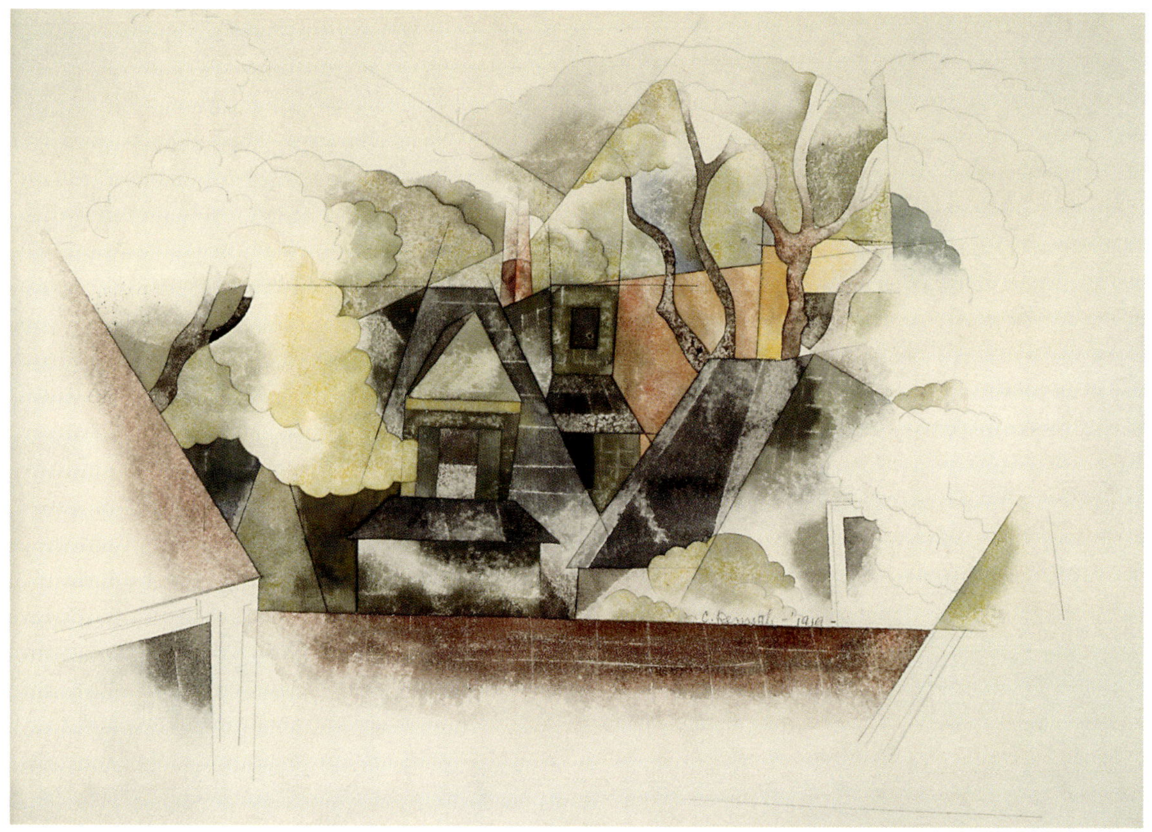

Roofs and Tree Forms,
1919, watercolor on paper,
10 x 14 inches

Charles Demuth (1883–1935)

Born into a prosperous family of tobacconists, Charles Demuth graduated from Franklin and Marshall Academy in his native Lancaster, Pennsylvania, in 1901. In 1903, he began taking courses at the Drexel Institute of Art, Science, and Industry in Philadelphia. By 1905 he was enrolled at the Pennsylvania Academy of the Fine Arts, also in Philadelphia, where his teachers included Thomas Anschutz (1851–1912) and William Merritt Chase (1849–1916). He further expanded his artistic horizons with trips to Europe in 1905, 1907, and 1912–1914. Yet it was slightly later, while on excursions to Bermuda and Provincetown, Massachusetts, that Demuth developed what is now recognized as his signature style. Perhaps inspired by his traveling companion Marsden Hartley (1877–1943) and the cubist painter Albert Gleizes (1881–1953)—who joined the two in Bermuda—the artist rendered the vernacular architecture in both locales with a newfound attention to crisp lines and tonally modulated surfaces.

Roofs and Tree Forms is an elevated view of façades, roofs, and winding branches, with pencil notations indicating more foliage at top, far left, and right. Like pieces of a mosaic, the patterned forms in the flattened perspective fit together, their intricate modeling—as well as the juxtaposition of trees and roofs—recalling similar work by Paul Cézanne (1839–1906).[1] Localizing the passages of blotted watercolor in carefully parceled zones, Demuth emphasizes the hardness and angularity of manmade and organic materials alike. The grid, broadly conceived, was central to the cubist enterprise, and its presence is apparent here as well, holding in check the evenly applied washes. Indeed, so uniformly tinted is each zone that the forms—even the arterial trees—maintain a sculptural, almost metallic sensibility, granting stability to the kaleidoscope-like composition.

With its compressed geometries and reductive palette, *Roofs and Tree Forms* certainly suggests an awareness of cubist works from the period. For contemporary audiences, however, the watercolor might well have elicited the increasingly common classifications, *precision* and *precisionism*.[2] The latter term characterizes the industrial imagery, immaculate stillness, and precise modeling of form found in the work of several early twentieth-century American artists, including Charles Sheeler (1883–1965) and Niles Spencer (1893–1952). In the present watercolor, domestic architecture is rendered with the matter-of-fact linearity one might associate with a factory or mechanical processes. The tree limbs similarly appear less like vegetation than meandering electrical wires or cables. In these ways, Demuth demonstrates the manner in which artists grafted precisionist formal idioms onto *non*-mechanical imagery, even rural and natural subjects.

Demuth's watercolor also demonstrates how "precision" presented a way to imagine even picturesque, time-honored subjects like Provincetown, Massachusetts. By the time Demuth and Hartley began summering there in the mid-1910s, the town had long been popularized as a remote fishing community, a quaint tourist haunt with native folkways still intact. Earlier in the century, the Provincetown-based Cape Cod School of Art advertised the locale as the "oldest and most picturesque fishing hamlet on the New England coast."[3] Demuth was only one of many to envision the village through a modernist lens. Yet his views stand apart because, with minimal lines, colors, and patterns, they suggest the richness of landscape and an entirety of experience. The critic Helen Henderson (1874–1956) offered a similar assessment in a review of an early exhibition of Demuth's watercolors, writing that his "impressions" of Provincetown convey "an intimate knowledge of the whole village, country, peninsula."[4] *Roofs and Tree Forms* substitutes the part for the whole, and, in the process, captures the fleeting poetry of Provincetown.

LGM

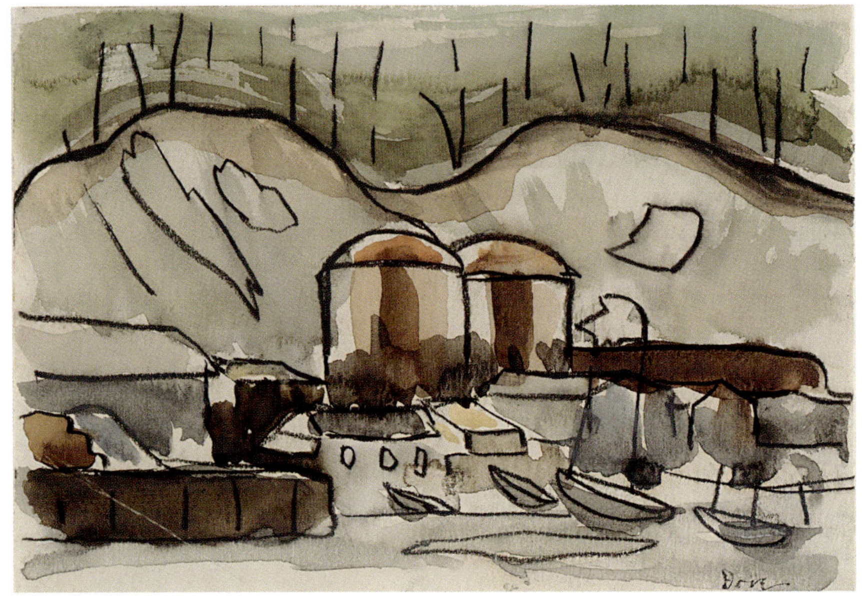

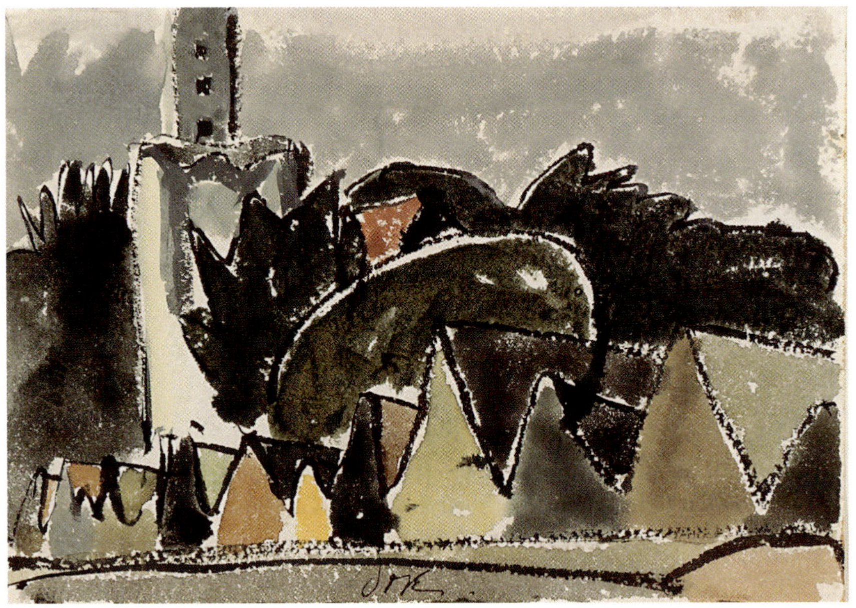

Gas Tanks and Sand Bank,
1932, watercolor on paper,
5 x 7 inches

From Lake, Geneva,
1938, watercolor on paper,
5 x 7 inches

Arthur Dove (1880–1946)

Like several of the other American artists in the intimate and supportive circle of the proprietary gallery owner Alfred Stieglitz (1864–1946), Arthur Dove found in the medium of watercolor a viable and inherently expressive mode for modernist experimentation. Perhaps because his own artistic origins were in photography, Stieglitz valued the so-called "minor" media and exhibited watercolors, drawings, and photographs alongside oils and sculpture regularly. "It is the spirit of the thing that is important," he once noted, a sentiment with which Dove undoubtedly would have agreed.[1]

Of the early American modernists, Dove was perhaps the most egalitarian in his use of materials. Among his earliest forays into a nature-based abstraction was a series of pastels known as *The Ten Commandments* (1911–1912), and many years later, in the mid- to late 1920s, he would incorporate a host of nontraditional materials in his Dada-influenced assemblages. Watercolor became a favored medium for the artist beginning in 1928, when he turned back to painting after the extended interlude of working with collage. For the next several years, Dove typically devoted the late spring, summer, and early fall months to his diminutive watercolor sketches, producing dozens of these small "ideas for paintings" each year.[2] Although most were executed as potential studies for larger compositions in oil, Dove clearly viewed them as independent works of art, regularly titling and signing them and exhibiting them at Stieglitz's gallery, An American Place, throughout the 1930s. Attesting to their importance in the artist's oeuvre, Duncan Phillips included a large group of watercolors in his 1937 retrospective of Dove's work held at the Phillips Memorial Gallery. In the accompanying catalogue, Phillips praised these "abbreviated notes from nature," calling attention to their delicate calligraphy and subtle washes of color.[3]

As might be expected, the subjects of the watercolors duplicate those found in the artist's oil paintings and record the habitual sites—both natural and manmade—of his immediate environs. *Gas Tanks and Sand Bank* reveals the felicitous commingling of nature and machine found in much of Dove's work and visually registers his delight in the varied shapes and colors of a working harbor. *From Lake, Geneva* was painted after the artist's move, along with his second wife, artist Helen Torr (1886–1967), to his hometown of Geneva, New York, in 1933. Prompted by his mother's death that year, the financially strapped Dove returned to the small lake town to help settle family business and found himself immersed once again in the familiar terrain of his youth.[4] As he noted in a letter to Stieglitz in 1937, the artist owned a small boat and often was on the water sketching by the very early hours of the morning.[5] *From Lake, Geneva* records the jagged regularity of rooftops along Lake Seneca's shoreline, as well as the looming tower-like presence of the town's recently built flour mill, a hulking monument that appears prominently in other of the artist's watercolors and oils from this period. Each of the Snowiss watercolors reveals Dove's mellifluous use of line, and together they demonstrate the artist's ability to manipulate the medium of watercolor with washes of pigment ranging from nearly opaque to virtually translucent. And we might agree with Lewis Mumford (1895–1990), who once noted that Dove "is most himself when he is most spontaneous, as in the small watercolors."[6]

JHR

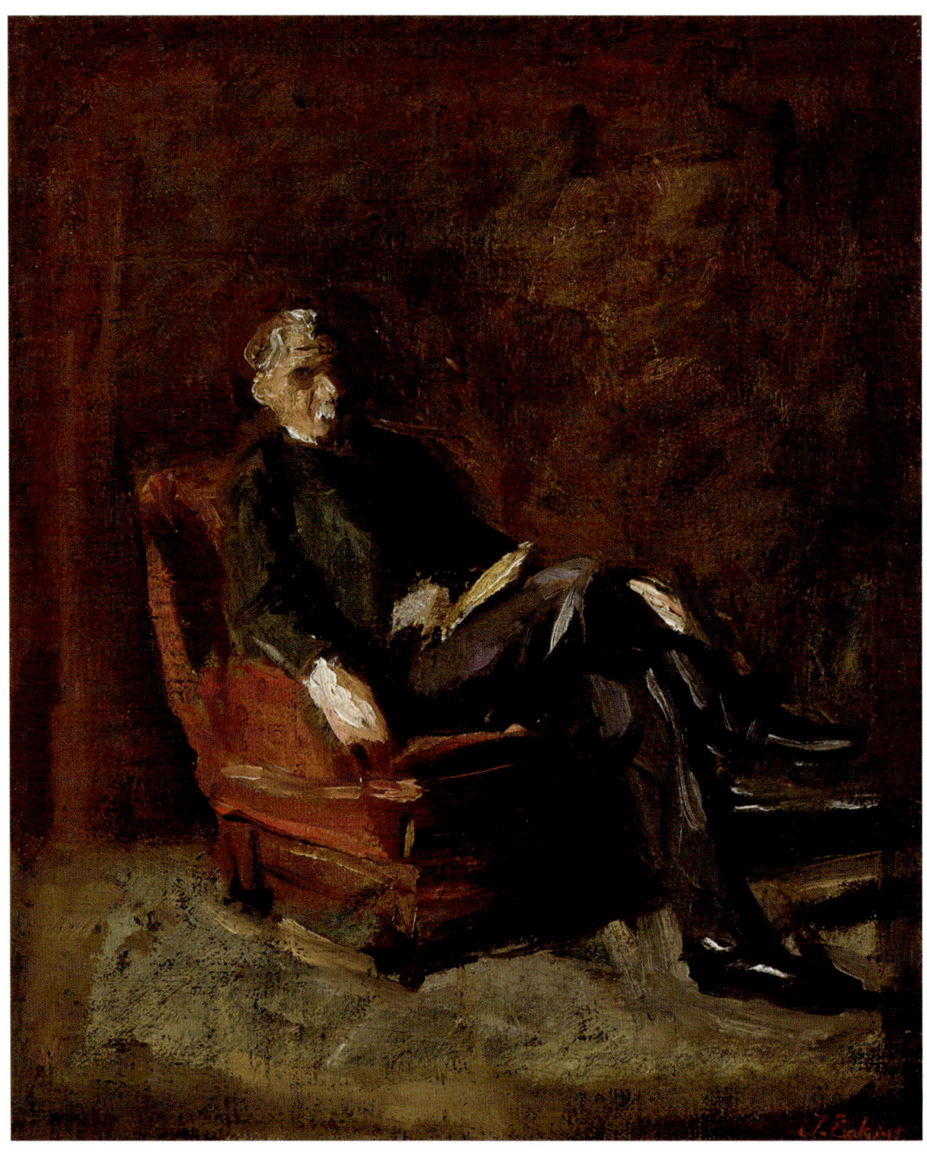

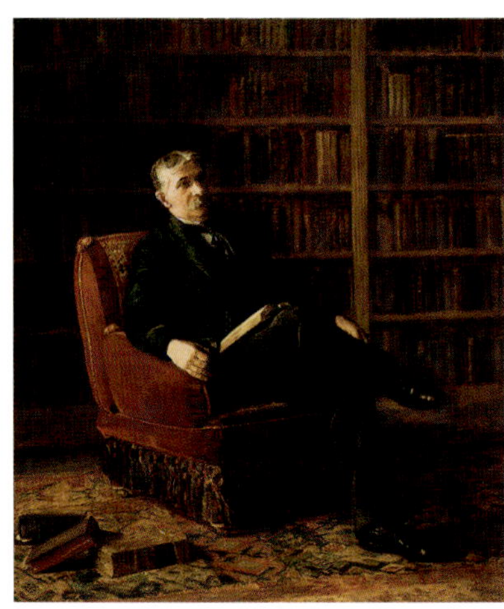

Preliminary Sketch for the Portrait of Riter Fitzgerald,
c. 1895, oil on canvas,
13 x 10 1/2 inches

Riter Fitzgerald,
1895, oil on canvas,
76 1/4 x 64 1/4 inches

The Art Institute of Chicago, Friends of American Art Collection, 1950.1511.

Thomas Eakins (1844–1916)

Frequently embroiled in controversy stemming from his unconventional artistic practice, Thomas Eakins found a staunch defender in Philadelphia journalist and art critic Riter Fitzgerald. *Preliminary Sketch for the Portrait of Riter Fitzgerald*, an expressive study for the full-length portrait of Fitzgerald, serves as evidence of the methodical preparations Eakins undertook when composing large works.[1] The sketch is also indicative of the artist's innate ability to envision the final effect of a painting during the earliest stages of its development.

After studying under the tutelage of Jean-Léon Gérôme (1824–1904) at the Ecole des Beaux-Arts in Paris, Eakins, a lifelong Philadelphia resident, began his teaching career at the Pennsylvania Academy of the Fine Arts in 1873.[2] By 1879, he was promoted to professor of painting and drawing and attained the distinguished position of director in 1881.[3] Shunning traditional teaching methods, which favored drawing from plaster casts and clothed figures, Eakins restructured the curriculum to include anatomy lessons, dissection, and drawing from nude models.

Eakins' teaching methodology proved contentious, ultimately leading to the end of his tenure at the Academy in 1886. *The Philadelphia Evening Item*, the newspaper founded by Riter Fitzgerald's father, Thomas Fitzgerald, praised Eakins' departure: "Professor Eakins … has proved from the first a mistake …. We admire Mr. Eakins for one thing, and that is his resignation from the Academy. For some time the trouble in regard to his being there has been increasing in the Life Class, and now it culminates with Mr. Eakins retiring, which is a wise movement on his part."[4] Although he was soon teaching at institutions such as the newly formed Art Students League of Philadelphia and the Women's Art School of the Cooper Union, criticism of his methodology persisted, and Eakins' opportunities dwindled. He ended his teaching career by 1897, devoting full attention to his own work.

The balance of Eakins' oeuvre consists of portraits of family members, friends, and respected colleagues. Financially secure throughout his lifetime, Eakins was able to paint subjects of his choosing; just a fraction of his output consisted of commissions.[5] As *The Pennsylvania Museum Bulletin* explained in its March 1930 edition, "Insipid pettiness did not appeal to him, neither would he endeavor to flatter his subject in any way, nor was he attracted by the sensuous or unclean, but it was always character, character, character."[6] The straightforward nature of his painting style occasionally met with disapproval, causing a number of portraits to go unclaimed by their owners.[7]

Riter Fitzgerald did not count himself among Eakins' dissatisfied patrons. He instead heralded his own portrait in the *Evening Item*, claiming it was "undoubtedly one of the finest portraits Eakins ever painted."[8] Believing that "the brush is a more powerful and rapid tool than the point or stump," Eakins composed *Preliminary Sketch for the Portrait of Riter Fitzgerald* with rapid impasto brushstrokes.[9] The work is indicative of his intuitive compositional decisions and reveals that the artist envisioned Fitzgerald's thoughtful pose from the portrait's inception. The final work, now in the collection of the Art Institute of Chicago, is a direct descendant of the sketch. The mottled brown background has been replaced by bookshelves that Fitzgerald described as "colored with that harmony which imparts an agreeable sensation to the observer."[10] The critic's face and hands, now clearly delineated, have retained the vibrant highlights found in the sketch. While the diminutive study gave way to a monumental painting, the essence and character of the final product is clearly evident in this first and most basic study of Riter Fitzgerald.[11]

JD

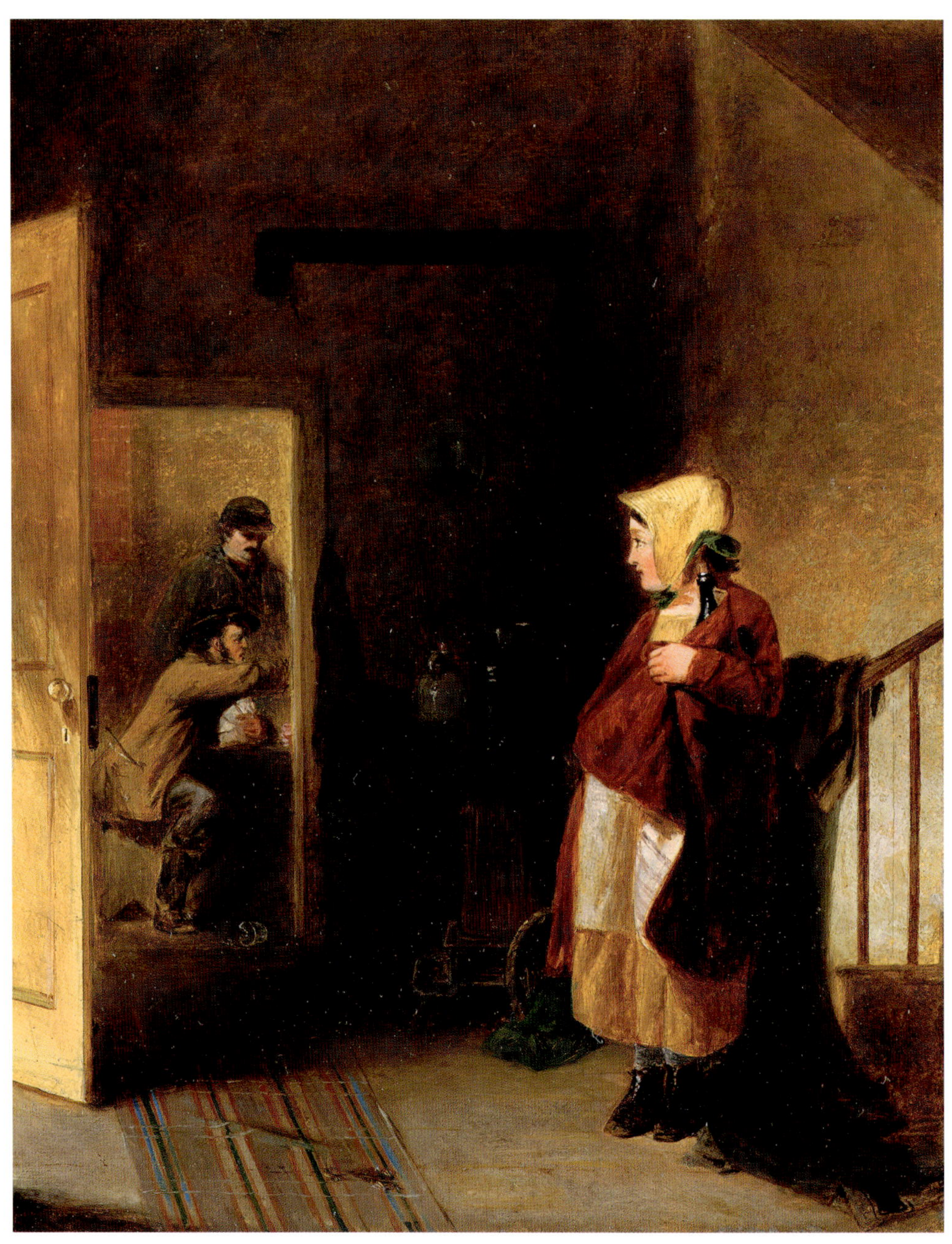

Waiting,
c. 1855–1860,
oil on panel,
14 3/4 x 11 1/2 inches

Francis William Edmonds (1806–1863)

That Francis William Edmonds produced fewer than sixty known paintings during his lifetime is not surprising. The Hudson, New York, native established a solid reputation within the elite art circles of New York City while simultaneously cultivating a successful, yet time-consuming banking career. Edmonds' provocative canvases, clearly influenced by seventeenth-century Dutch genre paintings, offer a glimpse of amusing domestic scenes, touching familial relationships, and, as in the case of *Waiting*, the occasional moral dilemma.

Edmonds displayed unusual artistic talent at a young age, prompting his parents' attempt to apprentice him to Philadelphia engraver Gideon Fairman (1774–1827) when he was just 15 years old. The apprenticeship fees proved prohibitive, however, forcing Edmonds to look elsewhere for employment. With the help of an uncle, Edmonds was hired as an underclerk at the Tradesman's Bank of New York City in 1823.[1] Although his profession kept him engrossed in the world of finance, Edmonds managed to continue his artistic pursuits by supplying designs to wood engravers.[2] In 1826, he attended evening drawing classes at the Antique School of the National Academy of Design and first exhibited his work there in 1829.

A new appointment at the Hudson River Bank in 1830 temporarily curtailed Edmonds' artistic activities, and he did not exhibit at the National Academy again until 1836.[3] During the late 1830s, Edmonds produced numerous paintings for Academy exhibitions and by 1840 was elected a full academician. He exhibited infrequently after 1846, having been sidetracked by business responsibilities and a number of posts with such artistic organizations as the Apollo Association, the National Academy of Design, and the Artists' Fund Society. After accusations of embezzlement forced him to leave the banking industry in 1855, Edmonds co-founded a bank note engraving business and rededicated his efforts to painting.[4]

Edmonds' style and subject matter are clearly indebted to seventeenth-century Netherlandish genre scenes, which were readily available to a receptive American audience through engravings. While a doctor-recommended sojourn in Europe from 1840 to 1841 served to improve his health after the death of his wife, it also provided the artist with the opportunity to view the major art collections of London, Paris, and Rome firsthand. Not surprisingly, Edmonds gravitated to works by Dutch painters Gabriel Metsu (1629–1667) and Adriaen van Ostade (1610–1685), both of whom specialized in anecdotal genre scenes.[5]

Edmonds relied on the compositional and thematic formulas that proved successful to these artists, supplemented with the occasional addition of moralizing overtones. In *Waiting*, Edmonds creates an intriguing scene of uncertainty and tension. A young woman stands transfixed in a dramatic light streaming in from the open door. H. Nichols B. Clark has suggested that the woman gathers her cape about her midriff and cradles a bottle of wine in a manner that alludes to a possible pregnancy. She gazes apprehensively toward two men who are actively engaged in a heated game of cards, their relationship to the woman unclear. A broken glass resting on the floor next to the seated card player confirms that something in the dreary stage-like setting is amiss. Clark asserts that an additional layer of moral uncertainty is raised by Edmonds' ambivalent portrayal of military figures. The dignified portrait of a soldier appears on the wall of the room where the young woman waits. The soldier in the back room, however, is engrossed with gambling. His participation suggests a tarnishing of the honorable reputation of the soldier in antebellum America.[6]

JD

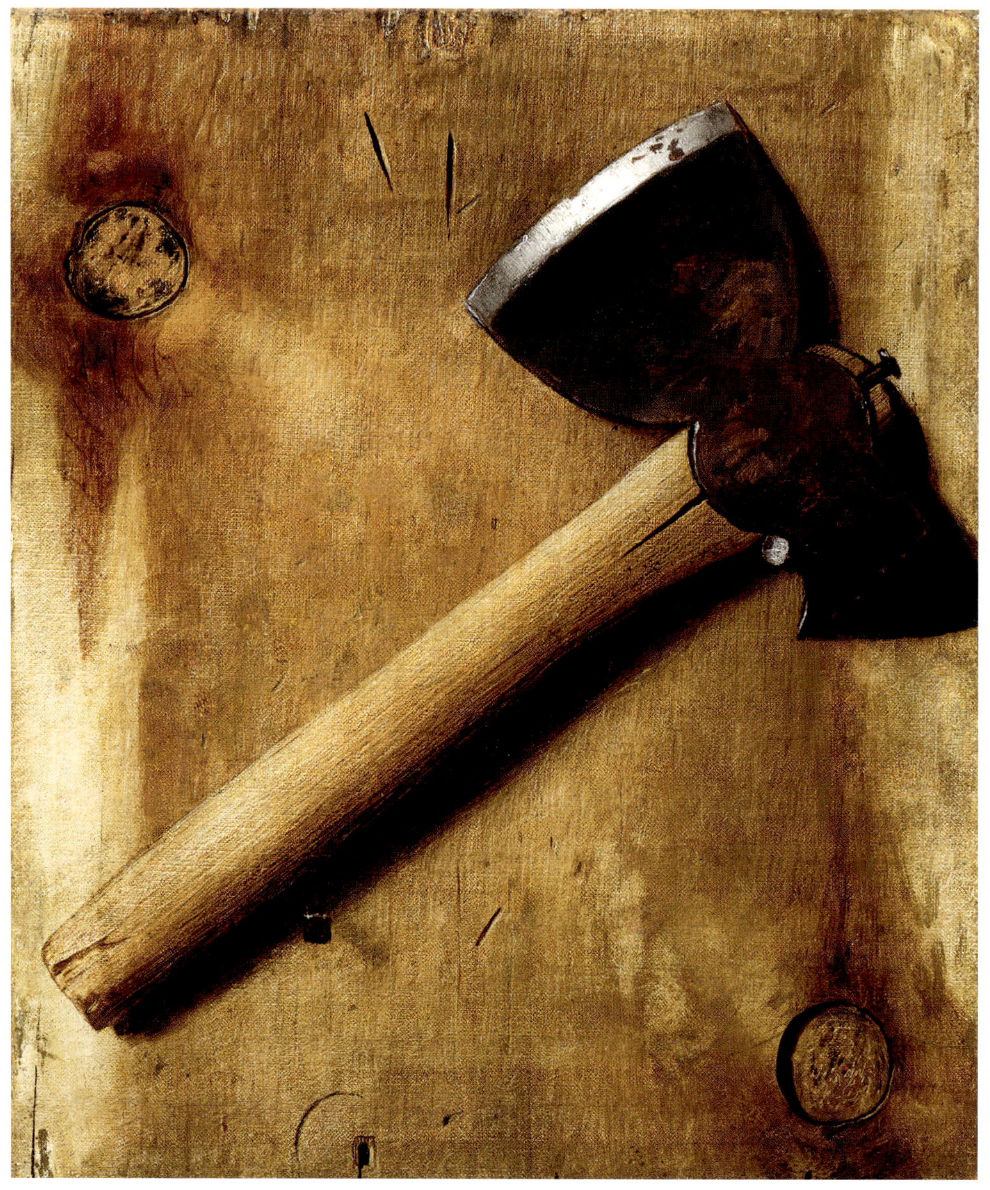

Hatchet,
c. 1888, oil on canvas,
12 1/8 x 10 inches

De Scott Evans (1847–1898)

Although trompe l'oeil painting is highly esteemed today as a vital and beguiling aspect of late nineteenth-century American art, such was not always the case. Seemingly lacking in heady content and clearly deriving its style from a slavish and unrevealing mimesis of nature, the "fool the eye" still life was critically discredited as a minor genre ironically in the midst of the heyday of its production. Denigrated by erudite aesthetes, the trompe l'oeil still life nonetheless appealed to and was collected by a largely middle-class audience that delighted in its deceptive optical trickery. De Scott Evans, known in his time as a genre painter and portraitist, owes his present-day revived reputation to the generally accepted supposition that he on occasion painted remarkable trompe l'oeil still lifes for an eager clientele.

Born David Scott Evans in Boston, Indiana, the young artist received formal artistic training in Cincinnati in the mid-1860s and by 1873 was chairman of the Fine Arts Department at Mount Union College in Alliance, Ohio.[1] The following year, Evans, who by then had adopted the professional name "De Scott," opened a studio in Cleveland and in 1877 left for Paris to pursue further academic training with the famed French painter William-Adolphe Bouguereau (1825–1905). When he returned to the States in 1878, Evans settled in Cleveland and became a founding member and co-director of that city's Academy of Art. By 1887, the artist had moved to New York City, where for the next decade he continued to exhibit regularly at the National Academy of Design and to produce rather cloying and derivative pictures of elegant young women in beautiful interiors. It is in New York as well that Evans purportedly began producing the trompe l'oeil pieces for which he is best known today. His life was tragically cut short in 1898 when, en route to Paris to complete a decorative commission, he and his daughters were drowned in the shipwreck of the French steamer *La Bourgogne*.

Much of the confusion surrounding Evans' still-life paintings derives from the artist's apparent use of pseudonyms ranging from "S. S. David" to "Scott David" to "Stanley S. David." In 1971, art historians William Gerdts and Russell Burke attributed two nearly identical paintings of pears suspended from a string—one signed De Scott Evans, the other Scott David, an inversion of the artist's given name—to Evans, postulating that the use of the pseudonym for such "off-duty" works was a means of protecting his reputation from the critical opprobrium surrounding trompe l'oeil painting.[2] Since that time, additional fruit and nut still lifes, as well as three hatchet paintings—all variously signed but seemingly by the same hand—have come to light.[3]

The Snowiss picture is remarkably similar to the two other known hatchet pictures: *Hatchet on Wood* (Snite Museum of Art, signed D. Scott Evans) and *Washington's Hatchet* (private collection, signed (on card) Stanley S. David). Although unsigned, *Hatchet* bears the "salient stylistic characteristics" of the body of works now identified as Evans/David, including the unusual handling of the tacking edges.[4] To perpetuate the illusion that the tool is hanging on a block of wood, Evans typically left the canvas exposed on all four sides of the stretcher, visually simulating the appearance of saw marks (left edge), vertical wood grain (right edge), and even the accumulation of dust and dirt along the top edge. The "board" itself appears to have splits, chips, and knotholes, "imperfections" perfectly described by a masterful hand—be it that of Evans or the elusive S. S. David.

JHR

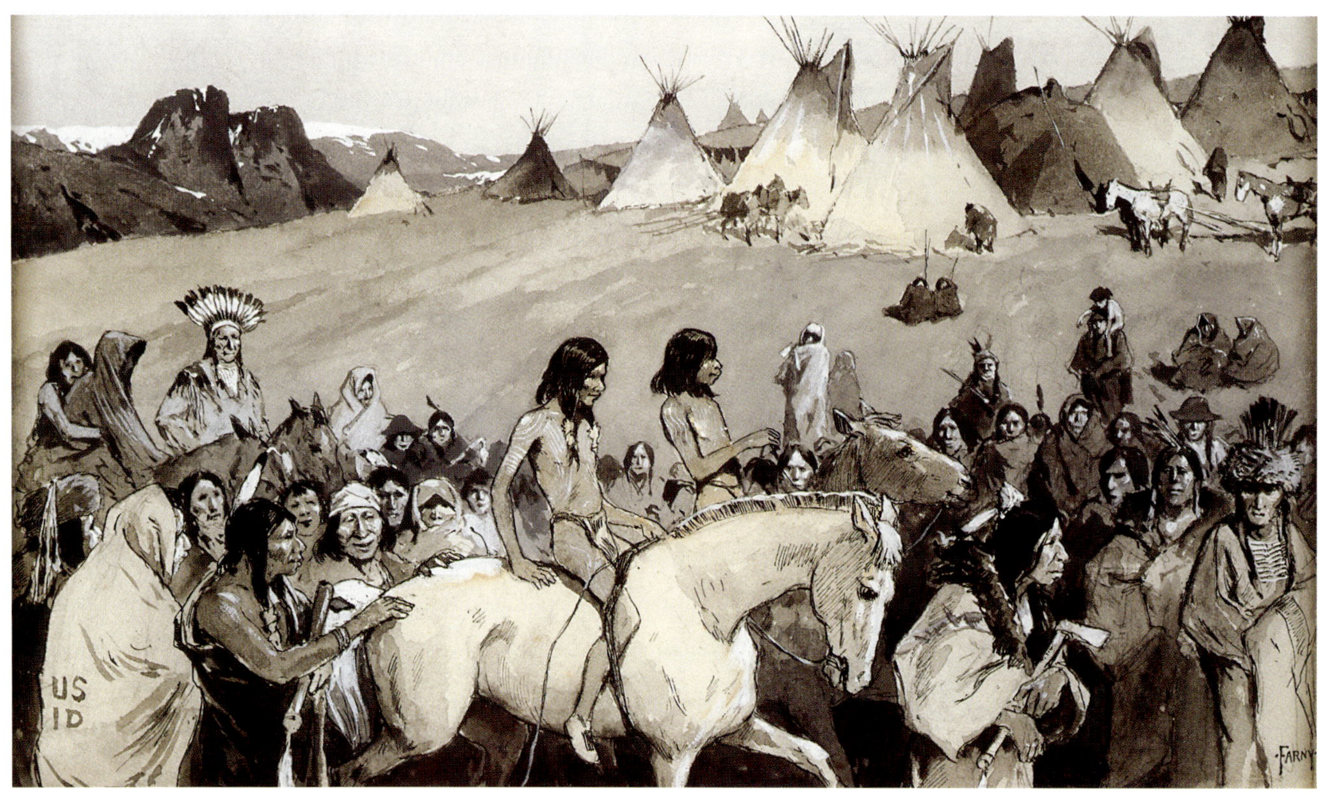

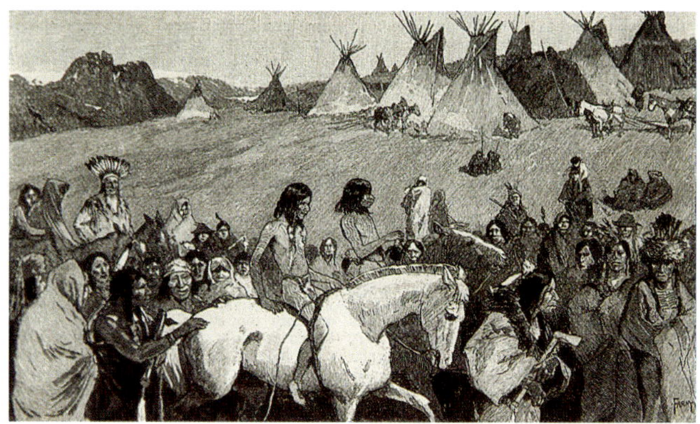

Indian Horse Race,
c. 1886, gouache on paper,
10 1/4 x 14 1/2 inches

"On the Way to the Starting-Point,"

Century Magazine,
January 1887.

Henry F. Farny (1847–1916)

For many artists in the late 1800s, the American West and its native inhabitants provided a rich source of visual and thematic material. Ironically, it was a native Frenchman, François Henri Farny, who would become one of the most successful delineators of American Indian life in the years surrounding the closing of the frontier at the end of the nineteenth century.

Farny was born in Ribeauville, France, and immigrated with his family to America in 1853. After settling for a few years in Warren County, Pennsylvania, the family moved further westward to Cincinnati, Ohio, where Farny would ultimately reside and establish his artistic career. By the mid-1860s, Farny was contributing illustrations to *Harper's Weekly*, and it was at this time that he anglicized and reversed his *prénoms* and moved to New York to pursue employment with Harper Brothers. European training soon beckoned, and by the fall of 1867, Farny was studying painting in Italy. Although at the time Farny expressed a desire to become a portrait painter, his studies would soon continue under the supervision of the landscape painter Hermann Herzog (1831–1932) in Düsseldorf. Farny returned to Europe on two other occasions in the 1870s, spending much of his time in Munich, where he drank in the painterly aesthetic of the Munich School. Farny's mature style would represent a successful amalgam of this European training, namely a precise drawing technique emblematic of Düsseldorf and the more sketch-like, painterly approach heralded in Munich.[1]

Farny's concentrated interest in Native Americans first became evident around 1880, the year he apparently began collecting Indian artifacts in his Cincinnati studio. The artist made his first trip west—the first of at least three during the next decade—in 1881 to the Dakota Territory, and it was on this trip that he began his practice of amassing on-the-spot sketches, photographs, and artifacts for later reference material.[2] Farny's paintings would soon captivate an American public eager to glimpse details of Native American life observed firsthand, prompting one writer to note that the painter had "struck an artistic bonanza."[3] Farny continued to be much in demand as an illustrator and provided both *Harper's Weekly* and *Century Magazine* with "spunky little sketches in black and white … to liven up" numerous published narratives of treks to the West.[4] Farny's gouache sketches intended for publication were typically executed in grisaille (shades of gray), which permitted both a wide tonal range and easy transcription into black-and-white engravings.

Indian Horse Race is one such gouache drawing and was published with the caption "On the way to the starting-point" in a January 1887 *Century Magazine* article written by C. E. S. Wood, the adjutant general, or scribe, for a government expedition to the remote northwest in 1879. Wood's article, "An Indian Horse-Race," is a detailed eyewitness account from this trip of a highly competitive race among rival tribes in the Wenatchee and Chelan territories. Although Farny's rendition is faithful to many of the particulars of the narrative (the riders' lariat-tied legs, for instance), it is doubtful that the artist, who favored depictions of Plains Indians, ever encountered the native cultures described in Wood's account. Editorial comments on the margins of the gouache confirm the disjunction between text and image. "These Indians mentioned in article never saw an agent nor lived on a reservation," noted the editor, who, likewise, in his marginalia called for more evidence of "fir covered mountains—the country just the opposite of the plains." While the visual reference to government-issued blankets is omitted in the engraved illustration, the reproduction otherwise follows the specifics of Farny's gouache, reminding us that such "firsthand" accounts of the era are often tempered with artistic—and editorial—license.

JHR

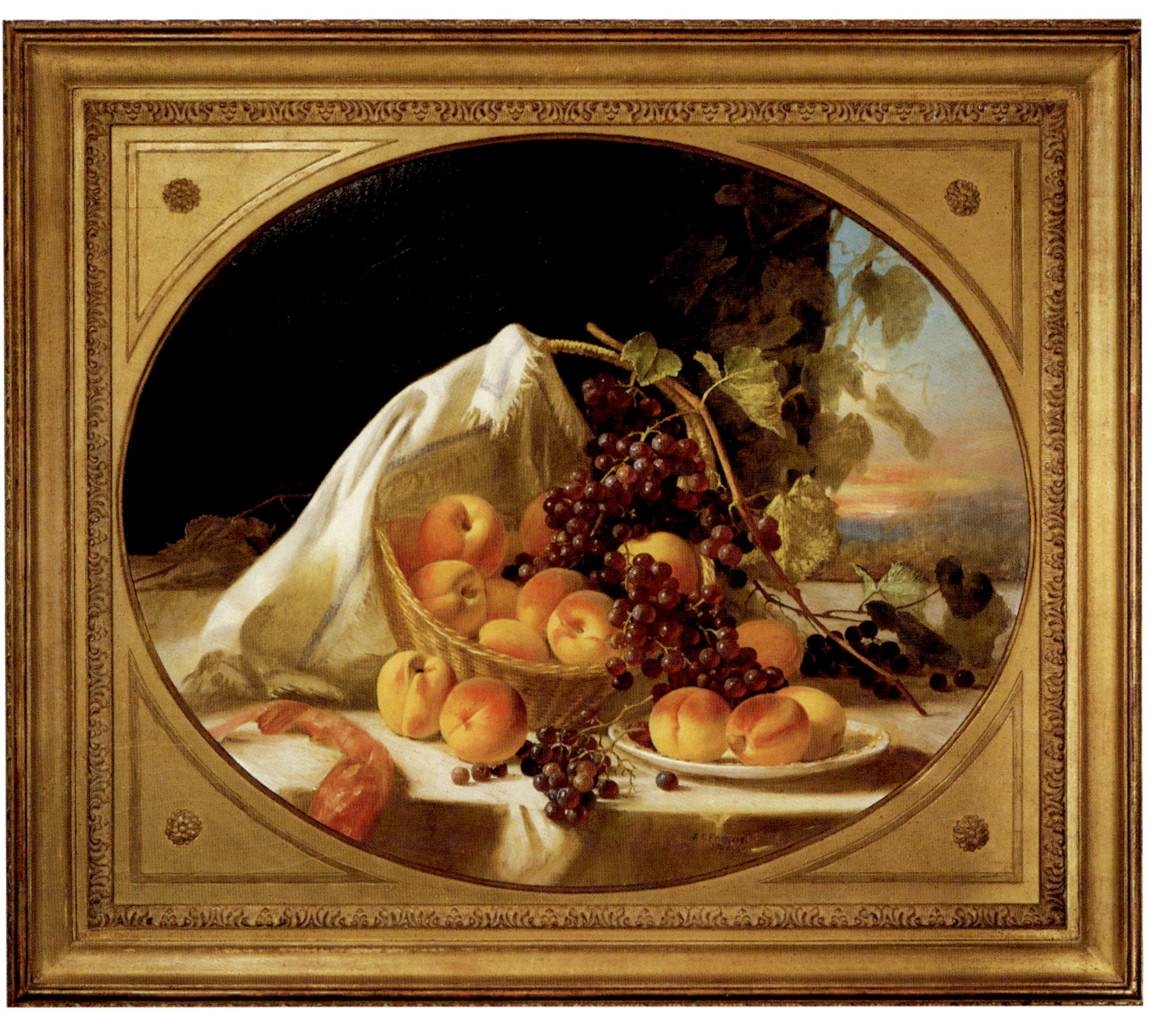

Still Life: Peaches and Grapes,
1860, oil on canvas,
24 5/8 x 29 1/2 inches

John F. Francis (1808–1886)

Born in Philadelphia in 1808, John F. Francis was the son of French parents who passed away during his youth.[1] Little is known about his upbringing, education, or initial interest in painting as a profession. The technical proficiency found in his early works, however, suggests that he studied with an instructor, perhaps at the Pennsylvania Academy of the Fine Arts.[2] Although Francis began what would become a successful professional career as an itinerant portrait painter in the 1830s, it was not until the tastes of American art consumers began to shift at mid-century that he turned his full attention to still-life painting.

Francis proved successful as a portrait painter, securing multiple commissions in such Pennsylvania cities as Harrisburg, Lewisburg, and Bellefonte, and also managed to establish a reputation in states as distant as Ohio and Tennessee.[3] His sitters included notable figures like Joseph Ritner (1780–1869), Pennsylvania's governor from 1835 to 1839. A list compiled by the artist notes that he painted portraits of at least two additional governors, along with numerous judges, lawyers, and merchants.[4] Francis' work met with critical success and was featured in Philadelphia's Artists' Fund exhibitions of 1840, 1841, and 1844, as well as the Pennsylvania Academy of the Fine Art's annual exhibitions in 1847, 1855, and 1858.[5]

Francis' artistic specialty was threatened at mid-century by new photographic technology that offered quick and inexpensive alternatives to the painted portrait. In addition, still-life painting, long considered low on the hierarchical scale of artistic subject matter, rapidly gained favor as popular Victorian tastes demanded decorative objects for the home.[6] Francis gradually shifted his own practice away from portraiture during the 1850s, dedicating the rest of his already successful career to the production of still life.[7]

Francis relied on a select number of compositions that, with minimal variation, constituted the bulk of his still-life vocabulary. His dessert, luncheon, and fruit displays are most often arranged on simple tabletops in nondescript interiors. As is the case in *Still Life: Peaches and Grapes*, devices such as cloth-draped baskets and white china trimmed with gold display a bountiful array of foodstuffs. These lush compositions are frequently placed before a window offering a view of the surrounding landscape. A climbing vine masks the hard edge of the window frame, softening the juxtaposition of interior and exterior environments. While the tight brushwork of the carefully defined grapes, peaches, and woven basket is typical of Francis' early style, the loosely rendered landscape and foliage foreshadow the overall painterly quality of many of his later works.[8]

JD

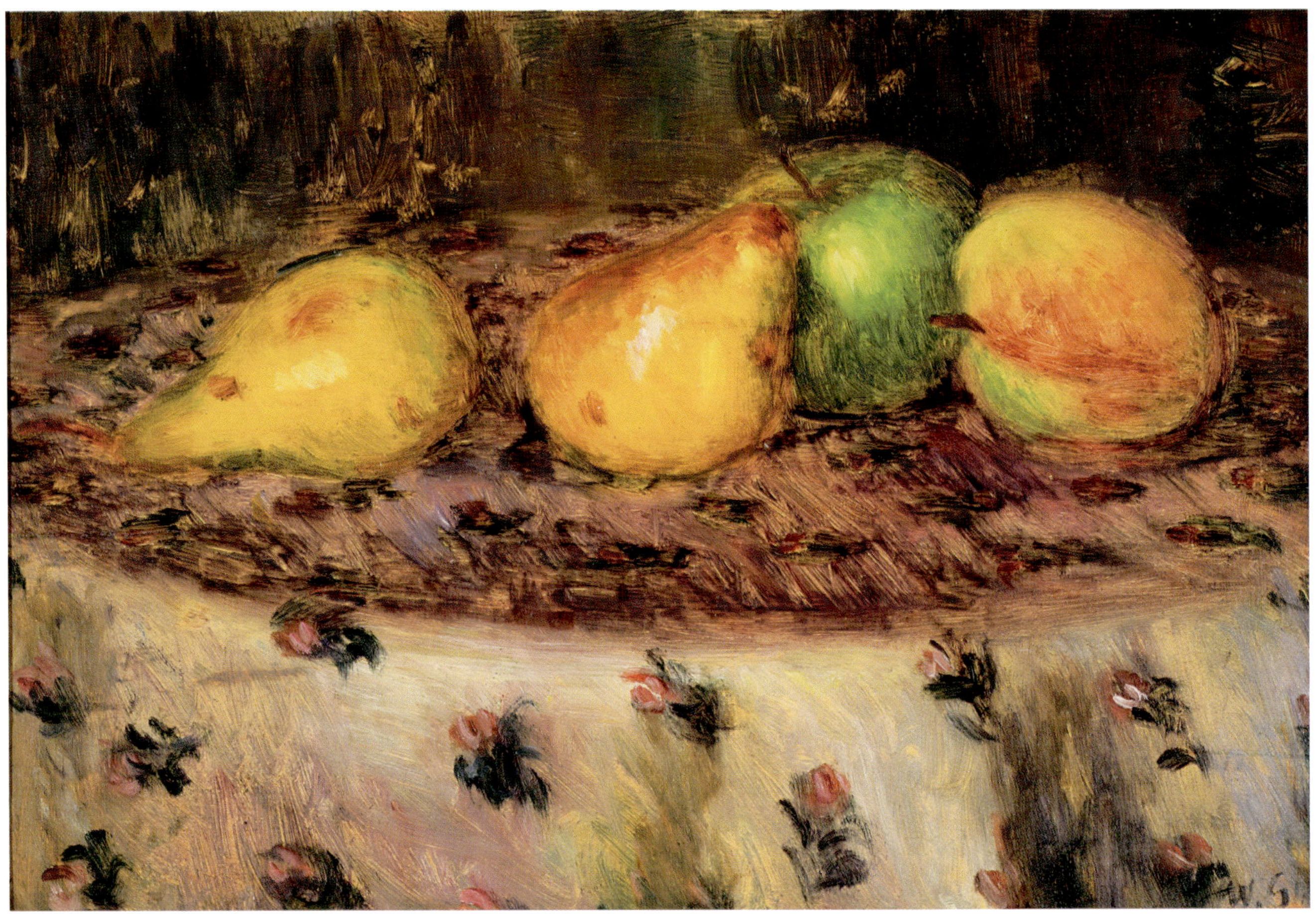

Four Fruits,
c. 1915–1920,
oil on panel,
9 1/4 x 13 1/4 inches

William Glackens (1870–1938)

In a career that spanned four decades, William Glackens gained renown for his contributions to several genres and themes, including illustration, still life, landscape, seascape, nudes, and portraiture. The artist was also known as the purchasing agent for his former schoolmate, the collector Albert C. Barnes (1872–1951). In February 1912, armed with $20,000 from Barnes, Glackens embarked on a month-long purchasing excursion to Paris, where he bought several impressionist and post-impressionist paintings. Of all the art works finding their way into Barnes' home in Upper Merion, Pennsylvania, those by Pierre-Auguste Renoir (1841–1919) must have made a particularly strong impression on artist and collector alike. Indeed, Glackens played an instrumental role in bringing several hundred paintings by the French master to the Barnes collection.[1] The two men shared what one may call a Renoir-mania, and works like *Four Fruits* offer an opportunity to explore the manner in which the American artist appropriated and ultimately elaborated on the lessons offered by the French painter.

In its loose modeling, sensual surfaces, and swirls of paint, *Four Fruits* evokes any number of still-life paintings by Renoir. Particularly Renoir-esque is the placement of the glistening pears and apples on the purple tablecloth in the foreground; neither cramped nor confined, the fruit are nonetheless in close proximity to the beholder. Yet it is here, in the compact foreground, where the analogy to French impressionism stops. Glackens introduces a new sense of drama to the picture plane. By capturing the seeming palpable textures of the fruit, as well as the reflective properties of the skin, Glackens simultaneously appeals to the senses of vision, touch, and taste. Adding a measure of compositional give-and-take, the floral motifs on the tablecloth provide a decorative foil to the more solidly conceived fruit forms above. The artist usually painted his floral and fruit still-life images not outdoors, but in the artificial studio environment.[2] Yet in *Four Fruits* the apples and pears are so vigorously modeled that, although removed from their natural setting, they appear teeming with life.

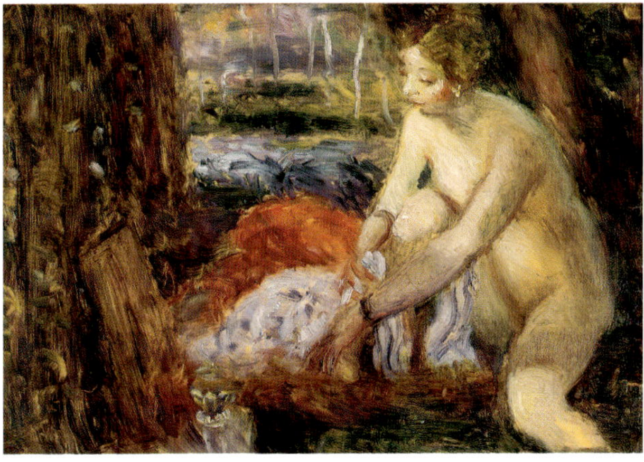

Glackens typically worked in oil on canvas; on those rare instances when he used wood panel, however, he often took the opportunity to paint on both sides. This is the case with *Four Fruits*, on the verso of which Glackens depicted a nude woman in a forest glade, drying her leg, presumably after bathing in the nearby lagoon. With her exposed flesh and elongated limbs, the bathing subject—identified as the biblical heroine Susanna—evokes similar works by Renoir, including *Small Blue Nude* (1878–1879, Albright-Knox Art Gallery), and a painting from Barnes' collection, *Female Bathers in the Forest* (c. 1897). As with *Four Fruits, Susanna without the Elders* also recalls the French painter's work in its loose but accurate draftsmanship. It was Barnes, however, who observed a subtle but crucial difference between Glackens and Renoir, noting that although similar, the American artist animated the picture plane with a new sensibility of "gesture and movement."[3] On both recto and verso, Glackens articulates his distinct style by way of rich coloration, prominently featured subjects, and a carefully conceived compositional structure.

LGM

Susanna without the Elders,
c. 1915–1920, oil on panel (verso)

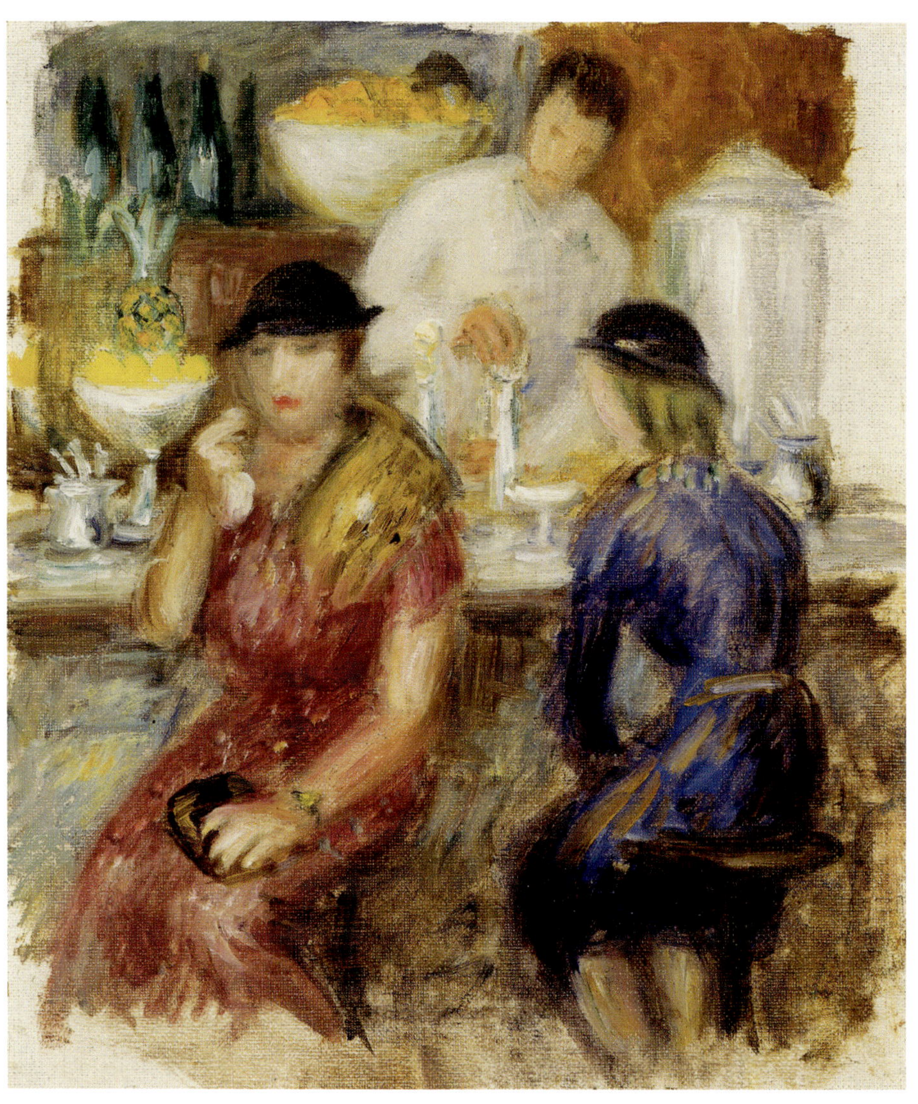

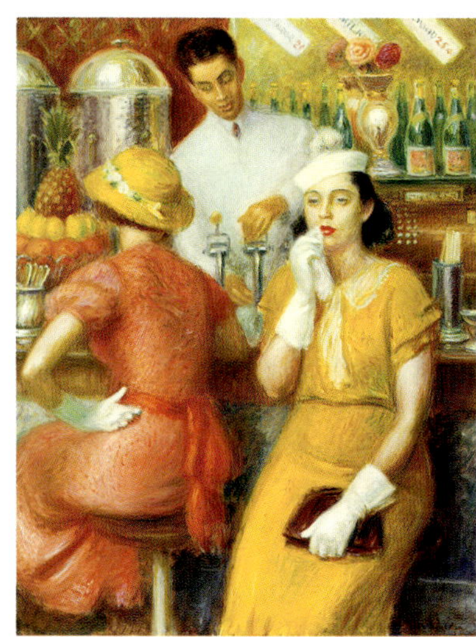

Study for The Soda Fountain,
1935, oil on canvas,
14 1/8 x 11 3/4 inches

The Soda Fountain,
1935, oil on canvas,
48 x 36 inches

Courtesy of the Pennsylvania Academy of the Fine Arts, Philadelphia, Joseph E. Temple and Henry D. Gilpin Funds, 1955.3.

William Glackens (1870–1938)

Throughout his oeuvre, William Glackens modeled forms with a vibrant painterly looseness. The recurring sketch-like quality surely owes as much to his early work as a Philadelphia artist-journalist as it does to his innovative assimilation of French impressionism into his creative process. In his early illustrations for the *Philadelphia Record, Philadelphia Public Ledger*, and *Philadelphia Press*, rapidly executed, on-the-spot sketches were transformed into reproductions complementing the text; these images brought to life the details and inherent sentiment of myriad newsworthy events. With a quickly applied brush and dynamically conceived composition, a work like *Study for The Soda Fountain* similarly transforms an everyday urban ritual into a psychologically charged genre scene, one that displays a keen understanding of human behavior.

Glackens' *Study for The Soda Fountain* is a preliminary oil sketch for a larger painting of the subject from the same year, now in the Pennsylvania Academy of the Fine Arts. He made several changes in the finished painting, including reversing the placement of the female figures, tilting the soda jerk's head to the left, adding a second coffee urn, and changing the color of the dresses. Yet, with the urns, the central placement of the spigots, and the compositionally stabilizing counter, the works also contain their share of similarities. Indeed, in its expressive lines and undulating textures, and the pyramid formed by the figural arrangement, the final work closely resembles the earlier study. As with artists past and present, Glackens produced numerous oil, pencil, and pastel studies for several paintings; oil sketches like *Study for The Soda Fountain* invite us to treat the graphics and studies on an aesthetic and intellectual par with the paintings for which the artist is best known.

Stylistically and thematically, the sketch recalls contemporary paintings by Isabel Bishop (1902–1988), Edward Hopper (1882–1967), and Guy Pène du Bois (1884–1958). Glackens was something of a veteran New York artist when he painted *The Soda Fountain* in 1935, and art historian William Gerdts has speculated that he explored the subject to "prove himself against newer figures" in the New York art world.[1] Indeed, the work could scarcely be more "up-to-date" in capturing the spectacle of American modernity between the World Wars. In the 1920s and 1930s, well over 100,000 soda fountains could be found in department stores, hotels, drugstores, theatres, and trains; new to the 1930s, however, was the streamlined design of stainless steel appliances and utensils, as evidenced in the shiny coffee urn and spigots in Glackens' painting.[2]

Perhaps most modern in *Study for The Soda Fountain* is the presence of the two women. Soda fountains had long served as community gathering points, where people from different socioeconomic classes could interact. By the 1920s and 1930s, as increasing numbers of women entered the workforce, the fountain became known as an acceptable place for women to socialize, even to flirt. Capitalizing on the establishment's appeal to female employees in factories and offices alike, Walgreens offered a special "shop girl's lunch" at its soda fountains.[3] In presenting well-dressed women as consumers, Glackens joined other American painters in depicting the "new woman," the autonomous—if controversial—individual found in restaurants, banks, theatres, and other public spaces.[4] With *Study for The Soda Fountain*, Glackens demonstrates his ongoing fusion of contemporary life and time-honored artistic conventions.

LGM

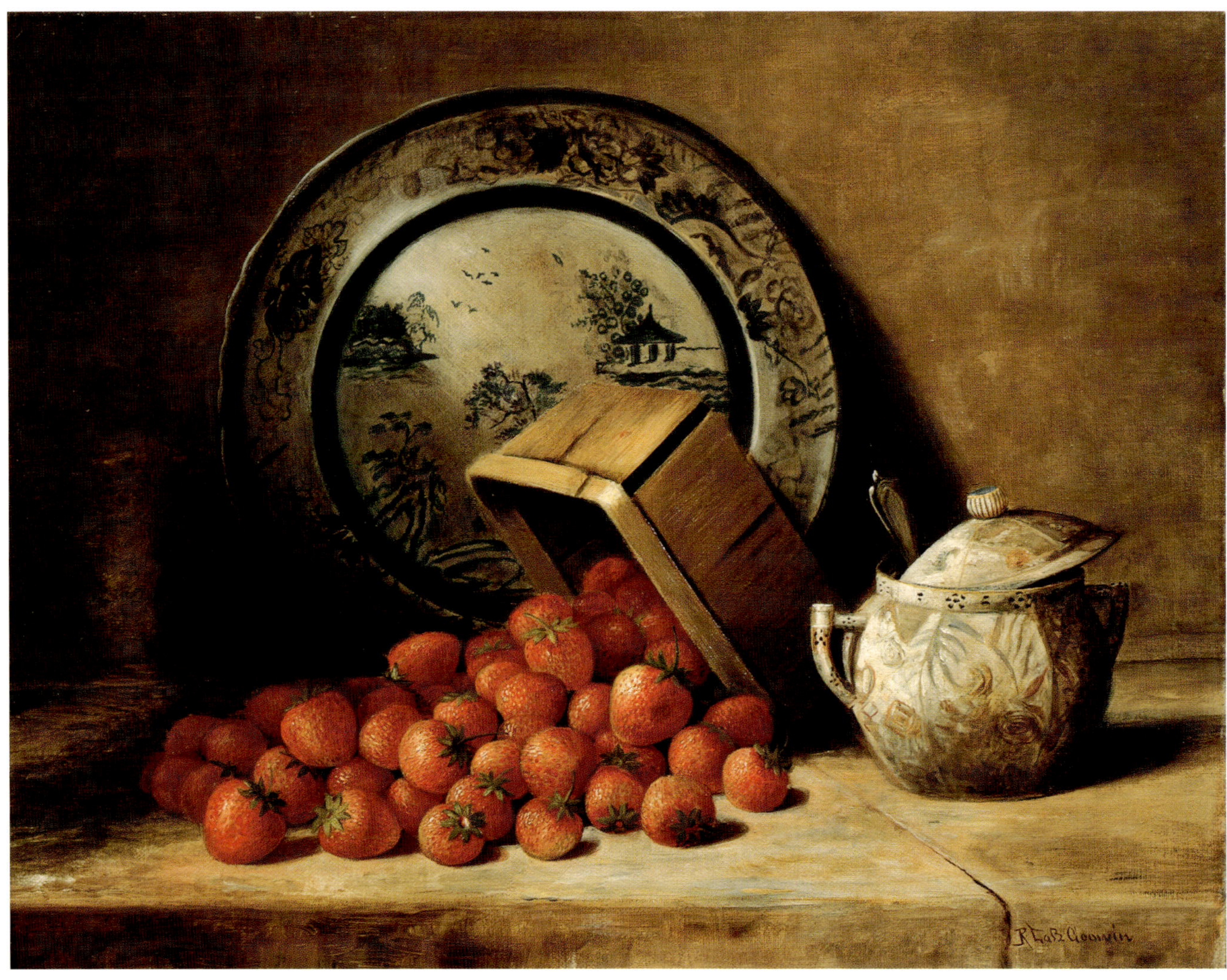

Still Life with Strawberries,
c. 1885, oil on canvas,
16 x 20 inches

Richard La Barre Goodwin (1840–1910)

Richard La Barre Goodwin was born in Albany, New York, the son of a prolific portrait painter by the name of Edwin W. Goodwin (1800–1845).[1] The young Goodwin followed in his father's footsteps and plied his trade as an itinerant portrait painter in western and upstate New York for well over twenty years at the outset of his career. Although the precise date remains unclear, Goodwin began painting still lifes in the 1880s, probably in response to the successful trompe l'oeil paintings of William Harnett (1848–1892). In the tradition of Harnett's famed painting *After the Hunt*, 1885, Goodwin specialized in cabin-door still lifes featuring spoils of the hunt. Goodwin ultimately made his reputation with a work titled *Theodore Roosevelt's Cabin Door* (Museum of Arts, Springfield, Massachusetts), painted in 1905 and inspired by the display of the original presidential relic at the centennial celebration of the Lewis and Clark expedition in Portland, Oregon. During the last twenty years of his life, the artist moved frequently, residing for a few years at a time in Washington, D.C., Chicago, Colorado Springs, Los Angeles, and Portland.

Still Life with Strawberries features objects that seem far more luxurious and precious than the braces of game populating Goodwin's more familiar hunting pictures. The prominently displayed plate appears to be an example of blue-and-white Chinese export porcelain from the eighteenth century, although the casual treatment of the decoration on the rim suggests that it may be of later Western manufacture. The United States had first begun trading with China in February 1784, when the American clipper *Empress of China* first left New York for Canton. Often used as non-spoiling ballast for more expensive luxury items such as tea and silk, export porcelain nonetheless satisfied the growing American lust for "chinaware." The china trade peaked in the early years of the nineteenth century but continued for several more decades as Americans sought to adorn their homes with a bit of *chinoiserie*.

The desire for *japonica*, however, took hold in this country only after the extensive display of Japanese decorative objects at Philadelphia's Centennial Exposition in 1876. Western manufacturers soon capitalized on the Victorian "Japan craze" and began manufacturing items, such as the sugar bowl depicted in the Goodwin, emulating Japanese decorative motifs. Although these "exports" were clearly mass-produced, they nonetheless satisfied a taste for the beautiful craftsmanship and graceful design associated with pottery of the Far East. Goodwin's still life, like the elegant objects it describes, probably met a similar demand for refined works of art for the home; and much like the Japan-crazed collectors of the era, its owner was assured of being among "the most cultivated, artistic people."[2]

JHR

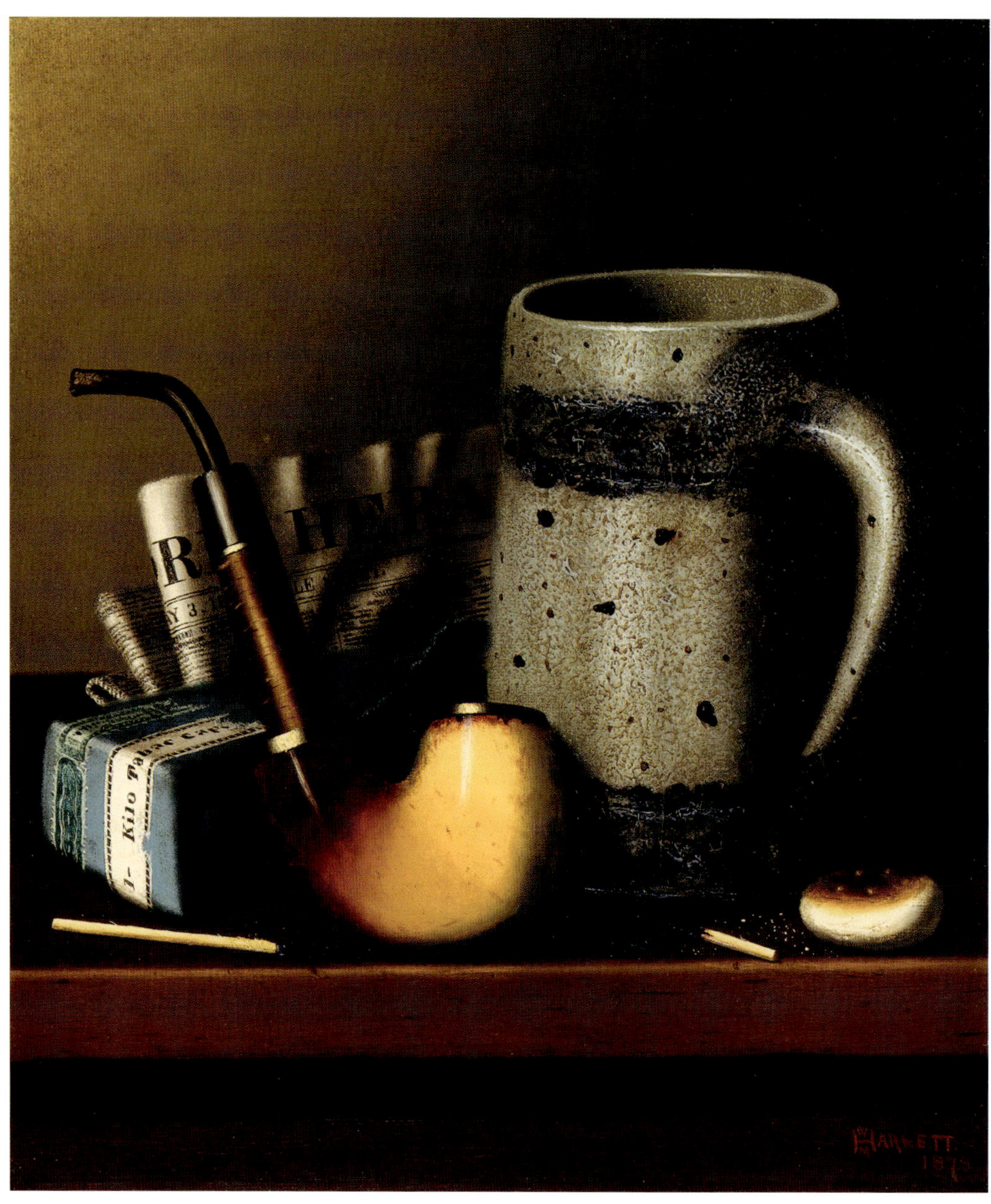

Still Life with Mug, Pipe, Tobacco, and New York Herald,
1878, oil on canvas,
12 1/4 x 10 1/4 inches

William Michael Harnett (1848–1892)

Although his work was largely forgotten after his death and not rediscovered until the 1930s, William Michael Harnett was the undisputed leader of American trompe l'oeil painting in the last quarter of the nineteenth century. Succinctly defined as "illusionism carried beyond convincingness to deception," trompe l'oeil painting was first practiced in this country by Charles Willson Peale (1741–1827) as early as the end of the eighteenth century. The artist's son Raphaelle (1774–1825) continued the tradition into the 1820s, but the practice appears to have largely ceased with his death. While highly prized today and, indeed, widely popular with the general public in its own day, trompe l'oeil painting was in many ways a marginal enterprise whose practitioners were both socially and ideologically outside the artistic mainstream.[1]

Born in Clonakilty, County Cork, Ireland, in 1848, Harnett came to Philadelphia with his family the following year. In an effort to support his mother and siblings after his father's death in the early 1860s, Harnett worked as an engraver of steel, copper, and ultimately silver, acquiring a technical precision that would serve him well in his later meticulously illusionistic work. Harnett began attending classes at the Pennsylvania Academy of the Fine Arts in 1866 and by 1869 had moved to New York to continue his studies at the Cooper Union and the National Academy of Design. By 1875, the budding artist was no longer practicing the engraver's trade and, having opened a studio, was already producing trompe l'oeil pictures. The following year, Harnett moved back to Philadelphia, returned to classes at the Academy, and soon earned a reputation for his remarkable dexterity as a crafter of illusionistic still lifes.[2]

Still Life with Mug, Pipe, Tobacco, and New York Herald is one of many "mug-and-pipe" pictures painted by the artist in Philadelphia in the late 1870s.[3] All are essentially variations on a theme consisting of a simple tabletop and a limited cast of objects: a roughly glazed beer stein with bands of blue at the bottom and below the lip; a folded newspaper with masthead partially revealed; a container of tobacco (often an oblong package with revenue stamps and label reading "I—Kilo Tabac Caporal"); matches, both burnt and unburnt; small, round biscuits; and a pipe, typically a meerschaum.[4] According to Harnett, such objects were the only things he could afford as a young artist: "I could not afford to hire models as the other students did, and I was forced to paint my first picture from still life models. These models were a pipe and a German beer mug."[5] Like the others of its type, the Snowiss still life features noticeably built-up areas of pigment, particularly the match heads and the highlights on the pipe and mug, which stand out in sculpted relief against the otherwise smooth surface of the painting.

In recent years scholars have become increasingly interested in the content of these "bachelor's still lifes," which appear to have been produced for ready sale to prosperous businessmen either for display in offices or in the more private setting of a billiard or smoking room.[6] The objects so exquisitely described in these works are utterly quotidian, the stuff of daily life, and their assembled presence bespeaks a familiar ritual of leisurely edification. By 1880 the circulation of newspapers in the United States had reached more than 3.5 million per day, and their consistent incorporation in Harnett's work suggests a highly literate audience immersed in the country's financial and cultural affairs.[7] The mastheads, however, may also symbolize something far less progressive and even traditional, for in their dated ephemerality they call to mind the transient pleasures of the *vanitas*, or *memento mori* still life—prosaic reminders of the fleeting nature of human existence.[8]

JHR

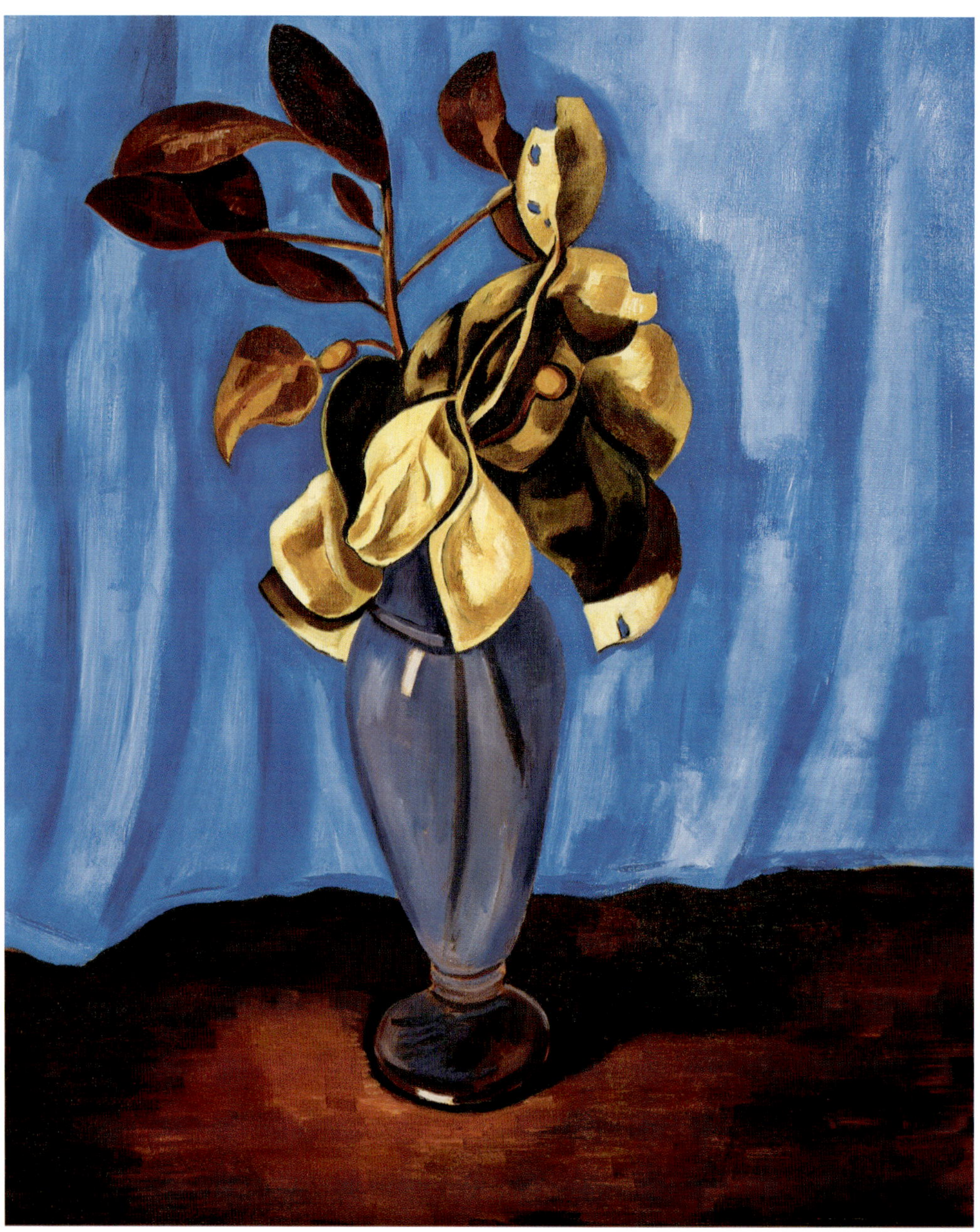

Purple Vase,
c. 1925, oil on canvas,
31 3/4 x 25 inches

Marsden Hartley (1877–1943)

As one of the central players in the circle of artists promoted by Alfred Stieglitz (1864–1946), Marsden Hartley helped to introduce an American audience to recent developments in European modernism through his "cosmic cubist" paintings of the early teens. After several years of aesthetic and personal retrenchment back in the United States in the years prior to and following World War I, Hartley spent much of the 1920s in Europe moving peripatetically, as was his nature, between Paris and Berlin with a lengthy stay in southern France beginning in 1925. An auction of Hartley's works facilitated by Stieglitz at the beginning of the decade had raised sufficient funds to support the artist's habitual wanderlust for a time. In early 1924, Hartley sailed to New York to work out an arrangement with a syndicate of four businessmen who would provide the artist $2,000 a year in exchange for ten paintings for a period of four years. The venture had been suggested to Hartley by William Bullitt (1891–1967), future American ambassador and husband to Louise Bryant (1885–1936), whom the artist had renewed contact with in Paris a year-and-a-half earlier.[1] With the logistics of the syndicate arranged, Hartley returned to Europe and by the summer of 1925 had settled in a small stucco house in Vence, France.

Purple Vase appears to date from about this time, its ambitious size suggesting a period of self-assurance and relative financial ease. The painting shares little in common with the cubist-inspired works from earlier in the decade, nor does it reveal the smaller scale and lightened palette of the still lifes produced a few years later. Indeed, the work represents a remarkable and assured merging of monumentality and elegance and may, in fact, be one of a group of still lifes completed in Vence that Hartley characterized as "at their best."[2]

Hartley's artistic output from the 1920s is dominated by landscape and still life, a seemingly objective interlude in a career otherwise devoted to explorations of personal subjectivity and the imagination. In a famous essay penned in 1928, Hartley commented on his shift away from subjective expressionism. "I am interested then only in the problem of painting, of how to make a better painting according to certain laws that are inherent in the making of a good picture—and not at all in private extraversions .... I would rather be sure that I had placed two colors in true relationship to each other than to have exposed a wealth of emotionalism gone wrong in the name of richness of personal expression."[3] Although the pierced leaves in the Snowiss picture hint at an "unknown symbolism," still life was clearly for Hartley a means of avoiding autobiographical content in a period marked by both personal and aesthetic self-doubt.[4]

The original owner of *Purple Vase* was Adelaide Kuntz, a close personal friend and supporter of Hartley, who first met the artist in Aix-en-Provence in 1927. She and her son, who later inherited the picture, dined with Hartley in New York just weeks before his death.

JHR

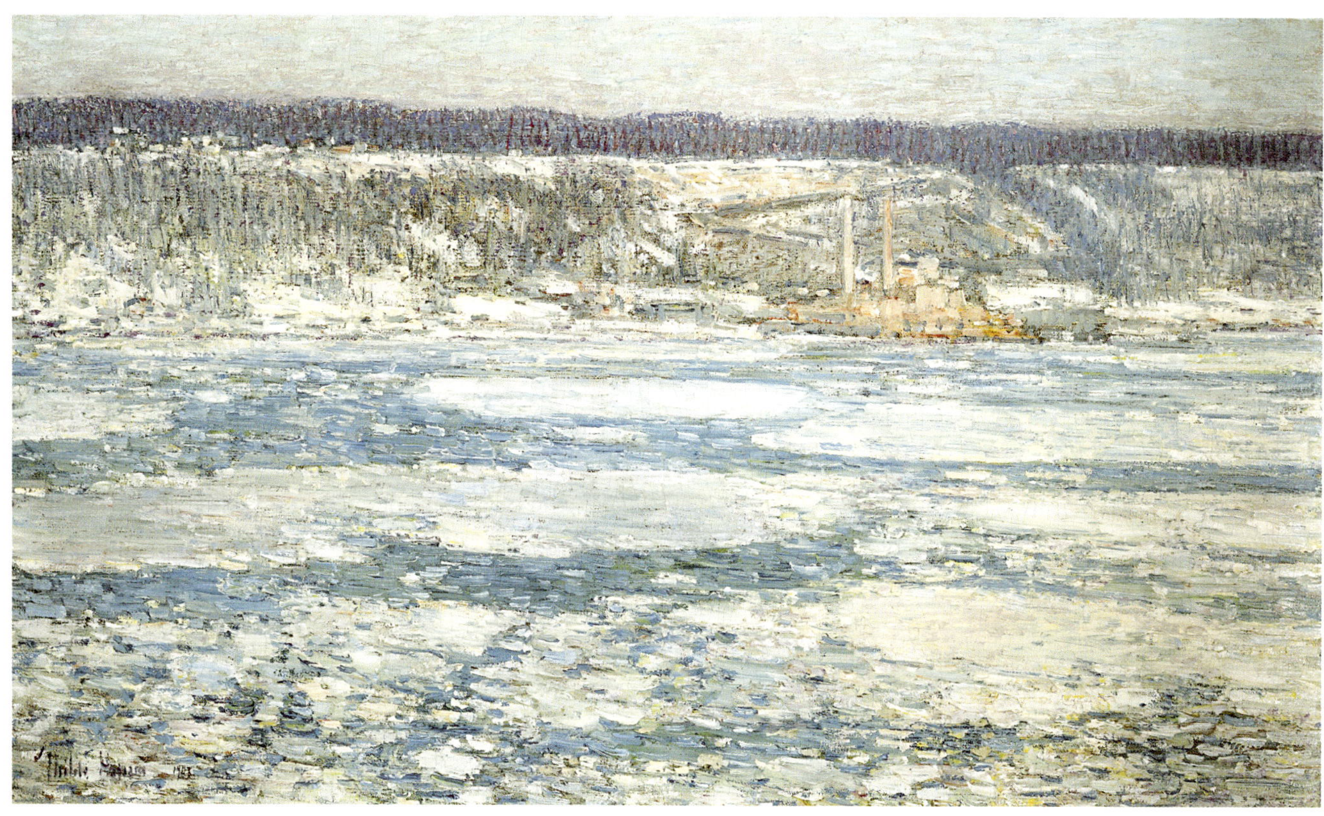

Ice on the Hudson,
1908, oil on canvas,
20 x 33 inches

Childe Hassam (1859–1935)

As one of the foremost American impressionists of his time, Frederick Childe Hassam achieved considerable critical and professional success by the end of the nineteenth century. Born in Dorchester, Massachusetts, a suburb of Boston, he was apprenticed in his late teens to a wood engraver and soon was able to support himself as a free-lance "draughtsman" and illustrator of children's stories. In the early 1880s, Hassam attended art classes and evening lectures at the Lowell Institute as well as the Boston Art Club. Although he had dabbled briefly in oil painting prior to that time, his first solo exhibition in the fall of 1882 featured recent watercolors, many of which were executed *en plein air* the previous summer in Nantucket. The following year Hassam left for Europe, and it was about this time that he dropped the prosaic "Frederick" from his signature, opting for the more romantic and distinctive moniker of "Childe."[1]

A second trip to Europe in 1886, this time with a wife to accompany him, resulted in additional training at the Académie Julian in Paris, where he studied with the French artists Gustave Boulanger (1824–1888) and Jules-Joseph Lefebvre (1836–1911), and exhibited at the Salons of 1887 and 1888. Several paintings by Hassam would also be included in the American section of the Paris Exposition Universelle in 1889, the year he returned to the United States to pursue his profession. Settling in New York City, the logical choice for an ambitious young artist, Hassam soon forged a career built around images of bustling cityscapes and picturesque New England settings, all rendered in a conservative, yet highly appealing impressionist style. During the ensuing decades, Hassam was an active member of such professional organizations as the Society of American Artists, the American Watercolor Society, and the New York Watercolor Club, and in late 1897 participated in the formation of the secessionist group known as The Ten American Painters, or The Ten. Despite this moment of apparent rebellion, Hassam was elected a full academician at the National Academy of Design in 1906, a testament to the institutional approbation of American impressionist painting by this date.

Ice on the Hudson was painted toward the end of a decade of prosperity and professional successes for Hassam, who continued his practice of wintering in the city and spending the rest of the year in various New England haunts until his move to East Hampton in 1919. By 1908, Hassam's interest in depicting urban genre scenes had abated somewhat, and a literal distance from the city—both in terms of a higher vantage point and selection of subjects from outlying areas—is evident in many of the canvases from this period.[2] In *Ice on the Hudson*, which was presumably painted during the winter months, Hassam stretches the definition of "picturesque" subject matter to include an industrial site viewed across the river along the Palisades in New Jersey. As in much of Hassam's work after the turn of the century, the two-dimensional surface of the painting is emphatically reiterated, here through the decorative bands of the composition and the encrusted tesserae-like brushstrokes particularly evident in the immediate foreground. In *Ice on the Hudson*, industry and nature coexist peacefully, united by a tapestry of snow and the subtle palette of a winter day.

JHR

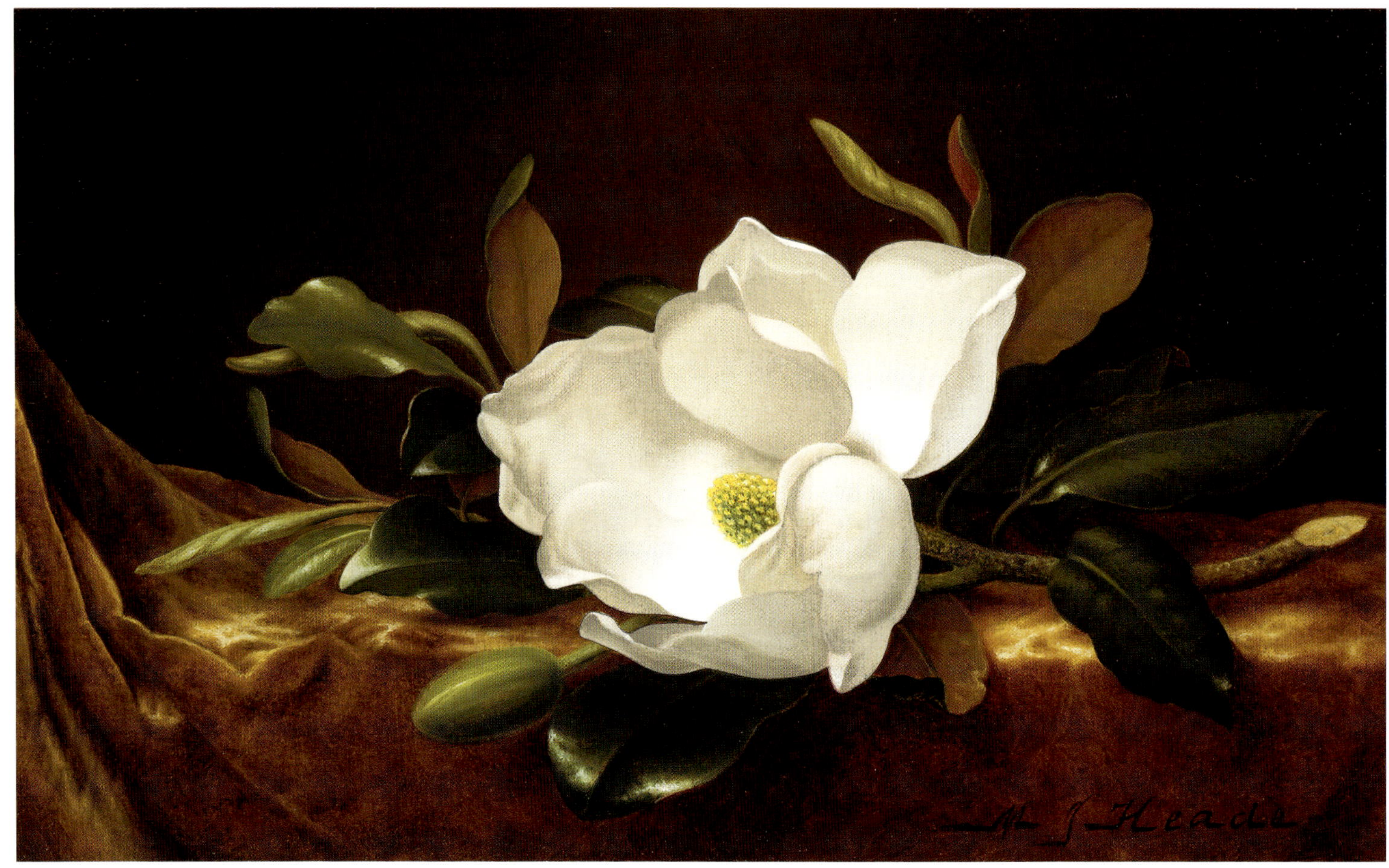

Magnolia Grandiflora on a Brown Velvet Cloth,
c. 1885–1895, oil on canvas,
13 3/4 x 21 1/2 inches

Martin Johnson Heade (1819–1904)

Born in Bucks County, Pennsylvania, Martin Johnson Heade spent much of his long and peripatetic life traveling around the globe searching for inspirational artistic motifs. After having trained for a brief time with local artist Edward Hicks (1780–1849), Heade went abroad to continue his studies and thereafter commenced an itinerant career as a portrait painter that led him from Philadelphia and New York to St. Louis and Chicago through the 1850s. By 1859, the artist had taken up residence in the recently constructed Tenth Street Studio Building in New York, and in the company of leading Hudson River School artists like Frederic Edwin Church (1826–1900) and Sanford Robinson Gifford (1823–1880), began to devote his artistic energies to landscape painting. As would be true throughout much of his career, Heade adapted the prevalent style of the day to his own personal vision, producing the luminous salt marsh and coastal paintings for which he is well known today.[1]

Although highly accomplished as a landscape painter, Heade was equally adept at the art of still life and began working seriously in the genre in the 1860s. Among Heade's most beloved still lifes are the magnolia paintings done after his move to St. Augustine, Florida, in 1883. Newly married that year, the 64-year-old artist settled happily in this southern resort town and as an avid naturalist delighted in the exotic flora of his new surroundings. *Magnolia Grandiflora on a Brown Velvet Cloth* is one of a dozen or so horizontally formatted depictions of the lush flower "reclining" on luxurious supports of blue, red, or brown velvet.[2] John Baur famously described the magnificent blossoms "startlingly arrayed on sumptuous red velvet like odalisques on a couch," and, indeed, as William Gerdts has noted, there is in these pictures an "erotic and exotic parallel" to the reclining nude of the Western tradition.[3]

Six of the known magnolia still lifes, including the Snowiss picture and those in the collections of the Museum of Fine Arts, Boston, and the Museum of Fine Arts, Houston, feature the same left-facing blossom,[4] all presumably based on a single sketch made directly from nature.[5] In contrast to the painterly strokes of the brown velvet support, the white blossoms and shiny green leaves are rendered in a meticulous illusionistic style that by the late 1880s was certainly outmoded. Never critically celebrated in his day, the magnolia pieces are nonetheless among the crowning achievements of Heade's career and nineteenth-century American still-life painting.

JHR

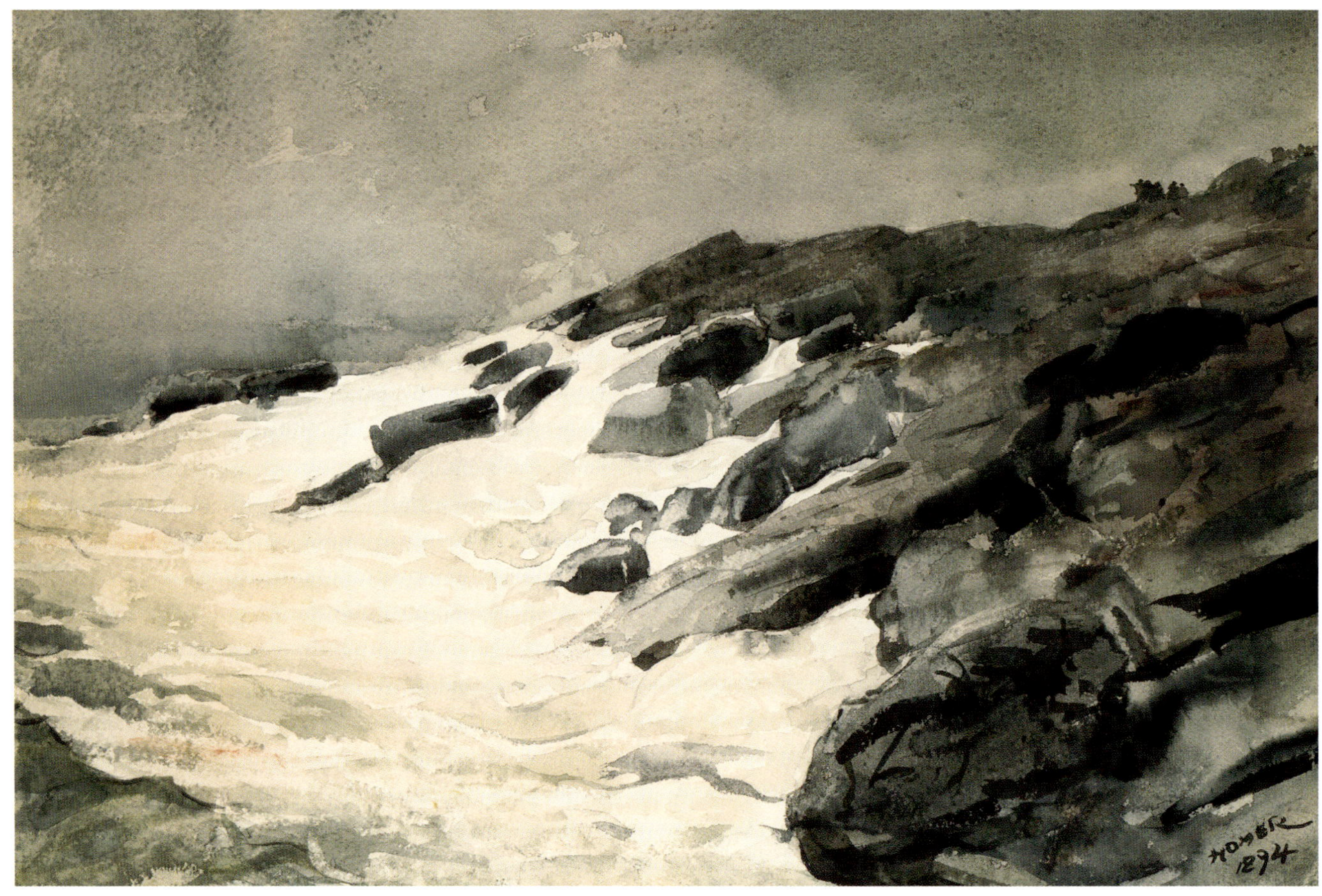

Sea and Rocks During a Storm,
1894, watercolor on paper,
14 1/2 x 21 1/4 inches

Winslow Homer (1836–1910)

The rugged peninsula of Prout's Neck, Maine, located a short distance from Portland, became Winslow Homer's permanent residence in the mid-1880s and served as an endless source of inspiration for his mature oil paintings and watercolors. Homer's relatives first vacationed at Prout's Neck, a sparsely populated region occasionally visited by summertime tourists, in 1875. By 1883, family members had constructed two homes on land overlooking the ocean. Homer moved to Prout's Neck from New York City later that year, just months after returning from a two-year sojourn in northern England, where he experimented with his ever-evolving watercolor technique.[1] While the rest of his relatives departed the area for warmer climes as summer gave way to autumn, Homer remained behind, converting a carriage house on the family property into his permanent residence and studio.[2]

The artist's powerful renderings of the Maine coastline evolved from his careful study of the region's ever-changing weather conditions. *Sea and Rocks During a Storm* captures the cold, unpredictable character of High Cliff, an intimidating outcropping of rock at Prout's Neck.[3] Aggressive yet thoughtfully placed brushstrokes define the rocks and suggest a foamy sea in retreat after assaulting the shore. The scene is evidence of Homer's ability to evoke tactile, olfactory, and auditory senses along with that of sight, confirming Lloyd Goodrich's observation that "he makes us feel the sheer physical force of the wave, the solidity of the rock, the shock of their collision. We seem to smell the salt and hear the roar of the breakers; we know the dread of fog and gale, and the vast loneliness of the ocean."[4]

Homer regularly included a human presence in his paintings. Many works feature men who hunt, fish, and log; monumental women loom large, wielding heavy baskets and fishing nets. This example, however, acknowledges nature's ability to supplant mankind's drive to control earth and sea. An oppressive range of gray tones in the upper right-hand corner of the painting traps a group of figures between heavy sky and battered granite. They huddle together against the wrath of the storm at a seemingly safe distance from the churning water. Although one of the figures motions toward the Atlantic, the gesture seems impotent in comparison to the power of the brooding ocean and darkened sky. In *Sea and Rocks During a Storm*, Homer pays homage to the fierce and unpredictable environment that both intrigued and inspired him for more than twenty-five years.

JD

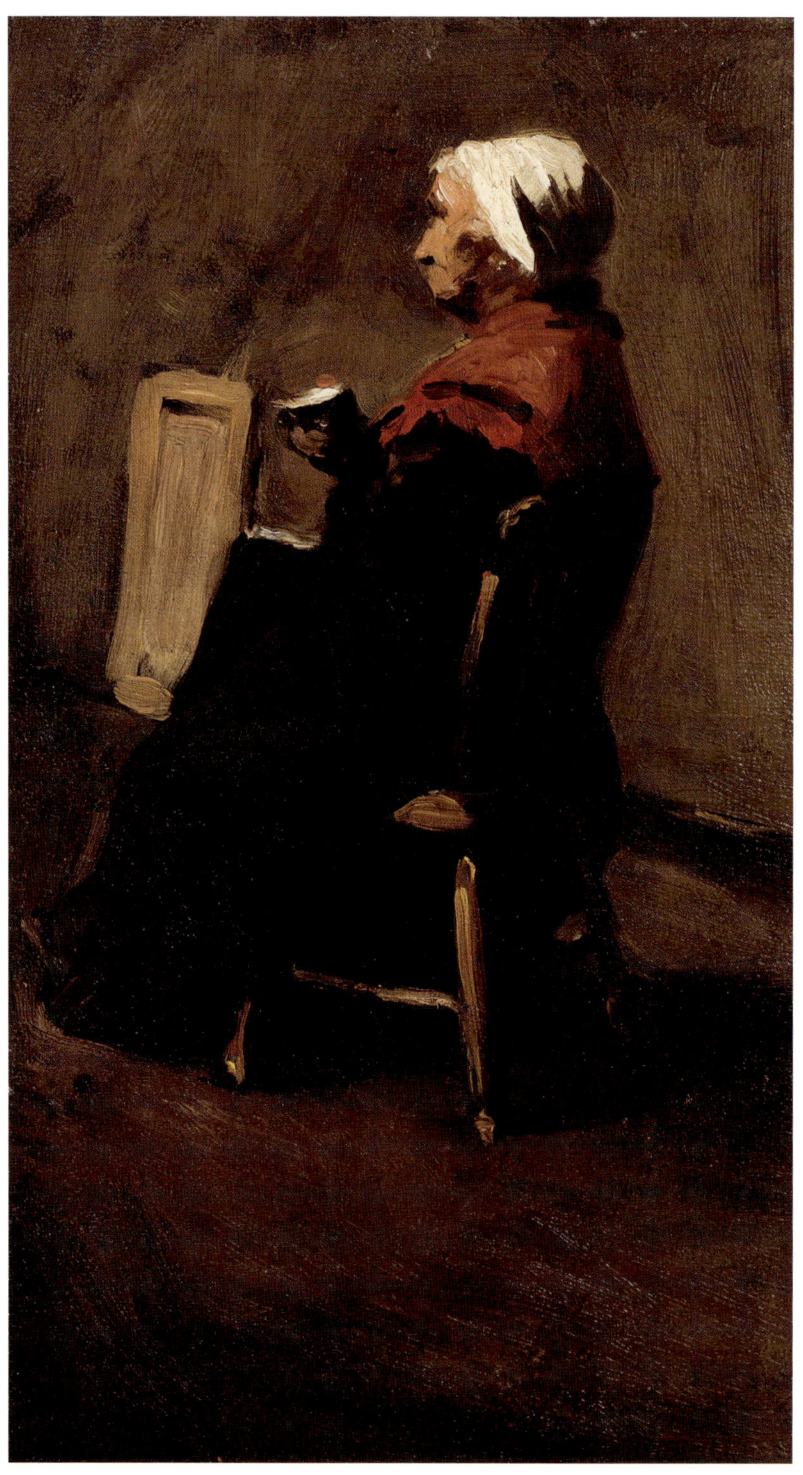

Old Lady on a Chair,
c. 1901, oil on canvas,
18 x 10 inches

Edward Hopper (1882–1967)

Edward Hopper continues to enjoy a reputation as one of America's preeminent painters of the twentieth century. Best known for his stark renderings of silent storefronts and under-populated urban interiors, Hopper captured the bland ordinariness of modern American life in a laconic realist style as sparse as the content of his paintings.

Hopper was born in the small Hudson River town of Nyack, New York, and grew up there in a middle-class family headed by the proprietor of a dry goods store. As a child, Hopper demonstrated a notable interest in drawing and, in 1899, after graduating from high school, entered the Correspondence School of Illustration in New York. The following year he continued to study illustration at the New York School of Art, commonly known as the "Chase School," so dubbed because of its illustrious founder, William Merritt Chase (1849–1916). Beginning in 1901, Hopper enrolled in painting classes and for the next five years pursued his studies under the tutelage of Chase, Robert Henri (1865–1929), and Kenneth Hayes Miller (1876–1952). After several extended trips to Europe, Hopper settled in New York and began a career as a commercial artist and illustrator in 1910. By 1924 at the age of 42, Hopper was able to quit his commercial work and pursue a career as a full-time artist, thanks largely to the critical and financial success of his etchings of modern urban life and a series of lyrical watercolors produced in Gloucester, Massachusetts. Although watercolor would continue to figure prominently in his work until the mid-1940s, much of Hopper's professional career would be devoted to the penetrating depictions of anonymous yet familiar scenes of American life, primarily in oil, for which he is best known.[1]

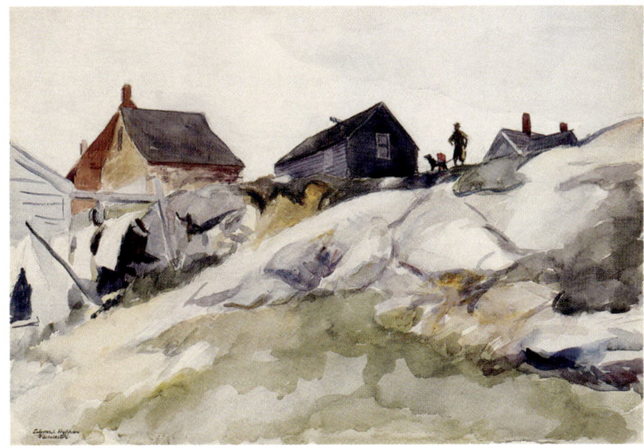

Old Lady on a Chair is an early oil by the artist dating from Hopper's student days at the Chase School.[2] Signed on the verso, this small study was most likely produced in an illustration class before Hopper switched to painting classes with Chase in the fall of 1901.[3] Its dark tonalities and broadly laid on brushstrokes may bespeak the influence of the school's founder and anticipate the gritty realist canvases of his other important mentor, Henri. While *Old Lady on a Chair* is clearly a straightforward character study typical of training in the academy, it is nonetheless tempting to read into its portrayal of a solitary, self-absorbed figure a portent of the anonymous denizens occupying the stark theatres of his later canvases. Hopper himself once observed that "the germ of the later work is always found in the earlier."[4]

JHR

Rocks at the Fort, Gloucester,
1924, watercolor, 14 x 20 inches

Palmer Museum of Art, Gift of Alvin and Jean Snowiss, 94.20.

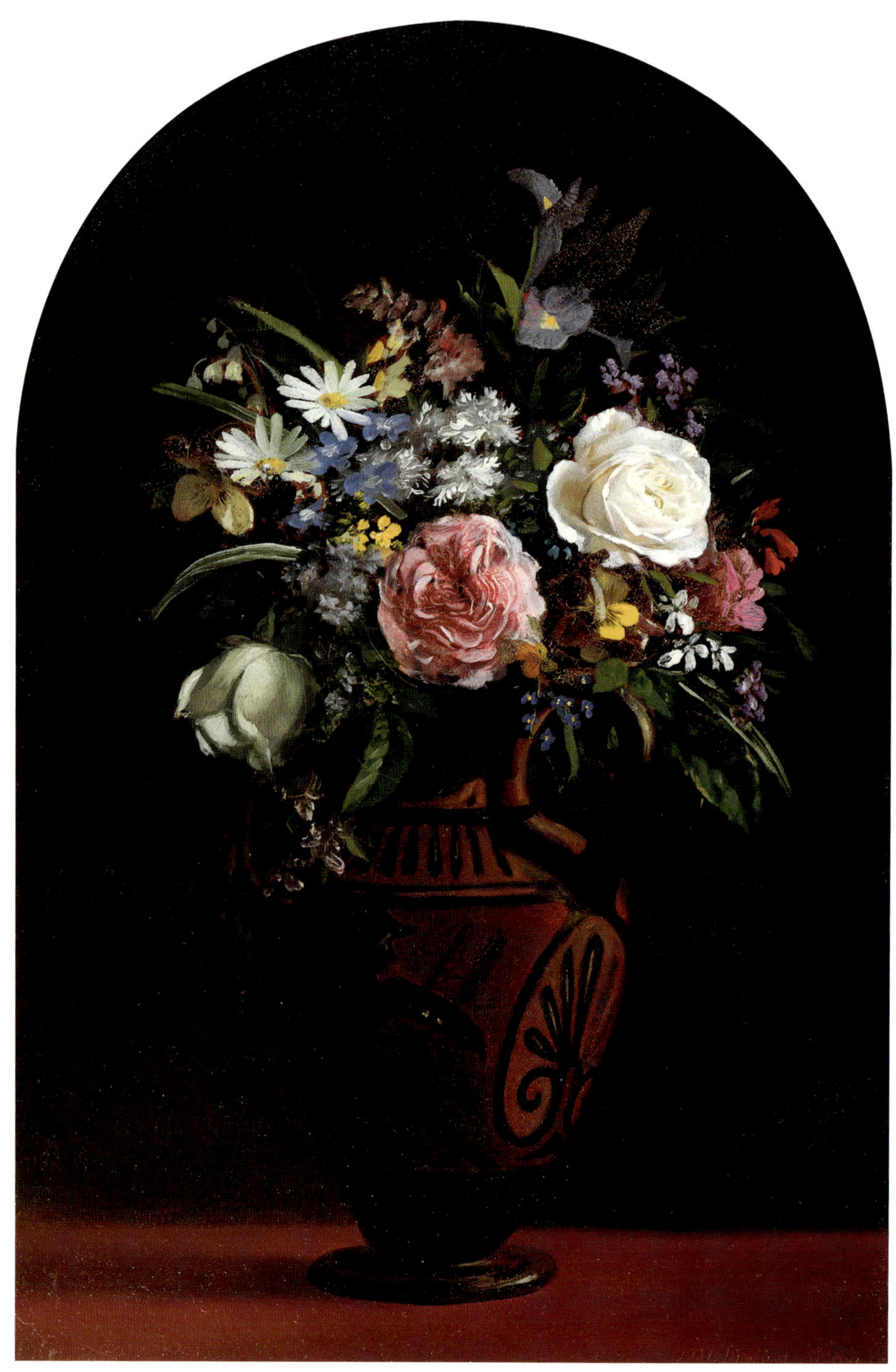

Flowers in a Vase,
1869, oil on panel,
17 1/4 x 11 inches

John O'Brien Inman (1828–1896)

John O'Brien Inman was the son of Henry Inman (1801–1846), an esteemed portrait painter and founding member of the National Academy of Design. Having trained as a young man with his father, Inman began his career painting portraits and miniatures in his studio on Broadway in New York City. During these early years, Inman also worked as an itinerant portrait painter, traveling primarily through the southern and western United States. Between 1855 and 1865, Inman worked periodically in New York, producing diminutive genre pictures, floral still lifes, and landscapes painted in the Adirondack Mountains. In 1853, Inman began exhibiting occasionally at the National Academy and was elected an associate member in 1865. The following year the artist moved to Europe, where he spent the next twelve years operating mostly in Paris and Rome. Although he did travel abroad again in the 1880s, Inman spent the final years of his life in New York State.[1]

Inman's floral still lifes have been characterized as "rather lush and Victorian," and undoubtedly *Flowers in a Vase* would have made a beautiful addition to any well-appointed nineteenth-century home.[2] With its emphasis on man-made objects as well as the products of nature, this painting qualifies as a modest "bric-a-brac" still life, a genre, which in its extreme manifestations, is a visual ode to collecting and ownership.[3] The "black-figure" amphora, a decorative homage to a ubiquitous neoclassical taste throughout much of the nineteenth century, serves a decidedly modern function in its housing of a resplendent summer bouquet of roses, daisies, and irises. Although *Flowers in a Vase* may have been painted on the Continent, its classicizing content undoubtedly appealed to a rising middle-class American audience eager to display its economic successes and growing cultural sophistication in the post-Civil War era.

JHR

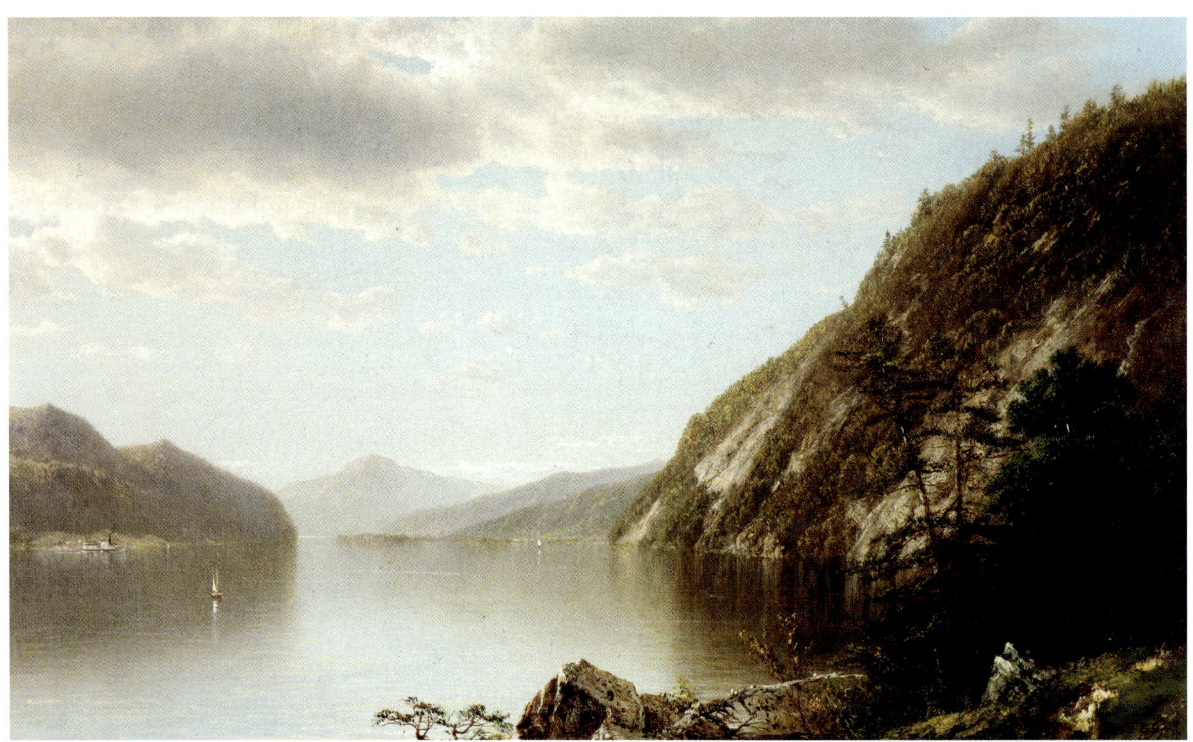

Rogers Slide,
Lake George, New York,
1870, oil on canvas,
13 1/2 x 21 3/8 inches

David Johnson (1827–1908)

Despite a long, productive, and varied career, "many small mysteries" surround the figure of David Johnson.[1] Details of Johnson's training are sketchy, and traditionally he has been characterized as largely self-taught. The artist, however, did study briefly with the landscape painter Jasper F. Cropsey (1823–1900) and appears to have been enrolled in the Antique School of the National Academy of Design for two years in the mid-1840s.[2] Residing in New York City for much of his life, Johnson was an active and prominent member of the Academy, having been elected to its ranks in 1861. His participation in the 1876 Centennial Exposition in Philadelphia and the Paris Salon the following year attests to his professional success. While Johnson has variously been characterized as a second-generation Hudson River School artist, a luminist, and a proto-Barbizon painter, what remains constant throughout his career of shifting aesthetic allegiances is an "acute attention" to the details of the natural world.[3]

Johnson's keen powers of observation are amply evident in *Rogers Slide, Lake George, New York*, a work painted in 1870 and signed with the artist's distinguishing monogram of interlaced initials. The painting is one of several works by Johnson featuring scenic Lake George, once a remote wilderness area near the Adirondack Mountains that by the mid-nineteenth century had become a picturesque destination for tourists and artists alike. As Gwendolyn Owens has noted, Johnson's paintings of the once unspoiled spot incorporate views from the many grand hotels dotting the lake's periphery at points of interest like Rogers Slide. Located south of Ticonderoga, the massive granite slide derives its name from the intrepid explorer Robert Rogers, who purportedly once evaded pursuing Native Americans by maneuvering its steep slope on snowshoes.[4] Clearly delighting in the sheer beauty of this natural wonder, Johnson nonetheless signals the site's transformation from wilderness to vacation spot by the inclusion of sailboats gliding gently across the lake's diaphanous surface. In the middle distance a steamship puffs merrily along, no doubt transporting pleasure seekers in search of respite from the city to this remote resort.[5]

In *Rogers Slide, Lake George, New York*, Johnson makes use of a favored compositional format in which a gently mountainous landscape and rocky shoreline enframe a wide expanse of resplendent water. The painting also reveals the artist's use of a varied technique, noticeably evident in the contrast between the lake's smooth and thinly painted surface and the broader, more viscous brushwork in the immediate foreground. As Owens has noted of similar Lake George paintings by Johnson, "the primary focus here is clearly on the luminous lake surface in the middle ground, which seems to open a transparent window on the world." That densely painted shoreline, she observes, offers the viewer his only resting place before his eye embarks on a "groundless voyage of reflection on the waters beyond."[6]

JHR

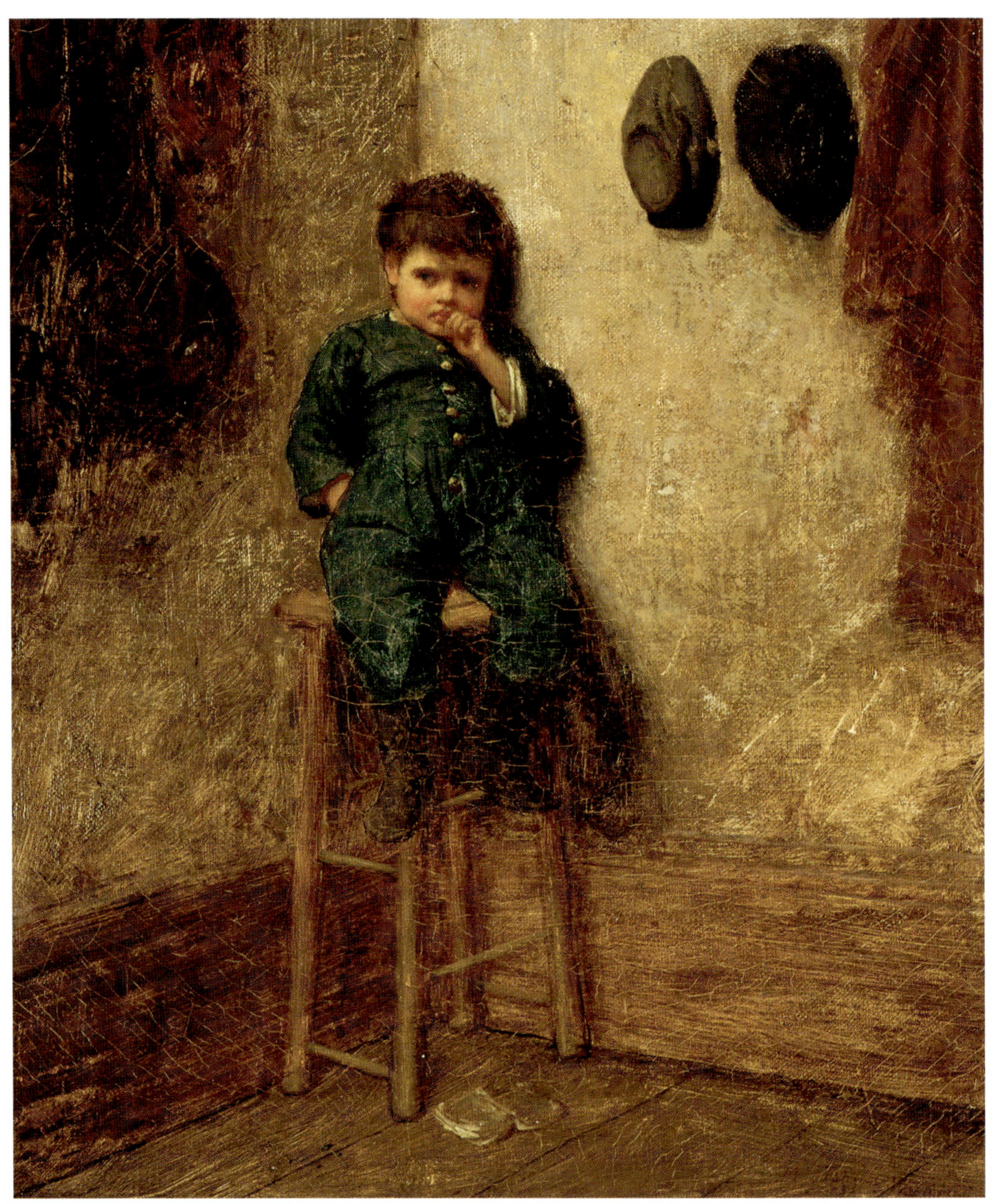

Little Boy on a Stool,
1860, oil on canvas,
12 x 10 inches

Eastman Johnson (1824–1906)

Waiting, leaning, sulking, pouting, crouching, and writing—playing musical instruments, warming their hands, and coyishly smiling—children assume a variety of colorfully charged moods and gestures in the work of the American genre and portrait painter Eastman Johnson. His images of youthful sitters tend to be either sentimentally exaggerated or psychologically intense. The child depicted in *Little Boy on a Stool*, however, straddles this fault-line. Wistful yet winsome, Johnson's protagonist appeals to seemingly opposing sensibilities. With the puffy cheeks, short stubby legs, and warm green coloration of his clothing, the figure appeals to our senses of sight and touch. Placed in a corner as if hiding or perhaps being punished, garbed in a confining outfit and averting the artist's gaze, the boy also appears, in effect, out of reach. At once posed and psychologically detached, the figure hovers between inward "absorption" and outward "theatricality."[1]

The little boy sits on a stool and leans against the walls in the corner of a typical mid-nineteenth-century architectural interior. He positions one hand in his pocket and the other at his mouth, as if wiping his lips or chewing on a fingernail. Flanked by hats and other articles, the child fixes his deeply inset eyes on a distant, unknown site. With the opened book below him—the placement of which suggests that it just fell from his hands—the subject appears lost in thought, oblivious to the presence of artist and audience alike. Earlier painters had certainly depicted discontent and mischievous children, but Johnson's suggestion of not only restlessness but also ennui is rare for the period. Suggestions of brooding psychological interiority were common in post-Civil War American art depicting children, but such license was unusual, if not daring, in 1860, when Johnson painted *Little Boy on a Stool*.[2]

In this same year, Johnson was riding the crest of popular and critical acclaim and was elected to full membership at the National Academy of Design in New York. Newly elected academicians were required to present a self-portrait upon their election into the prestigious institution, but Johnson also contributed the painting *Negro Boy* (1860, National Academy of Design), depicting a child seated inside a stoop, absorbed in the act of playing a fife.[3] Both *Negro Boy* and *Little Boy on a Stool* demonstrate the manner in which the artist sidestepped conventional attributes of race and childhood, effectively declaring his interest in investing his subjects with an underlying realism. In these paintings from the early 1860s, Johnson anticipates the probing and intensity of artists of the following decades, including Thomas Eakins (1844–1916) and Winslow Homer (1836–1910).

Particularly modern is Johnson's keen understanding of the relationship between the figure and the space it inhabits. The artist has positioned the child precisely at the meeting of the two walls. Enlisting architecture as an agent in suggesting the child's subjectivity, Johnson foreshadows late nineteenth- and early twentieth-century art historians and critics who emphasized bodily metaphors projected by the built environment.[4] Within the space of one square foot, *Little Boy on a Stool* evokes a wealth of mental activity and bridges the gap between a corner of a room and the corners of our imagination.

LGM

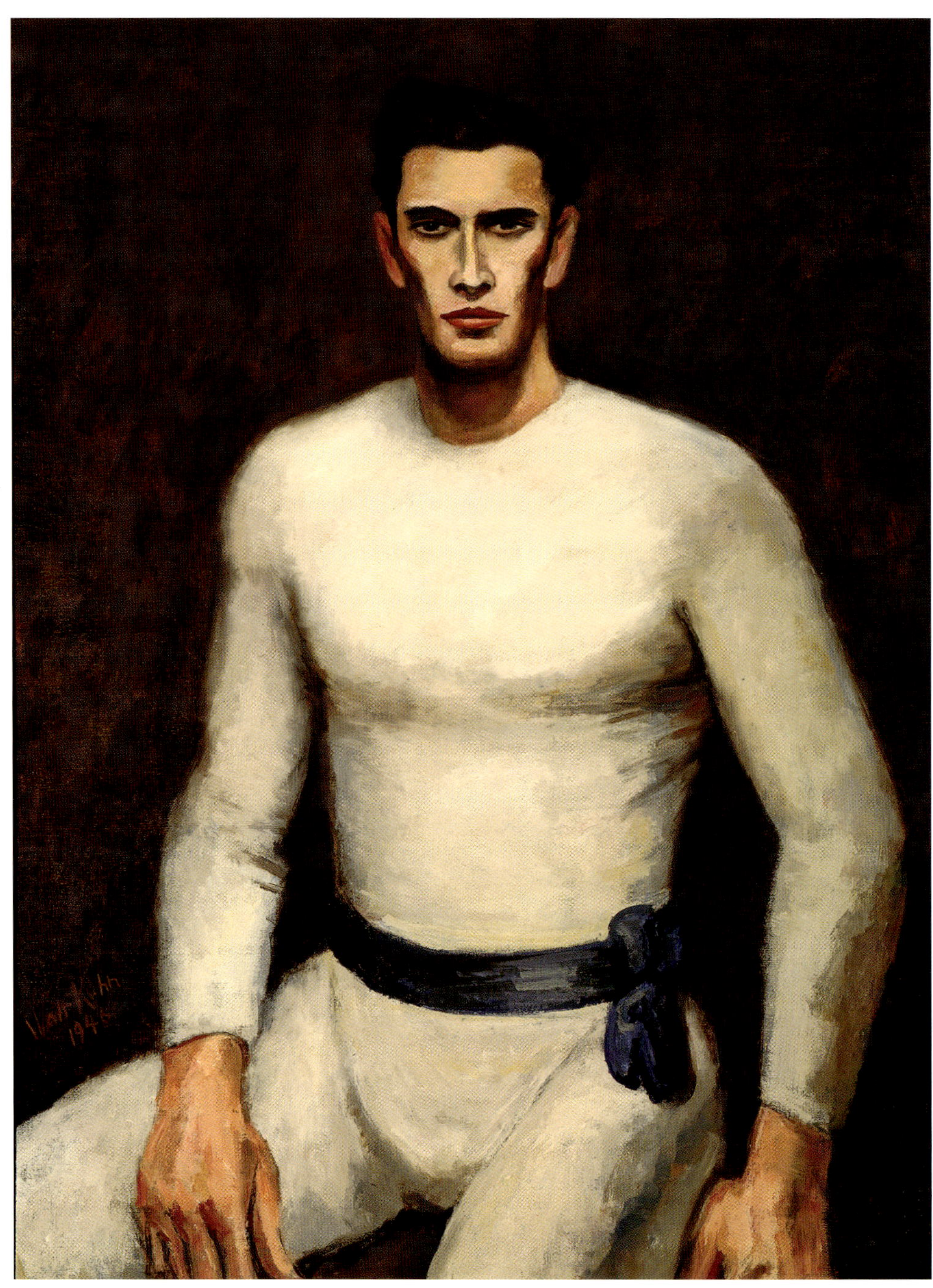

Rider with Blue Sash,
1946, oil on canvas,
40 x 30 inches

Walt Kuhn (1877–1949)

Walt Kuhn was the son of Bavarian immigrants who owned the International Hotel in Brooklyn, New York. By the age of 8, he was illustrating the colorful tales told to him by the sailors who frequented the establishment. At 15, he sold a drawing to *Truth* magazine, which became the first of many illustrations Kuhn marketed to the popular press.[1] A lifelong interest in the theatre, first cultivated by his mother when Kuhn was a young child, was rekindled when he was hired as a clerk for a sporting goods store. His duties included the delivery of rented costumes to local acting troupes. A subsequent stint as a bicycle shop owner and professional racer afforded him the opportunity to spend time backstage at the county fair sideshows that sponsored racing events.[2]

Beginning in 1898, Kuhn paid increasing attention to his latent artistic interests and attended an evening life drawing class in New York City. He moved to California in 1899, where he sold numerous illustrations to the *Wasp*, a popular weekly journal.[3] In 1901, Kuhn departed for Europe and studied at the Académie Colarossi in Paris and later at the Royal Academy in Munich. After returning to New York in 1905, he relied on his talent as an illustrator for income, contributing works to such periodicals as *Puck, Judge,* and *Life*. Kuhn's desire to establish a painting career took hold just as the Association of American Painters and Sculptors, headed by Arthur B. Davies (1862–1928), was formed. Kuhn served as executive secretary, playing a pivotal role when the association organized the Armory Show in 1913.

Although Kuhn established his reputation as a painter soon after the Armory Show, the highly particular artist, known to rework a canvas numerous times and destroy any work that failed to meet his stringent expectations, spent extended periods of time without significant income.[4] In order to support his family during these creative spells, he was once again drawn into the world of show business. He designed sets for musical revues and directed vaudeville and pantomime acts during the months he was not painting. In addition, the Union Pacific Railroad hired Kuhn to design the interior of their club cars, which he decorated with various show business accoutrements.[5]

Kuhn painted critically successful still-life compositions and landscapes throughout his career, but collectors and critics alike have consistently gravitated to his unforgiving depictions of circus performers, which, as *Newsweek* noted in 1941, were executed in a manner unique to the artist: "Unlike Watteau, Degas, and Toulouse-Lautrec, three of the many French artists who have been fascinated by theatrical folk, Kuhn doesn't paint performers at their glamorous best .... Instead, he likes to catch them off guard back stage."[6] Kuhn's solitary figures sport brightly colored costumes, which nonetheless fail to mask faces at once psychologically intense and emotionally detached. The subject of *Rider with Blue Sash* stares out from the canvas, his penetrating gaze emphasized by the shadows defining his taut jaw line and upper eyelids.[7] Kuhn executed the painting during a "creative storm" of activity that took place in 1946, a mere three years before the artist's precipitous slide into the depths of mental illness and death while confined to a sanitarium.[8]

JD

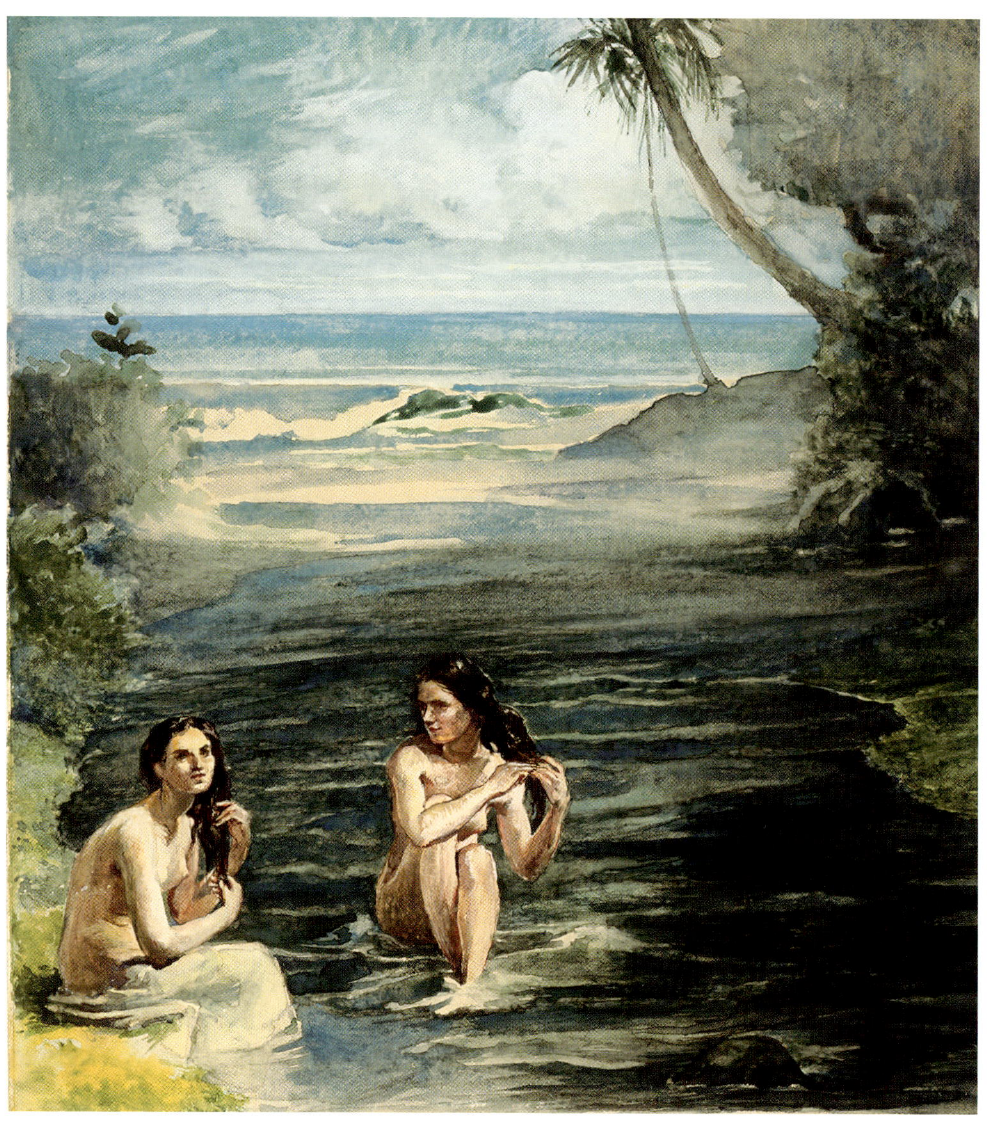

Women Bathing in Papara River,
1891, watercolor on paper,
16 3/4 x 14 1/2 inches

John La Farge (1835–1910)

Born in New York City to wealthy French immigrant parents, John La Farge was destined to lead a cosmopolitan life filled with the pursuit of cultural refinement and aesthetic beauty. His childhood lessons in drawing and watercolor came at the hands of his maternal grandfather and an unidentified English artist, and he was fortunate to be raised in the cultivated environs of a home boasting paintings by well-known European artists. Although he practiced law after finishing college, an extended trip to Europe in 1856 no doubt encouraged the budding artist to consider an alternative profession. During his time in Paris, La Farge moved in important literary and artistic circles and studied briefly with Thomas Couture (1815–1879).

After returning to New York in 1857, he continued to practice law but also took a studio in the recently constructed Tenth Street Studio Building designed by Richard Morris Hunt (1828–1895). At Hunt's urging, La Farge turned his attention fully to his artistic pursuits two years later and moved to Newport, Rhode Island, to study with the architect's brother, the painter William Morris Hunt (1824–1879). La Farge devoted the next several years to the study of landscape and still-life painting and was elected a full academician at the National Academy of Design in 1869. In 1876, the architect Henry Hobson Richardson (1838–1886) invited the artist to participate in the decoration of the interior of Trinity Church in Boston, and from that date on, La Farge would expend a great deal of energy on the creation of murals and stained glass for churches, public buildings, and private homes.

One scholar has noted that watercolor was the "first medium of [La Farge]'s youth and the favored medium of his old age."[1] An active exhibiting member of the American Society of Painters in Water Colors, La Farge used the medium for illustration, as well as in the preparatory process of much of his design work. The artist also clearly valued watercolor as a medium in its own right, and he devoted much of his late career to the production of large works suitable for exhibition. The portability of watercolor made it a favored medium for travel and enabled La Farge to produce works such as *Women Bathing in Papara River* during his extended sojourn to the Pacific in the early 1890s.

Along with his friend the historian Henry Adams (1838–1918), La Farge left for the South Seas during the summer of 1890 for a "year of recreation and idleness."[2] After visiting the Hawaiian and Samoan Islands, the two arrived in Papeete, the capital of Tahiti, in early 1891. Thanks to intrepid explorers like Louis Antoine de Bougainville (1729–1811) and Captain James Cook (1728–1779), Tahiti had long fascinated Westerners as an exotic Garden of Eden inhabited by a noble, yet primitive people.[3] Even by the end of the nineteenth century, relatively few Americans had ventured to the Tahitian Islands, and French artist Paul Gauguin (1848–1903) would not arrive there until days after La Farge's departure in early June. Disappointed by the colonial atmosphere of Papeete, Adams and La Farge traveled further down the coast to Papara, where they were housed by a native royal family.

Women Bathing in Papara River appears to have been painted during this visit and, with its fluid washes of evanescent color, is somewhat less finished than similar Tahitian works executed after the artist's return home. The image, which later served as an illustration in the artist's article "Passages from a Diary in the Pacific," published in *Scribner's*, features two statuesque light-skinned women bathing at the mouth of the Papara River where it met the ocean through a gap in the reef.[4] Like his written memoirs, La Farge's visual accounts of his Tahitian trip are filtered through a classical lens, and both make references to a lost mythical paradise extolled by artists and writers in the West. La Farge's luminous evocations of Tahiti, exhibited as part of the artist's *Records of Travel* in Boston, New York, and Paris in 1895, found ready buyers among American patricians whose Gilded Age lives, tarnished by the demands of modern civilization, were undoubtedly made better through such aesthetic visions of a distant and exotic golden age.[5]

JHR

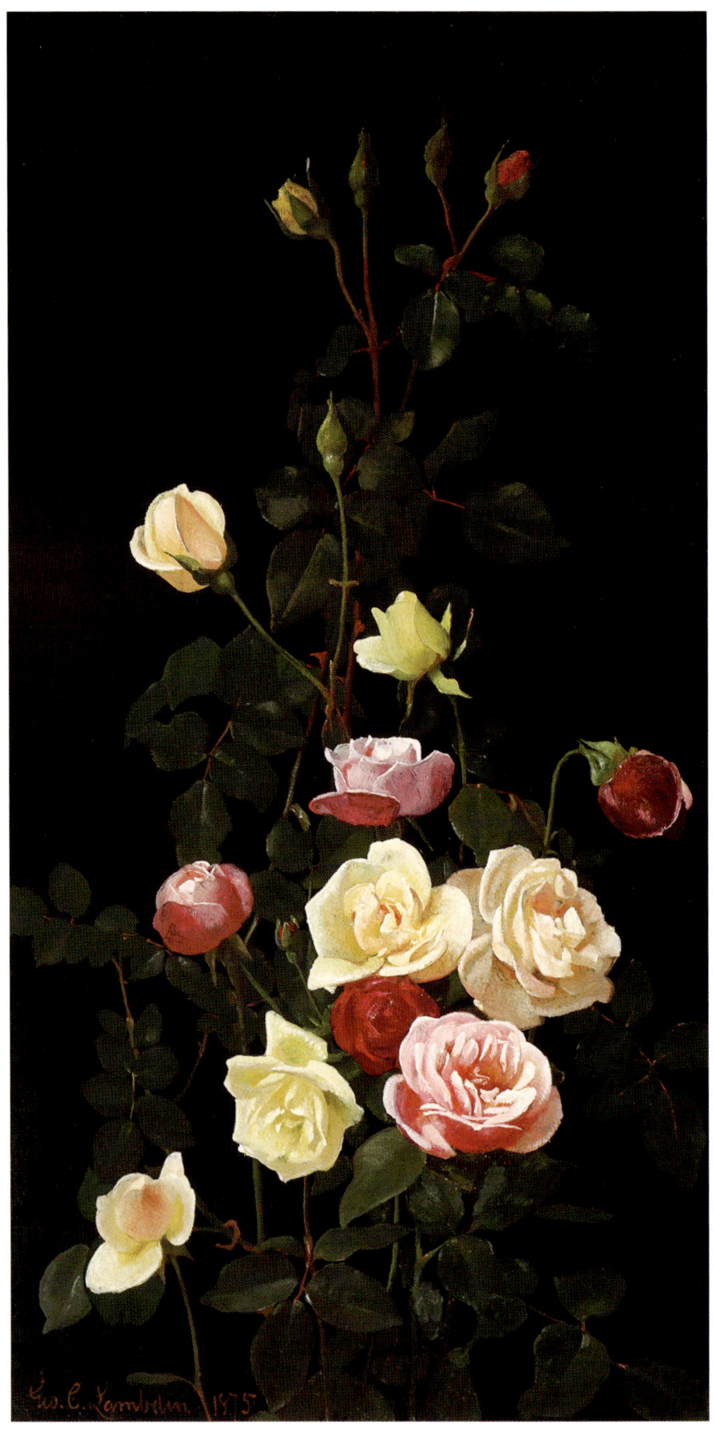

Still Life with Yellow and Pink Roses, 1875, oil on panel, 24 x 12 inches

George Cochran Lambdin (1830–1896)

As one of the founding members of the Germantown Horticultural Society, George Cochran Lambdin understood well the fragile splendor of flowers and devoted a significant part of his artistic career to capturing their evanescent beauty. Lambdin was born in Pittsburgh into an artistic family headed by the well-known portraitist James Reid Lambdin (1807–1889), who moved his wife and children to Philadelphia in 1837. After initial training by his father, the young artist spent two years studying painting in Munich and Paris in the mid-1850s. Except for a brief period in 1868–1870 in New York, Lambdin spent the remainder of his career in Philadelphia.[1]

Having established his reputation early on with sentimental pictures of children and Civil War soldiers, Lambdin began concentrating on flower paintings by the early 1870s and apparently met with immediate success. The artist was a frequent participant in the annual exhibitions of the Pennsylvania Academy of the Fine Arts, and inexpensive chromolithographs of "Lambdin's roses" were widely distributed by the Boston firm of Louis Prang, furthering the artist's reputation and popularity. An avid gardener himself, Lambdin resided in the Germantown section of Philadelphia, an area of the city noted at the time for its horticultural activity and, in particular, for nurseries devoted to the cultivation of new roses.[2] "There is probably no inanimate object in the world more beautiful than a delicately tinted Rose," the artist once wrote. "There is certainly nothing else which combines such beauty of form and color with such exquisite delicacy of texture and such delicious perfume."[3]

Lambdin's floral paintings fall into several distinct categories: the traditional tabletop still life; flowers growing in a natural or a greenhouse setting; and the more decorative arrangement, evident here, of flowers set against a dark background.[4] Many of these were prepared with black lacquer, and the enamel-like surface of these pieces creates a striking backdrop for the subtle, yet exquisite coloration of the roses.[5] Shown in virtually every stage of their life cycle—from bud through full bloom—the roses are described with the most delicate of painterly touches seemingly as fragile and lush as the flowers themselves.

JHR

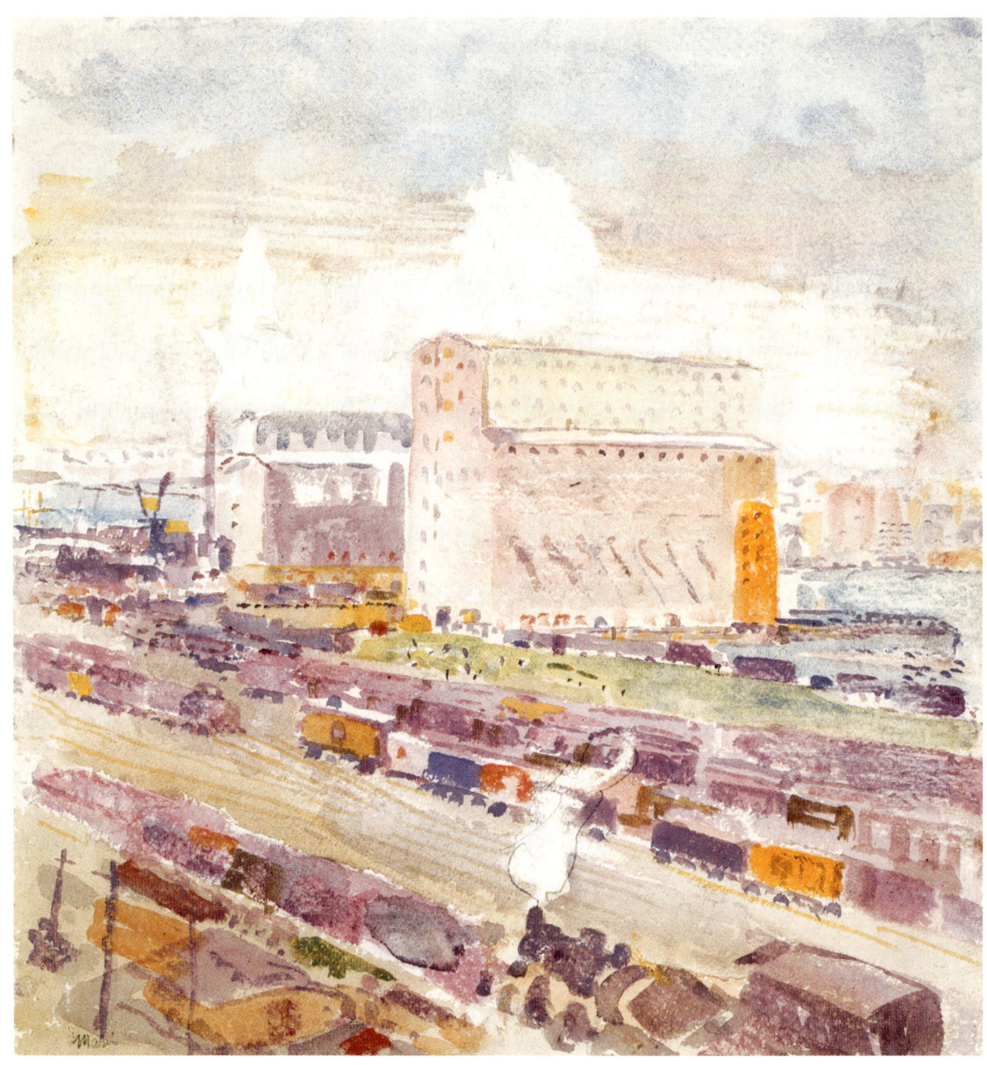

Weehawken Railroad Yards and Grain Elevators,
1910, watercolor and graphite on paper, 15 x 13 7/8 inches

John Marin (1870–1953)

John Marin was widely acclaimed in his lifetime and remains known today as one of America's most important early modernist painters. Firmly ensconced in the avant-garde circle of the aesthetic impresario Alfred Stieglitz (1864–1946), Marin enjoyed a long and productive career moving easily both in his life and in his art between the attractions of city and country. Drawn both to the expressive viscosity of oil paint and to the lyrical translucence of watercolor, Marin devoted some fifty years of his life to capturing the dynamism of the American scene from the bustle of New York City to the natural drama of coastal Maine.

Marin was born in Rutherford, New Jersey, in the latter half of the 1800s, three decades prior to the start of the century with which he is most assuredly identified. Raised in nearby Weehawken by his maternal grandparents and maiden aunts, the young Marin initially pursued architecture as a career and worked for a time in the 1890s as a draftsman for architects before setting up his own firm. By 1899, Marin had enrolled at the Pennsylvania Academy of the Fine Arts, where he remained for two years before continuing his studies at the Art Students League in New York. In 1905, the artist, now well over 30 years old, left for Paris to pursue an artistic career in the city where modernism in a wide range of arts was rapidly being defined.

While abroad Marin associated with a progressive group of likeminded expatriate artists including Max Weber (1881–1961), Arthur B. Carles (1882–1952), and Alfred Maurer (1868–1932), and ultimately joined them as part of the New Society of American Artists in Paris founded by Edward Steichen (1879–1973) in 1908. Through Steichen, the artist's early watercolors were brought to the attention of Stieglitz, and by 1909, Marin was showing at 291, the gallery through which the work of many European modernists and their American converts would be disseminated to the American public.

Weehawken Railroad Yards and Grain Elevators is one of several watercolor views of Weehawken painted in 1910—the year of his first one-man show at 291 and his definitive move back to this country.[1] Marin appears to have especially enjoyed this view of Weehawken's industrial forms set against the distant scrim of New York City just across the Hudson River. As Ruth Fine has noted, Marin's watercolors from this period range from highly descriptive views, such as this one, to more abstract evocations of the city's architectural forms. Marin appears to have worked this image so rigorously that the paper itself is rubbed away in areas of the sky and foreground smoke.[2] Although Marin claims not to have been aware of the work of Paul Cézanne (1839–1906) until 1911, John Baur has noted the post-impressionist qualities of this work, particularly its building up of forms in well-defined blocks of color, as well as its unusually high-keyed Fauve-like palette.[3]

JHR

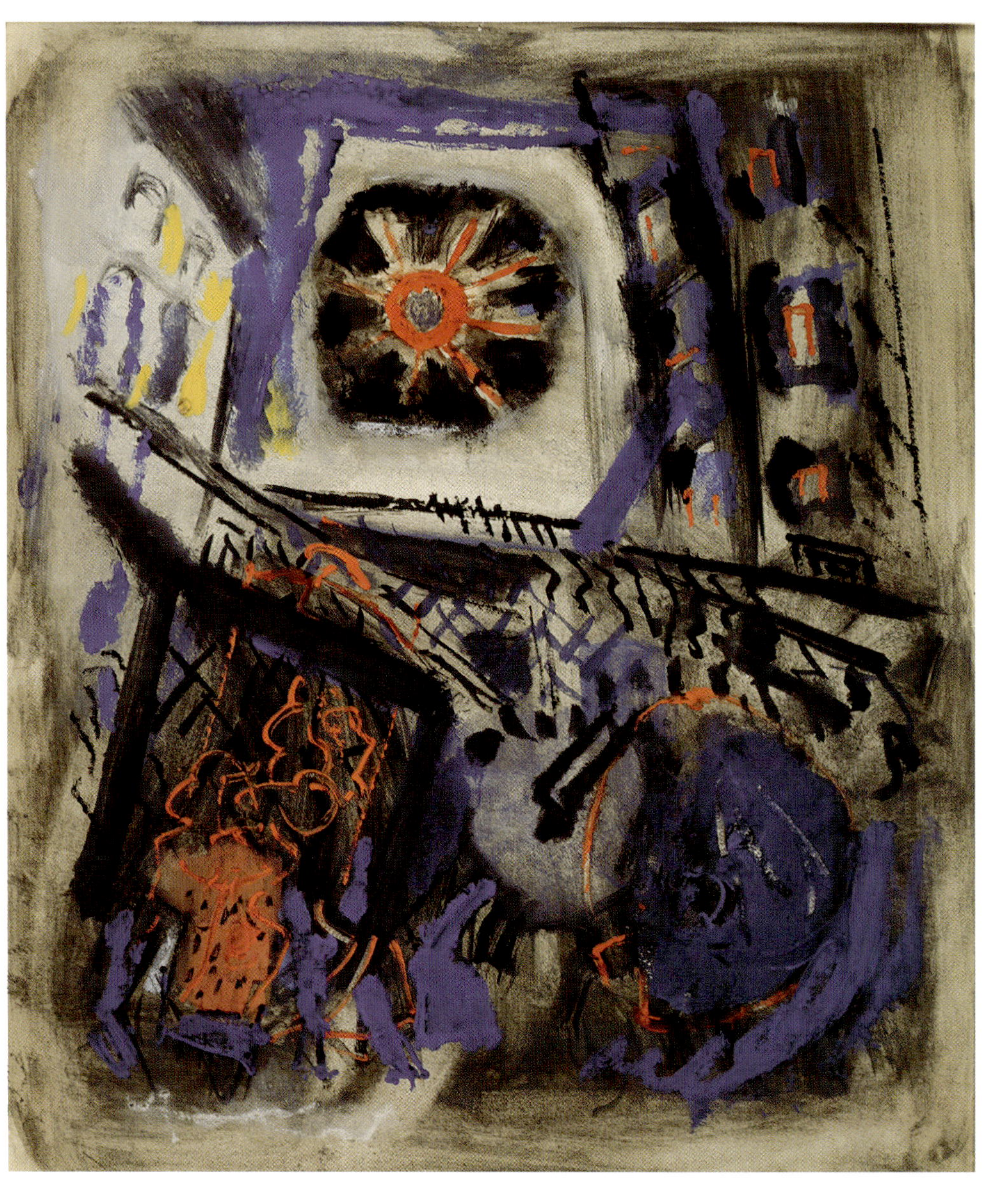

Street Movement, New York,
c. 1932, gouache on paper,
24 1/4 x 20 inches

John Marin (1870–1953)

For John Marin, New York was the quintessential modern city. Throughout his career he returned repeatedly to its dynamic forms, capturing the "tilt, color and sparkle" of its skyscrapers in a lyrical, cubist-influenced language of fractured, pulsating form.[1] From 1920 until the end of his life, Marin maintained a winter studio in Cliffside, New Jersey, occupying a modest home that allowed him easy access—both physical and visual—to the city.

Well known for his early modernist depictions of such noted monuments as the Woolworth Building and the Brooklyn Bridge, Marin was also drawn to the simultaneity and dynamism of Manhattan's city streets. *Street Movement, New York* was painted in the early 1930s when figural motifs were becoming increasingly apparent in Marin's work. A watercolor on the verso titled *Manhattan Movement* and dated 1932 prominently features a well-dressed female in the foreground set against a roughly delineated architectural backdrop.[2] *Street Movement, New York* derives much of its visual energy from the bustling movement of the foreground figures, presumably pedestrians and shoppers making their way through a crowded thoroughfare at the heart of the city. Barely legible, the figures are rendered in an audacious shorthand of calligraphic brushstrokes that vividly embody the "movement" of the painting's title. Marin included "movement" in the titles of at least 164 works, suggesting the word's potency as a signifier not only of urban modernity, but also of the "pulse and rhythm of life itself."[3]

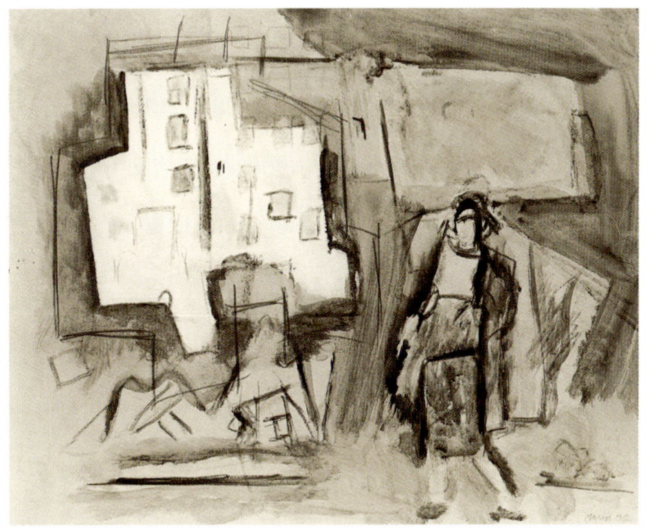

Beginning in the late 1920s, Marin returned to oil painting with great intensity, and this work's richly textured surface and areas of built-up impasto may be a result of that renewed interest. Ruth Fine, who included this work as well as the Snowisses' Weehawken watercolor in the National Gallery of Art's 1990 retrospective of the artist, characterizes *Street Movement, New York* as "extreme" in its brilliant coloration and "highly abbreviated suggestion of form." Fine notes the small piece of cardboard attached to the painting's surface, and suggests that the medium was squeezed with such haste directly from the tube that Marin neglected to remove the cap's inner lining.[4]

JHR

Manhattan Movement, 1932, watercolor on paper (verso)

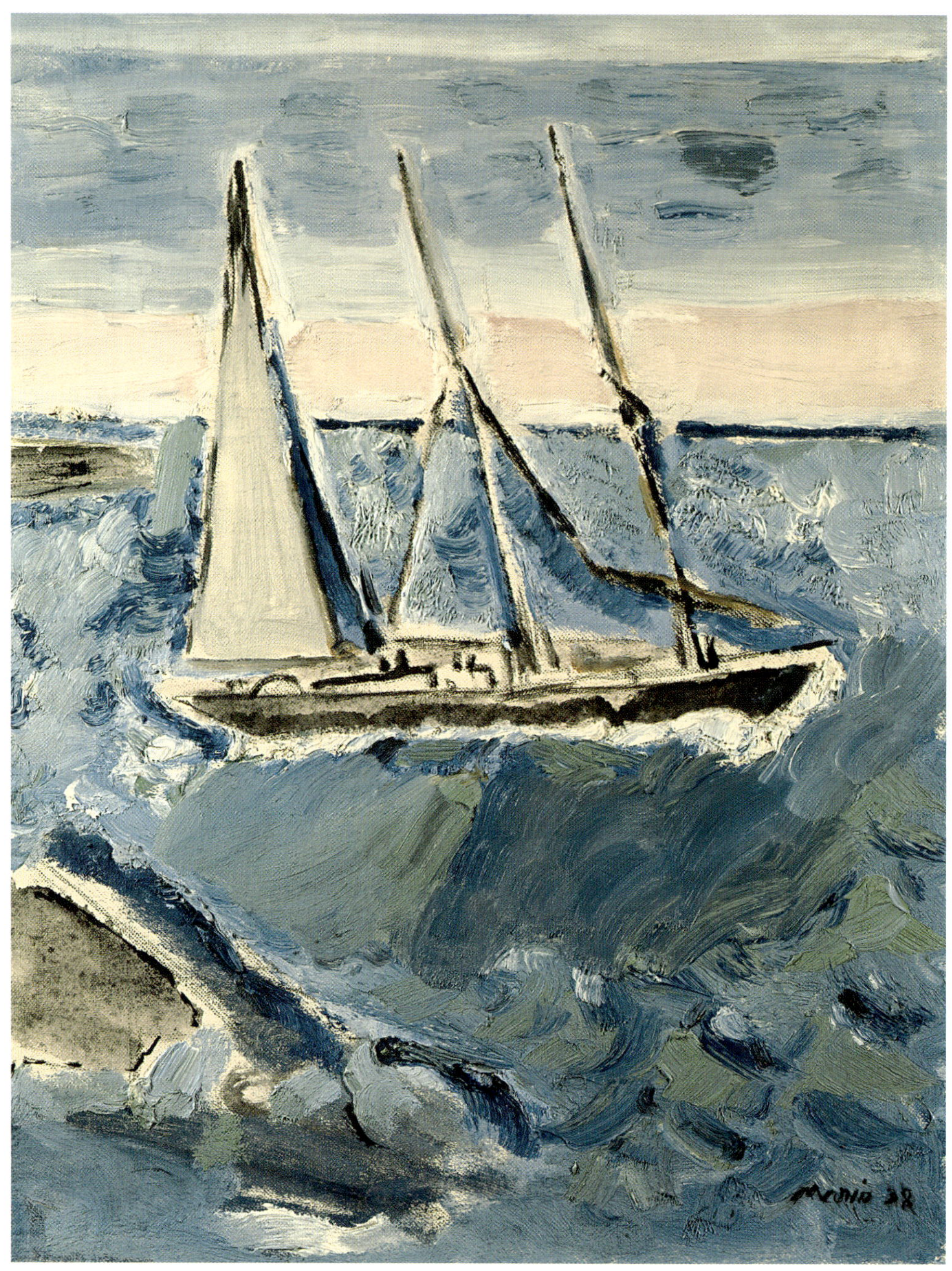

Sailboat and Sea, Maine,
1938, oil on canvas board,
16 x 12 inches

John Marin (1870–1953)

John Marin's infatuation with Maine began with a visit in 1914, early on in his professional career. He was so enamored with the place that he purchased an island off the coast of Small Point Harbor at about that time, apparently depleting a stipend provided by his dealer and friend, Alfred Stieglitz (1864–1946), for support of the artist and his pregnant wife. For the rest of his life, Marin returned to the coast of Maine regularly, typically spending the better part of the summer and fall months there. In 1933, Marin rented a house, which he purchased the following year, on Cape Split in Addison, Maine, a sparsely populated region at the easternmost reaches of the country. "The house is so close to the water," Marin commented, "I almost feel at times that I am on a boat."[1] From this remote vantage point at the edge of the sea, Marin painted some of the most expressive canvases of his career.

Throughout his lifetime, Marin was consistently lauded for his work in watercolor, and in 1927, Stieglitz characterized him as "probably the world's foremost watercolorist."[2] Marin, however, had painted in oils from the outset of his career, producing an important series of nearly abstract views of Weehawken, New Jersey, around 1916 and periodic canvases over the next decade and a half. Only later in his career did the artist consistently work in oil, and while Stieglitz and most critics were less than enamored of the artist's shift to the more viscous medium, Marin pursued its painterly possibilities with great determination. Marin seems to have found in the sea the perfect subject for his explorations on canvas, capturing its tempestuous mood shifts in a series of impassioned works.[3]

Marin often painted from the open porch of his Cape Split cottage, which, perched on rocks a short distance from the sea, afforded him a front row seat for one of nature's grandest shows.[4] For subject matter Marin didn't have to go very far, as he himself once noted. "I stick a boat in here and there from past experience of boats."[5] Marin's first biographer, MacKinley Helm, observed that lobstermen's motorboats would have been a more familiar sight to the artist than the three- and four-master schooners that sail in and out of the sea pictures of the 1930s.[6] Characterized by Helm as "the filling out of the present from past recollections," their presence may also suggest that eternal pitting of man and nature that lies at the heart of the American seascape tradition. *Sailboat and Sea, Maine* is painted in the spontaneous and energized manner typical of the artist's late oils, with every stroke of paint seemingly indicative of the sea's turbulent movements.[7] Areas of bare canvas alongside the foreground rocks and around the boat's edges adamantly confirm the reality of the canvas support and remind us that this powerfully swirling sea is insistently composed of pigment. "There now she moves, a painted boat in her paint sea—Her gray green paint Sea—a sea curling white about the boat—a sea curling white about the ledges-and if you put on the paint right it will find its own depth and if you paint that boat right it will tell its own story .... But again paint the boat right and forget the story, paint the sea right and forget the story."[8]

JHR

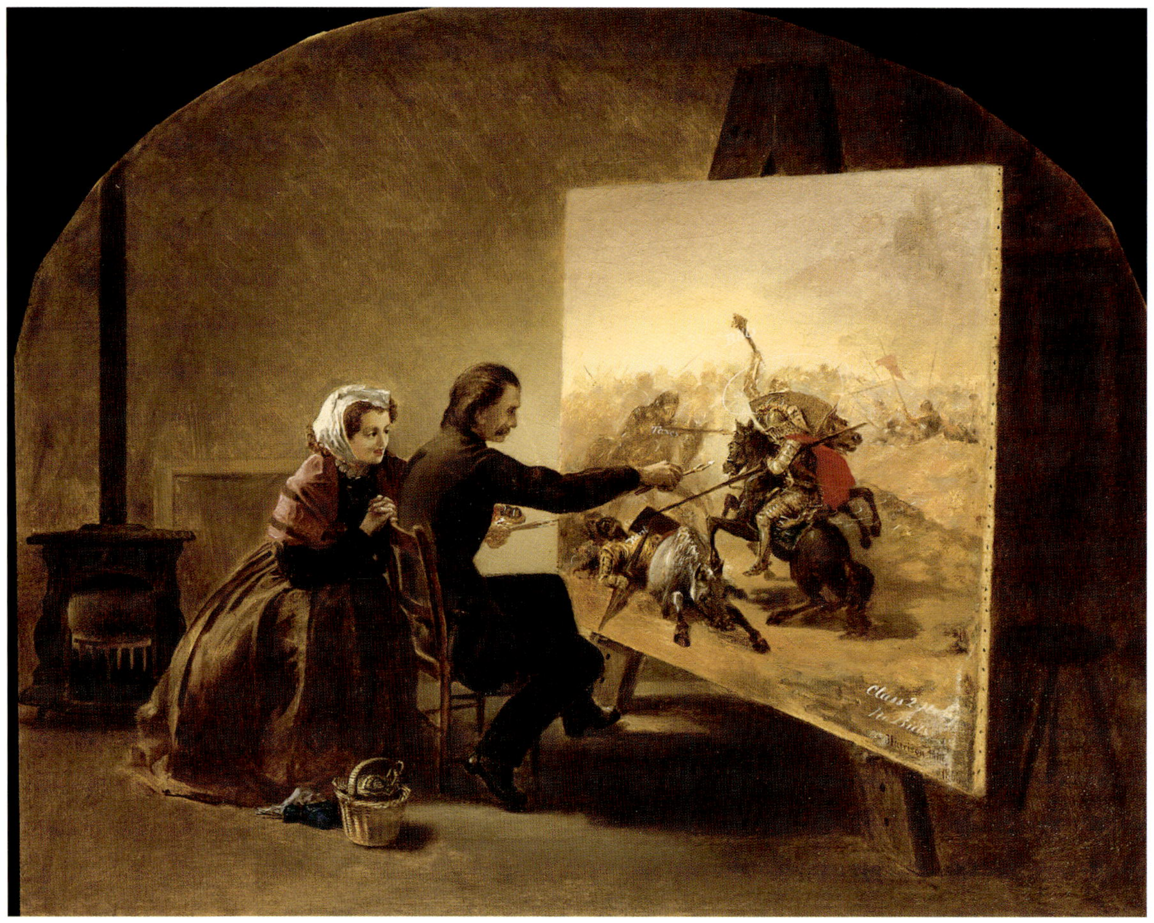

Artist Painting a Satirical Painting, c. late 1860s–1880s, oil on canvas, 20 x 24 1/2 inches

John Harrison Mills (1842–1916)

As a young man in his native Buffalo, New York, the painter and poet John Harrison Mills trained under the banknote engraver John Jamison (c. 1820–after 1860) and benefited from the guidance of two older, more seasoned artists, William Holbrook Beard (1824–1900) and Lars Gustaf Sellstedt (1819–1911).[1] Mills enlisted in the Union Army in April 1861 and contributed to the illustrated *Chronicles of the 21st Regiment*, documenting the Virginia campaigns of 1861 and 1862. By the end of the decade, the artist provided wood engravings for Mark Twain's *Sketches*. In the 1870s, after Mills moved to Colorado, engravings after his drawings appeared in such periodicals as *Scribner's* and *Frank Leslie's Illustrated Newspaper*. Much later in life, he exhibited works at the most eminent American art museums, including the National Academy of Design, the Pennsylvania Academy of the Fine Arts, and the Art Institute of Chicago.

Wounded at the Battle of Second Bull Run (1862), Mills found work after the war as an artist-correspondent for the *Buffalo Express*. From August 1869 through January 1871, Mark Twain also worked at the *Express*, and it is probably here that the men first met; our knowledge of Twain's work in these early years is in fact drawn in part from Mills' reminiscences.[2] It is significant that in Twain's first column for the newspaper—his "Salutatory"—he used the occasion to complain bitterly about the recently instituted federal income tax. In telling his readers what they might expect from him, he promised he would not curse, although, he added, the subject of taxation might test him: "I … shall never use profanity except in discussing house-rent and taxes."[3] The imposing of a federal income tax in 1863 was bitterly contested, reported, and debated in the *Express* and throughout the national press.[4]

Artist Painting a Satirical Painting is a critique of the controversial topic of taxation. Just to the right of a wood stove in a dimly lit studio, a fashionably dressed woman clasps her hands on a chair where an artist sits, apparently making finishing touches on a painting of a medieval battle. In the foreground of the canvas on the easel, a red-caped knight directs his spear at a similarly clad fallen figure, on whose chest is inscribed "Rent." Partly obscured by the large, centrally placed knight in red is another man on horseback, on whose raised spear is written "Bills." An additional rider, with the word "Taxes" on his chest, charges from the left, jabbing his lance into the red-caped knight, who may be seen as the hero, warding off the evil triumvirate of rent, bills, and taxes. Mills has enlisted medieval imagery to wage his social commentary, in much the same way Twain would in *A Connecticut Yankee in King Arthur's Court* (1889), perhaps the most notorious use of medievalism in American literature.

The Mills-Twain connection is complicated by the presence of the date 1866 in the lower right-hand corner of the painting on the easel. Indeed the author did not publish his medievalizing tales until much later. Yet, with the white chalk or paint at the end of his stick, the artist appears to be adding the words—"Rent," "Bills," and "Taxes"—to an already finished picture, transforming the history painting into a contemporary cultural critique. Given Mills' association with Twain in the late 1860s, as well as the contrast between the vivid white markings and the brown and yellow earth tones, it seems likely that, although the *pictured* canvas is dated 1866, the Snowiss painting was completed later. The artist may have produced the picture as late as the 1880s, when medievalizing social critiques—including those by his satirist-friend Twain—were popular.

Also complicating matters, the picture was probably intended as a commentary not only on taxation policies, but more likely, on the artistic profession. Following in the tradition of William Sidney Mount's *The Painter's Triumph* (1838, Pennsylvania Academy of the Fine Arts), Mills establishes the painter as a pictorial magician, concocting credible illusions much to the delight of the easily duped and engrossed visitor.[5] The fictive painter, much like Mills himself, entices and instructs his audience, blurring the line between artistic celebration and cultural critique.

LGM

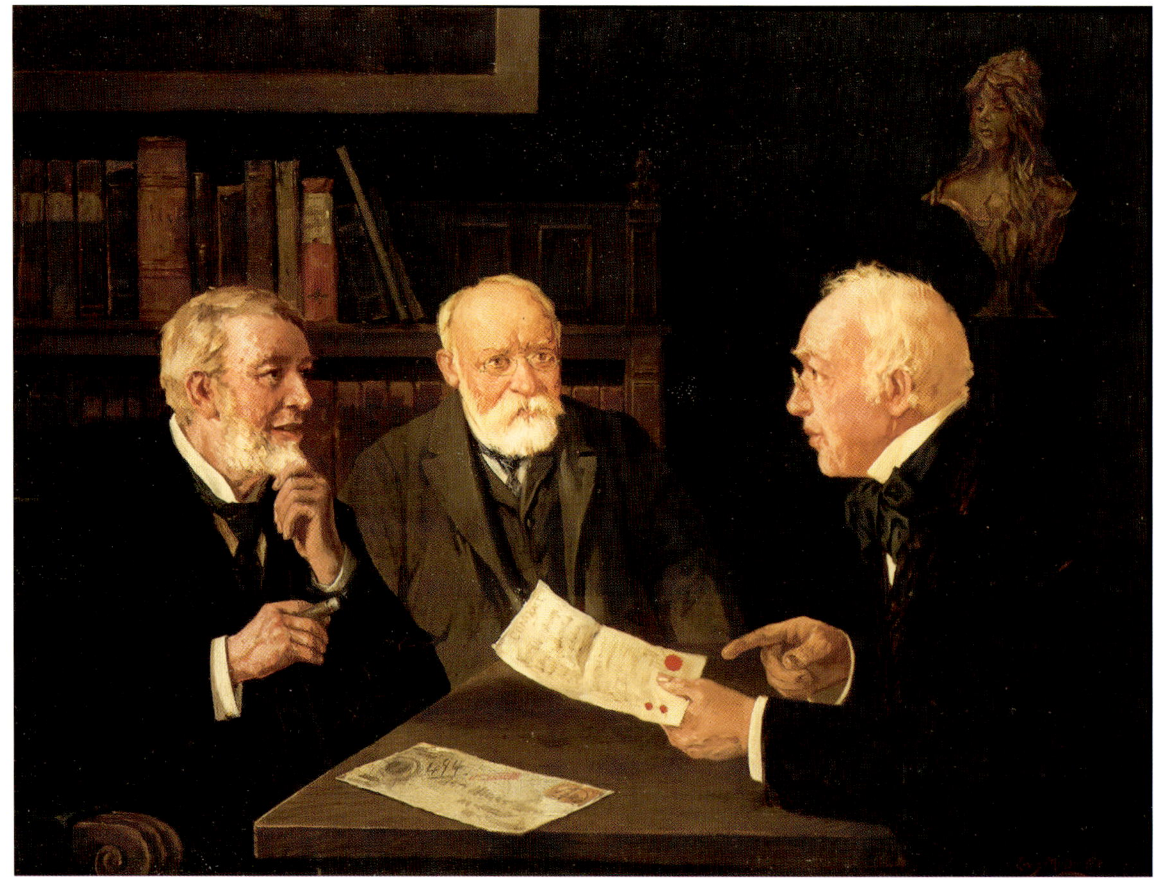

The Lawyers,
after 1895, oil on canvas,
20 x 26 1/4 inches

Louis Moeller (1855–1930)

Although little known today, Louis Moeller enjoyed a reputation as one of America's leading genre painters at the height of his career at the end of the nineteenth century.[1] Initially apprenticed to his father, a decorative painter of German lineage, Moeller continued his professional training at the Cooper Union and the National Academy of Design, two of the nation's most prestigious art schools, in the early 1870s. Like many ambitious American students, the young artist pursued further study in Europe, departing for Germany in the fall of 1873.

Moeller's destination was Munich, an important center for aspiring artists that rivaled Paris in attracting American art students in the decades following the Civil War. Moeller pursued academic training at the Munich Royal Academy and studied with Wilhelm von Diez (1839–1907), an artist whose tightly painted, small-scale genre scenes laid the groundwork for what would become a dominant artistic mode in Munich by the late 1870s.[2] According to Gerdts, Moeller also listed as his teacher Frank Duveneck (1848–1919), a renegade American painter whose bravura paint handling and dramatic use of chiaroscuro set him apart from the official, more highly finished mode promulgated by the Academy.

Moeller returned to New York City in 1882 after an extensive stay in Munich. The artist began exhibiting regularly at prominent venues such as the National Academy of Design and, occasionally, the Society of American Artists, and soon attracted positive attention both from critics and collectors for his modestly scaled, often anecdotal, genre paintings. Moeller quickly became identified with his favorite subject—which he repeated ad infinitum—namely, crusty old men involved in intellectual banter in richly appointed interiors. In *The Lawyers*, two white-haired codgers appear to debate the fine points of a legal contract, their concentrated expressions revealing what one contemporary critic characterized as an "intensity of mental action and life."[3] The carefully described setting, with its venerable old books and respectable bric-a-brac, provides the appropriate backdrop for what in its day was a quintessentially masculine encounter. A female in the form of a statue, typical of the kind of decorative bronzes marketed in Europe in large editions at the end of the nineteenth century, invades the sacrosanct domain, adding a humorous touch of feminine judgment to this scene of masculine negotiation.

Moeller continued to enjoy critical success well into the 1890s and was made a full National Academician in 1895. The "N.A." appended to his signature in this piece thus suggests its completion sometime after that date.

JHR

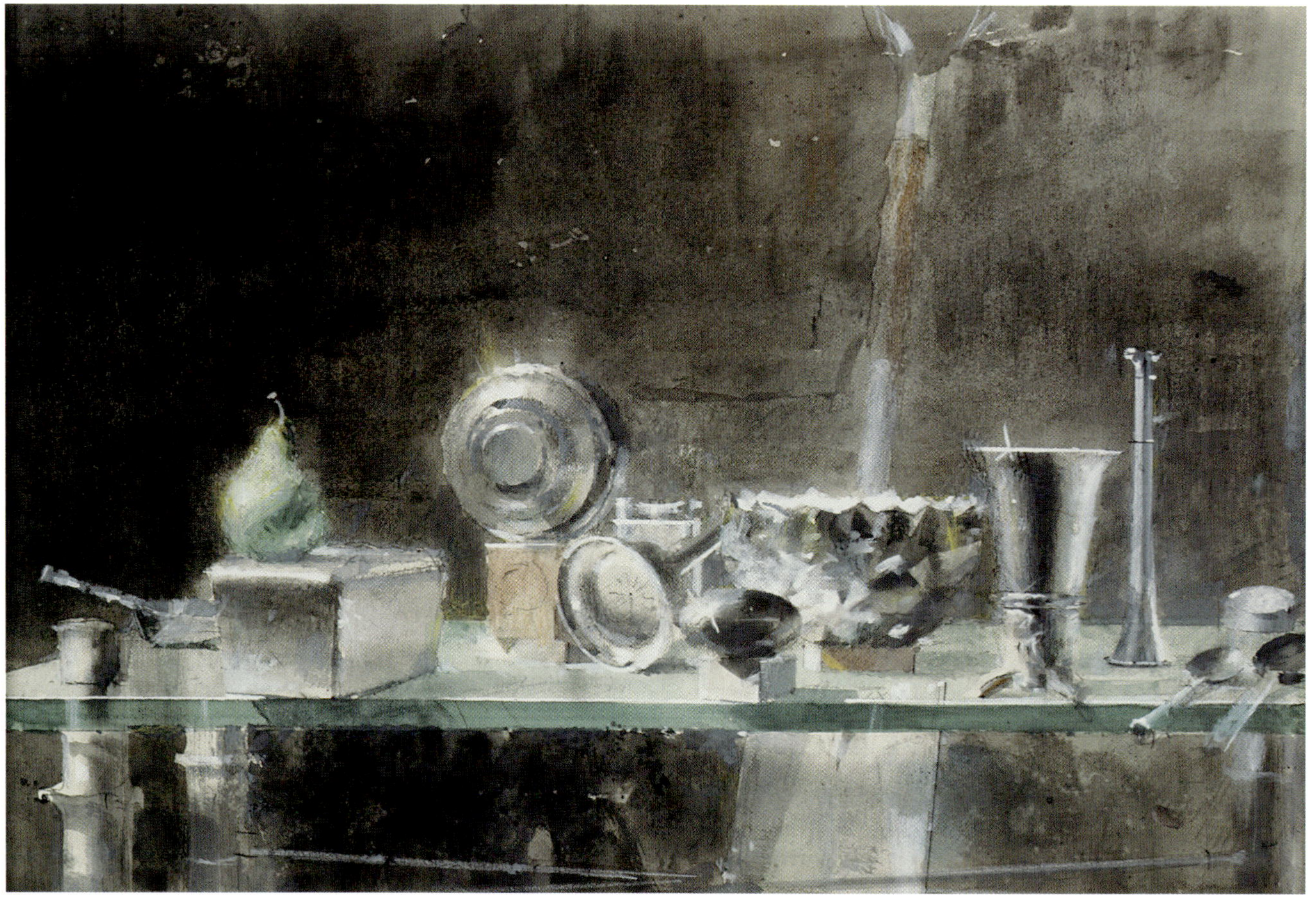

Study for Sound of Silver,
1965, gouache and
pencil on paper,
16 1/4 x 18 3/4 inches

Walter Murch (1907–1967)

Once characterized by a critic as "willfully marginal," Walter Murch has remained a somewhat anomalous figure in the history of post-war American art.[1] In 1984, long after the artist's death, Henry Geldzahler (1935–1994), an early champion of Pop Art and former curator at the Metropolitan Museum of Art, included Murch in an exhibition of overlooked talent titled *Underknown* at the alternative gallery P.S. 1. The artist's still lifes with their odd conjoining of the old and the new—with their Chardin-like reverence for humble objects and their persistent modernist facture—fail to fit neatly into the parade of avant-garde movements that in part defined the making of careers in the late twentieth century. Perhaps that explains why this "painter's painter," this man who was friends and colleagues with the likes of Arshile Gorky (1904–1948), Betty Parsons (1900–1982), and Barnett Newman (1905–1970), was and remains one of the century's best-kept secrets.

Murch was born in Toronto, Canada, and after a brief stint at the Toronto Conservatory of Music, matriculated at the Ontario College of Art in the mid-1920s. By 1927, the young artist had moved to New York City and found work as an assistant designer of stained glass, a job he held until 1931 when he left to become a graphic designer for Lord and Taylor's department store. During these early years, Murch continued his studies at the Art Students League and the Grand Central School of Art and studied painting privately with Arshile Gorky, an artist whose free handling of paint would soon ally him with the experimental artists known as the abstract expressionists. Equally influential on the young Murch was the work of the European surrealists, then au courant in several New York galleries, and that of their American counterpart, Joseph Cornell (1903–1972).

Scholars have noted that it was his friendship with Cornell that most likely led Murch to his own definition of art as "the manufacture of a completely useless thing," and that encouraged the artist to bring together mundane objects in seemingly illogical combinations.[2] In the early 1940s, Murch began to incorporate mechanical parts—clock mechanisms, locks, motors—in part influenced by commercial work he was doing for magazines like *Fortune* and *Scientific American*. "I think a painter paints best what he thinks about most," Murch once noted. "For me this is about objects—objects from my childhood, present surroundings, or a chance object that stimulates my interest, around which accumulate these thoughts."[3]

Study for Sound of Silver is a work from late in the artist's career and is clearly related to a finished painting of the same title formerly in the collection of Lee Ault.[4] Two years earlier in 1963, Murch had completed a work for a *Vogue* magazine commission titled *Midnight Portrait of Silver*, a similar still life dedicated to the sheen of metal and the exquisite tonalities of a host of disparate silver objects.[5] With a musical metaphor embedded in its title, *Study for Sound of Silver* trenchantly demonstrates Murch's belief that what ultimately carries meaning in a work of art is not the depicted objects so much as the formal elements, the "music of paint," as it were.[6]

JHR

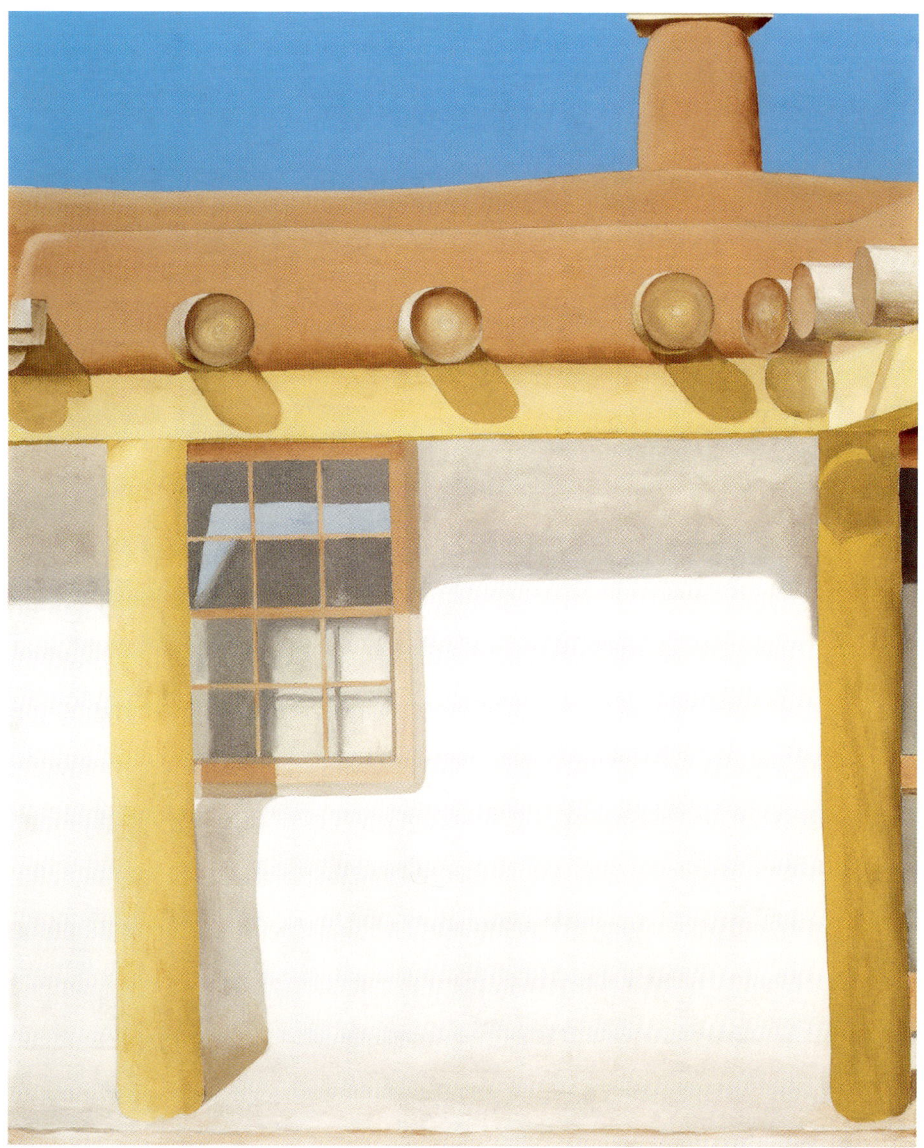

From the Patio No. II,
1940, oil on canvas,
24 x 19 inches

Georgia O'Keeffe (1887–1986)

For even the most casual student of American art, Georgia O'Keeffe hardly needs an introduction. O'Keeffe's work was first introduced to the public in 1916, the year a group of her charcoal drawings was shown at Alfred Stieglitz's 291 gallery in New York. Stieglitz (1864–1946), the noted photographer and ardent champion of American modernism, would later become her husband, and together they orchestrated a career that would catapult O'Keeffe to fame.

Before her "discovery" by the man who would become her husband and dealer, O'Keeffe trained with noted American artists Kenyon Cox (1856–1919) and William Merritt Chase (1849–1916) at the Art Students League. The teacher who most greatly influenced her, she acknowledged, was Arthur Wesley Dow (1857–1922), with whom she studied at Columbia University Teachers College beginning in 1914. Dow's approach, with its mingling of Eastern and Western aesthetic concepts, had one "dominating idea," O'Keeffe recalls, "to fill a space in a beautiful way."[1] Heeding this advice and drawing inspiration from a wide range of sources, including Japanese prints and modernist photography, O'Keeffe went on to receive critical acclaim for her signature flower abstractions, which she began producing in the early 1920s. Not so much copies as pictorial "equivalents" of nature, O'Keeffe's paintings throughout her career remained grounded in the objective world, drawing their potency from their abstemious, yet trenchant interpretations of nature's complex vocabulary.[2]

O'Keeffe spent the final decades of her life in New Mexico, moving there permanently in 1949, a few years after Stieglitz's death. Many years earlier, in 1917, the artist had visited the state on a trip with her sister, noting "I loved it immediately. From then on I was always on my way back." Hailing from Wisconsin and having spent a number of formative years as a young art teacher in Texas, O'Keeffe identified with the vast, sparsely populated expanses of the western landscape, delighting in the region's brilliant light and exotic artifacts. Beginning in 1929, the year she was a guest at the Taos home of socialite Mabel Dodge Luhan (1879–1962), the artist spent several months every year almost without exception working in New Mexico.

In 1940, O'Keeffe bought an adobe house called Rancho de los Burros—the first home she ever owned—on Ghost Ranch, a 21,000-acre property west of Taos owned by Arthur Pack, founder of *Nature* magazine.[3] Located in the Chama River Valley, the modest U-shaped house was situated on an isolated portion of the ranch at the foot of magnificent striated cliffs and rugged hills. The views from Rancho de los Burros inspired some of the most dramatic landscapes of the artist's career. The simple adobe house also inspired introspective works such as *From the Patio No. II*, one of two versions of the subject painted in 1940.[4] With all references to the surrounding majestic scenery cropped away, the painting derives its visual potency from the simple massing of architectonic, sun-drenched forms and the inherent geometry of the articulated parade of supporting beams. Anticipating the extreme economy of form in her virtually abstract *Patio Door* series (1946–1960), completed at her second home in nearby Abiquiu, *From the Patio No. II* succinctly encapsulates the artist's unique sensibility—"spare, tactile, sculptural, with a relation between outside and inside that speak[s] at once of her need for privacy and her openness to the natural world."[5]

JHR

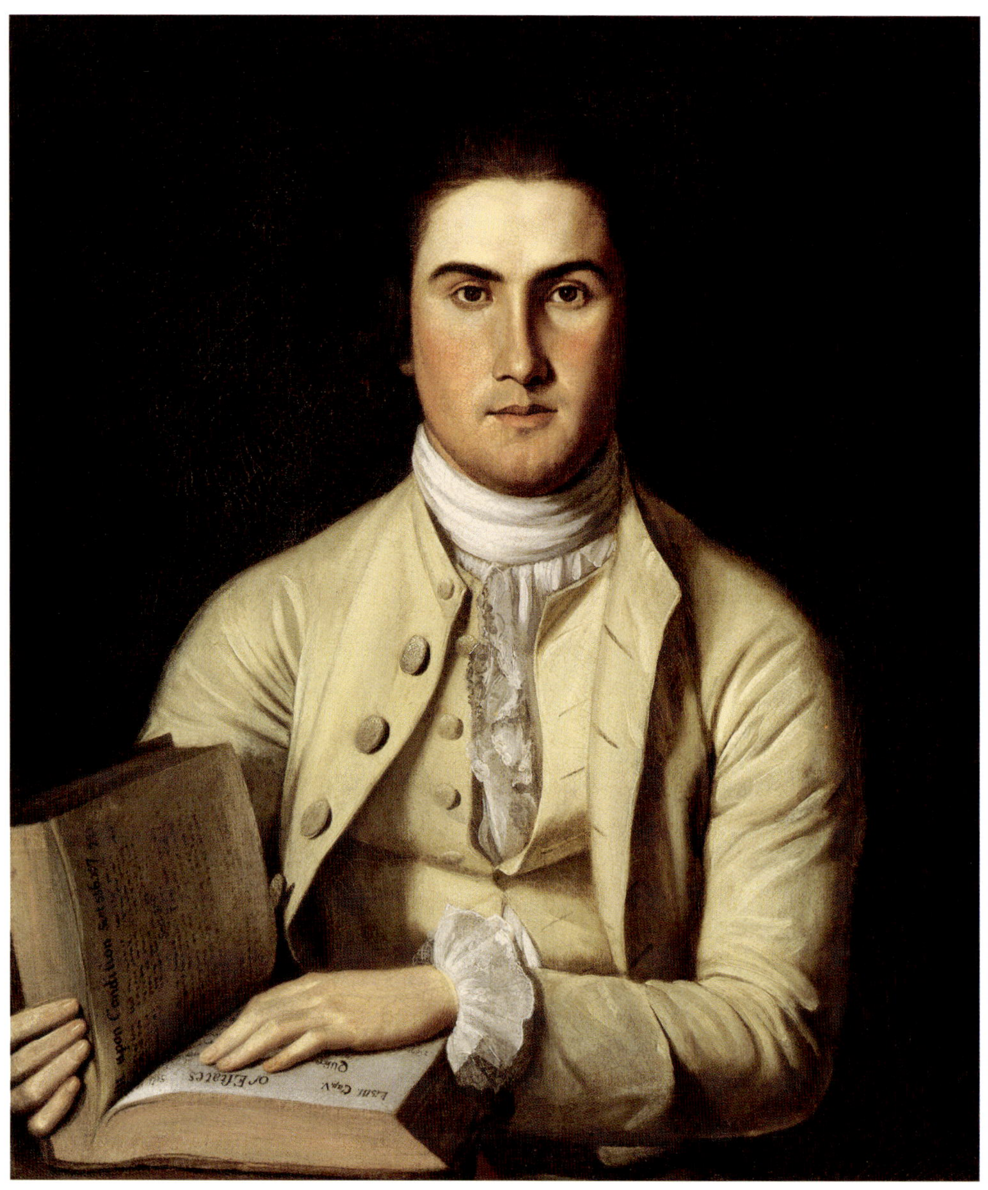

Judge Benjamin Mackall,
c. 1770, oil on canvas,
25 x 30 inches

Charles Willson Peale (1741–1827)

It was Charles Willson Peale's contention that "the great book of nature may be opened and studied, leaf by leaf, and a knowledge gained of the character which the great Creator has stamped on each being."[1] From his earliest portraits, Peale demonstrated his belief that simplicity of composition and fidelity to nature permitted the true disposition of distinguished subjects, such as Judge Benjamin Mackall, to emanate from each canvas.[2]

Peale, a sign painter and proprietor of a saddler's shop in Annapolis, Maryland, during the early 1760s, became intrigued with portraiture after viewing likenesses in Virginia that were "miserably done."[3] Prompted to commence another profession, he received instruction from the established Maryland portrait painter John Hesselius (1728–1788), and sought out John Singleton Copley (c. 1738–1815) during an extended stay in Boston in 1765. Peale, sponsored by a number of distinguished Maryland gentlemen, traveled to England in 1767, where he studied painting for two years under Benjamin West (1738–1820).[4] Peale quickly established himself as a respected limner upon his return to Annapolis in 1769, executing Judge Benjamin Mackall's portrait shortly thereafter.[5]

Brandon Brame Fortune asserts that "[Peale's] portraits were to be exact and 'true,' not only for his own artistic integrity, but so that the painted faces would express the virtues of their subjects."[6] The portrait of Benjamin Mackall is an early example of Peale's straightforward style. The artist likely considered Mackall, a respected judge of the appellate court in Calvert County, Maryland, and proprietor of God's Grace plantation, to be a man of ideal character and deserving of a portrait that would serve as an appropriate reflection of his nature. The unobtrusive background and pointed light source direct attention to the sitter's visage as he gazes outward in a beneficent manner. Mackall's hand rests gently on a book, which has been opened to a page outlining estate law. In a letter to patron and friend John Beale Bordley, Peale described a change in the portrait that further eliminated artifice: "I have improved Mr. Machol's [sic] picture very much by changing the wig for hair."[7] This simple depiction of Mackall exemplifies Peale's developing tendency to express the merits of his sitters without unnecessary embellishment.

JD

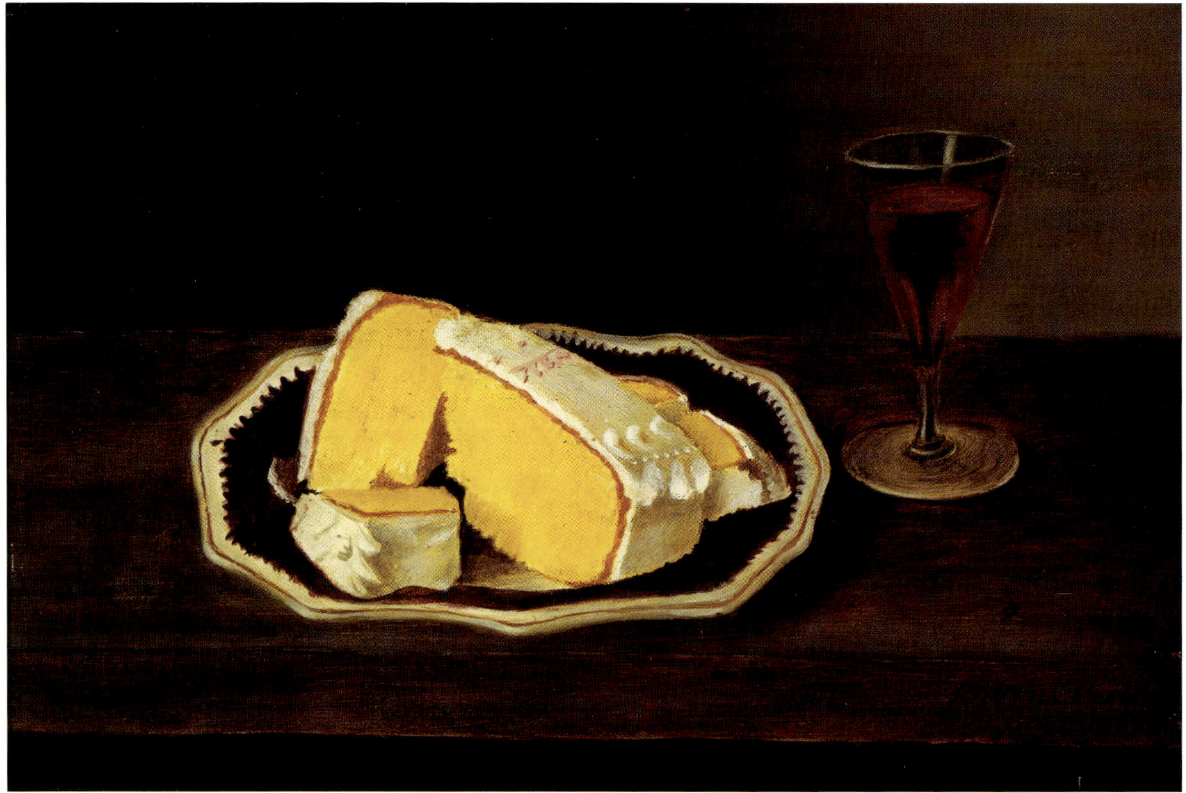

The Artist's Last Birthday,
1865, oil on canvas,
9 1/2 x 13 1/4 inches

Rubens Peale (1784–1865)

Rubens Peale may best be known to art lovers as the bespectacled, seemingly quizzical young gentleman portrayed in the National Gallery of Art's *Rubens Peale with Geranium*, painted by his brother Rembrandt (1778–1860) in 1801. Born into a talented family of artists, yet hindered by poor eyesight, Rubens enjoyed a long career as a museum administrator before turning to painting late in life. The fourth son of the illustrious painter and museum entrepreneur Charles Willson Peale (1741–1827), Rubens did not receive the same artistic training acquired by his siblings and pursued the sciences instead. Elected a member of the Academy of Natural Sciences in 1813, Peale had succeeded his father as administrator of the Peale Museum in Philadelphia in 1810. Rubens was the perfect choice for overseer of the museum's collection, which represented a wonderful mélange of natural curiosities and manmade marvels, from mastodon bones to painted portraits of famous Americans. In 1822, Peale took over the upkeep of the Peale Museum operated by his brother Rembrandt in Baltimore, and three years later founded his own museum in New York City. Forced to sell his collection to P. T. Barnum (1810–1891) due to the financial panic of 1837, the destitute Peale retired to "Woodland Farm" in the hills of Pennsylvania near Schuylkill Haven in 1841, thanks to the generosity of his wife's family.

Peale managed the daily activities of the farm—and served as the local taxidermist—until 1855, the same year his daughter, Mary Jane Peale (1827–1902), returned home after studying art with her uncle Rembrandt. Under the tutelage of his daughter, the almost 71-year-old naturalist farmer began to pursue painting seriously, recording his comments on both the mundane workings of the farm and his artistic work in progress in his daily diary entries. During his brief ten-year career, Peale produced more than 130 paintings, which, according to his handwritten and self-maintained "List of Pictures," included landscapes, interiors, pictures of game birds, and still life, the latter of which dominated his output. Probably because of his lack of formal training, Peale often copied works of art by family members, particularly still-life compositions by his brother Raphaelle Peale (1774–1825) and his uncle, James Peale (1749–1831).

In the last six months of his life, Rubens produced several "cake and wine" pictures, perhaps as a kind of memorial to his wife, Eliza Burd Patterson (1795–1864), who died in September 1864.[1] Raphaelle Peale had presented the couple with a modest still-life painting, *Cake and Wine* (1813, private collection), in celebration of their wedding in 1820.[2] Just prior to his death in July 1865, Rubens produced several copies of the Raphaelle Peale still life for his children. *The Artist's Last Birthday*, which according to the artist's diary was commenced and completed in June 1865, seems not to be a copy of *Cake and Wine*, but rather a variation on its basic elements.[3] One month earlier, Rubens had painted another variation titled *Magpie Eating Cake* (1865, private collection), featuring the same plate and glass along with a foreboding English magpie nibbling at the cake's sugar icing. Cake and wine were typically served at weddings, as well as at funerals, and thus we might speculate that both *Magpie* and *The Artist's Last Birthday* were painted by the aged artist as he mourned his wife and prepared for his own departure from this world.[4] Peale spent the last several months of his life in Philadelphia with his daughter, and his last journal entries give the impression of a weakened man, somewhat lonely, yet still actively painting. Barely one month after completing *The Artist's Last Birthday,* Peale took ill at his easel and died later that day.

JHR

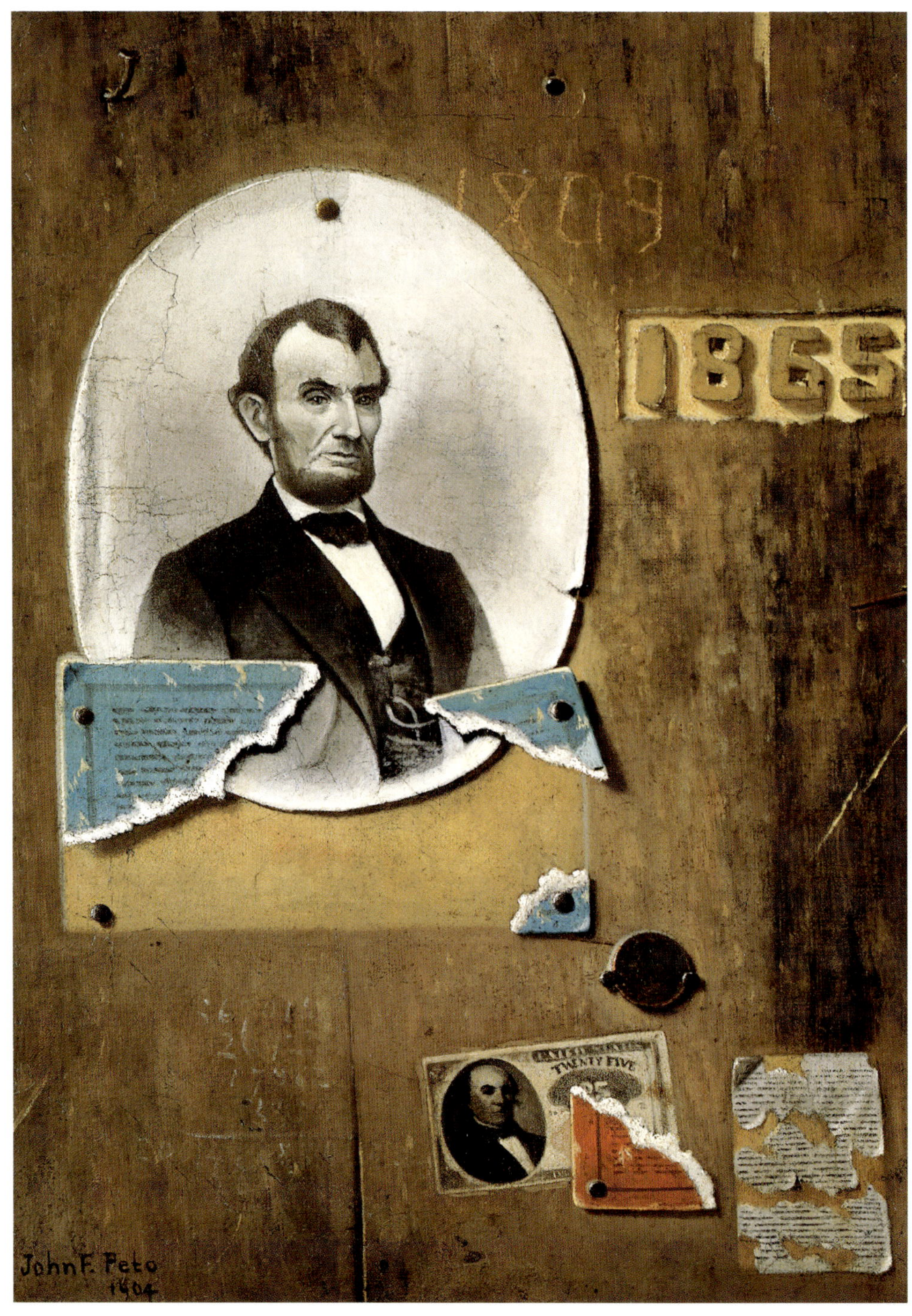

Lincoln and the 25¢ Note,
1904, oil on canvas,
20 1/8 x 14 1/8 inches

John Frederick Peto (1854–1907)

Trompe l'oeil painting almost by definition defies the indexical or autographic presence of an individual artist's hand. It is perhaps not surprising, then, that works by two of the genre's greatest practitioners, John Frederick Peto and William Harnett (1848–1892), were for several decades confused and misidentified. Peto, who never enjoyed the critical or popular success experienced by his slightly older colleague, led a reclusive life and practiced his trade of crafting illusions far from the centers of artistic production in this country for much of his career. Ever since the "rediscovery" of his artistic identity in the late 1940s, Peto has continued to emerge from the shadow of the illustrious Harnett, and his unique sensibilities and gifts as an artist have become increasingly clear to collectors and scholars alike.[1]

Peto's father, Thomas Hope Peto, worked as a gilder and picture framer in Philadelphia during the early years of his son's life, undoubtedly affording the young artist an important introduction to the world of picture making. Peto appears to have had little formal training, studying only for a short period in 1877 at the Pennsylvania Academy of the Fine Arts, where he exhibited periodically over the next several years. Peto maintained a studio in Philadelphia throughout much of the 1880s in a variety of locations, mostly on Chestnut Street in the city's art district. Many of the artist's canvases from this early period in Philadelphia, particularly in their choice of motif and compositional format, suggest the influence of Harnett, whom Peto had met in the late 1870s. In 1887, Peto married a young woman from Ohio and by the end of the decade had moved to Island Heights, New Jersey, a seaside resort where the artist lived in relative seclusion until his death.[2]

Lincoln and the 25¢ Note is an example of a vertical still life, a sub-genre of trompe l'oeil painting in which a variety of objects appear to hang from a wall or door whose surface is coterminous with the picture plane.[3] Since 1879, Peto had produced a variety of rack pictures, probably his most important contribution to the genre, in which a wide range of printed documents—letters, playing cards, clippings, advertisements—appear to be held in place by the crossed tapes of a letter rack. Here the objects, which are affixed by nails or some form of adhesive to a worn panel of wood, include an oval print of Abraham Lincoln (1809–1865), a well-known likeness that appears in some dozen canvases from the 1890s into the early 1900s. The painting also features the assassinated president's life dates, carved directly into the wood, an old coin, and a 25¢ note known as a "shinplaster." Such fractional notes were issued by the Federal government beginning in 1862 as a substitute for metal coins, which increasingly were in short supply. The note in the Snowiss picture was part of the fifth and final government issue (1874–1876) and depicts Robert J. Walker, secretary of the treasury from 1845 to 1849. By 1876, such "paper change" was virtually worthless (valuable only as a "shinplaster" or bandage), and Congress revoked its use as legal tender.[4]

Lincoln and the 25¢ Note was painted in Island Heights toward the end of Peto's career at a time when the artist was increasingly plagued by complications from a chronic kidney ailment known as Bright's Disease. Scholars have noted an introspective and melancholy tone in these late pictures, and John Wilmerding has suggested that the "obsession" with Lincoln imagery evident in these late canvases may reveal the artist's "apparent psychological association of the fallen president with his own late father" who passed away in the mid-1890s.[5] Whether or not this is the case, Peto clearly infuses the trompe l'oeil tradition with a sense of nostalgic longing, bathing his forms in a diffused "twilight luminosity" that reminds us that these objects are not so much illusions as painted signifiers of memory.[6]

JHR

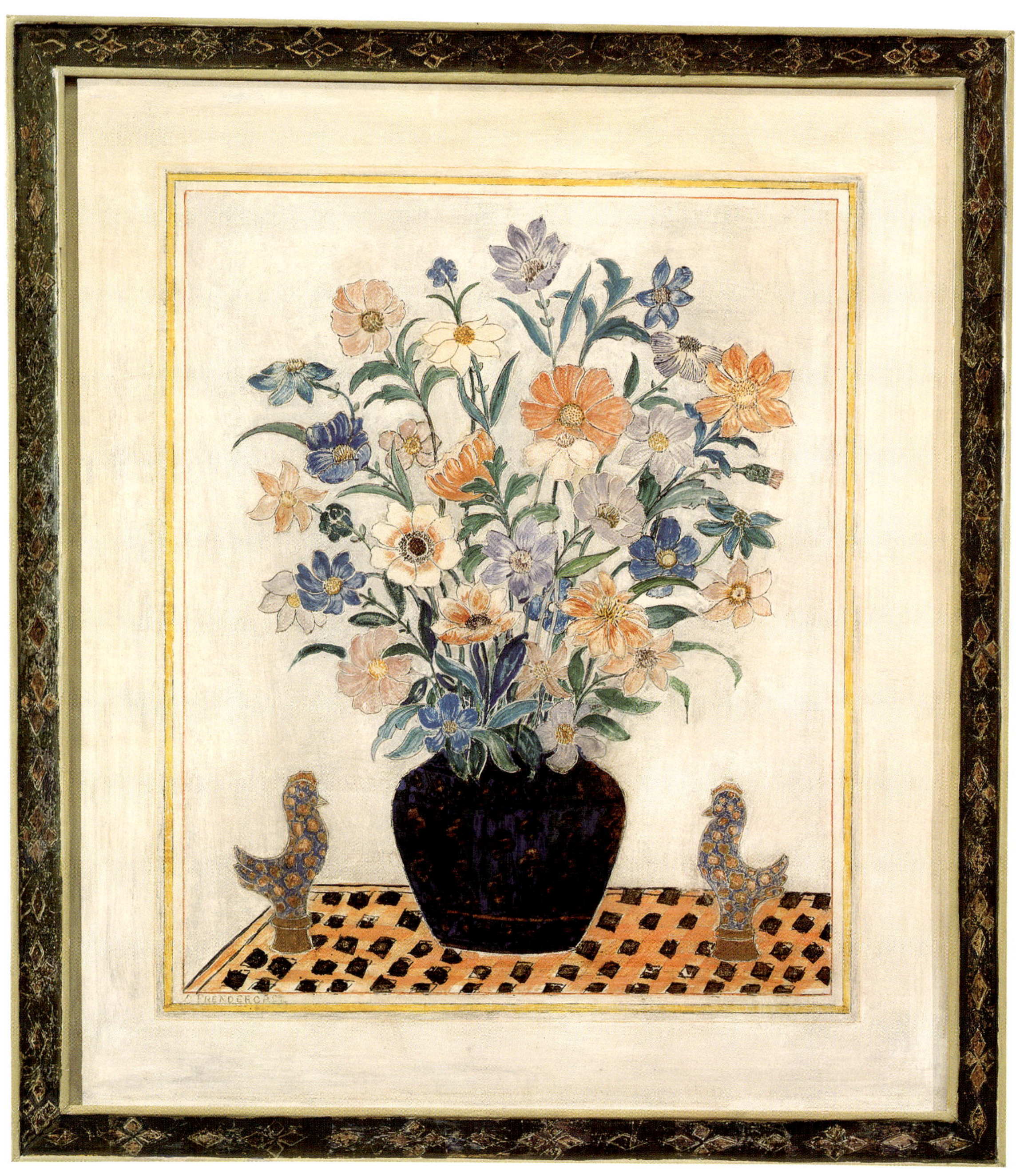

Blue Vase and Birds,
c. 1932–1935, tempera, gold and silver leaf on gessoed panel, 24 1/2 x 20 1/2 inches

Charles Prendergast (1863–1948)

Unlike his brother, Maurice (1858–1924), who appears to have known the trajectory of his professional career early on, Charles Prendergast realized a career as an artist fairly late in life. Not surprisingly, his output was quite small—barely more than 100 finished pictorial works. Yet, each of his panels, housed often in frames that he designed, is a testament to the consummate craftsmanship of a highly unique artist whose work resists easy categorization in the history of twentieth-century American art.

Both Prendergast brothers were born in St. Johns, Newfoundland, the only two children of six who survived into adulthood. The family moved to Boston in 1867, and Charles became an errand runner for the art gallery Doll & Richards in his teens before trying his hand at a variety of jobs. In 1890, Charles accompanied his brother to Paris and, after taking a few art classes, returned to Boston to take a job in a firm that produced decorative wood moldings. Although he probably began as a salesman, by 1894, he was ensconced in the "manufacturing" side of the business. By this time Maurice had returned from four years of study, and the two brothers began living together as they pursued their respective careers. Charles was soon making frames for his brother, other friends, and dealers, as well as for Boston's Museum of Fine Arts and private collectors, including Isabella Stewart Gardner (1840–1924). Not content to replicate established models, Charles designed many of the frames he carved for clients, and soon became well known and much sought after as an "artist-frame maker."[1]

In 1912, inspired in part by a trip to Italy the previous summer, Charles began making carved wood panels with pictorial elements defined in tempera and gilding, thus beginning, at mid-life, an alternate career as a painter. The stylistic and iconographic sources for these small panels, many of which were sacred in nature, were diverse and included medieval illuminations, Italian Trecento altarpieces, and Persian miniatures. As is evident in the rather self-conscious simplicity of these early incised, gessoed panels, Charles, like many of his contemporaries, was inspired by a varied range of what at the time were considered anticlassical traditions.[2] A growing taste for the art of so-called "primitives," particularly in the form of folk art, would preoccupy this country in the ensuing decades and helped provide an appreciative audience for this professional *naïf* whose techniques and materials were seemingly "pulled from the periphery."[3]

In a 1946 interview, Prendergast divided his work into three distinct phases: the early "celestial" period (1912–1928); the "transitional" years (1928–1932); and the "modern" (beginning in 1932).[4] *Blue Vase and Birds* dates from the very early years of the latter phase, a period marked by commonplace subjects and an emphatic simplification of pictorial design, and is one of several floral still lifes painted by the artist in the early 1930s.[5] The flower vase paintings were innovative within the artist's oeuvre in their inclusion of a self-mat, a wide border of gessoed panel, visually enframing the painted composition.[6] Like many of Prendergast's panels, the work in the Snowiss collection is housed in its original frame designed and painted by the artist. The decorative simplicity of the frame, the naïve treatment of space, and the hieratic composition, with its playful homage to the contemporary rage for Americana, all speak to the artist's sophisticated manipulation of the language of art in a decidedly folk dialect.

JHR

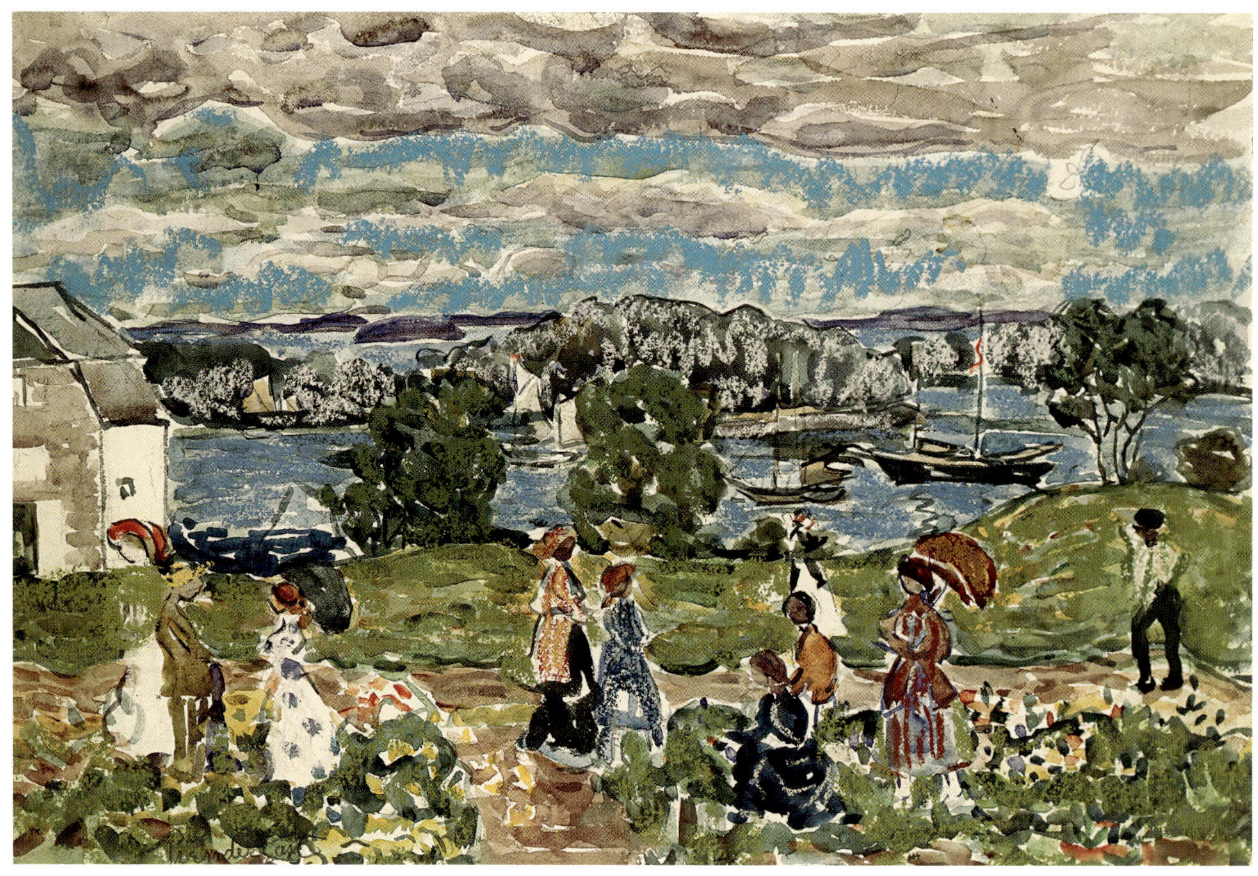

Massachusetts Shore,
c. 1910–1911, watercolor, pencil, and pastel on paper, 13 1/2 x 19 1/2 inches

Maurice Prendergast (1859–1924)

As a "lifelong habitué of seaside resorts," Maurice Prendergast built a career around the depiction of fashionably dressed men and women enjoying the natural beauty and social pageantry of the New England shore.[1] Prendergast was raised in Boston, along with his brother, Charles (1863–1948), a noted frame maker who would become an artist much later in life. As adults, the two often spent their summers on the coast. Boston directories from the late 1870s and early 1880s list a variety of jobs for Maurice, including "clerk," "designer," and "decorator," and it appears that his training as a young artist was largely directed toward the commercial spectrum.[2] In 1891, Prendergast embarked for Paris for what would be a four-year stay, enrolled at the Académie Julian, and was soon painting sights in the city as well as along the Normandy coast. After returning home in 1894, Prendergast gradually abandoned design work and began actively exhibiting watercolors of people at play near the sea, many of which attracted favorable criticism.

A later trip to Paris in 1907, during which he encountered a significant group of watercolors by Paul Cézanne (1839–1906), greatly impacted Prendergast's stylistic development. Much of the work produced in the next several years reveals an artist coming to terms with the heightened palette of the Fauves (whose paintings he also saw in 1907) and the formal lessons of Cézanne, who, he told a friend at the time, "will influence me more than the others."[3] In 1908, the artist exhibited a group of works painted in St. Malo the previous summer at the now-infamous exhibition of The Eight, held at the New York gallery of William Macbeth (1851–1917). Although not stylistically akin, the eight artists were united in their common stance against the restrictive exhibition policies of the academy and in their embrace of subjects drawn from modern life. Alongside his realist colleagues, Prendergast clearly stood apart as an artist in the modernist camp, prompting one critic to remark that his work on view was the result of an "explosion in a color factory."[4]

Massachusetts Shore is one of many watercolors with pastel overlay painted by the artist in the wake of his significant encounter with progressive European art. Its use of broken brushwork, especially in the foreground, anticipates the familiar mosaic-like application of paint found in his later works.[5] Familiar, too, is the subject of modern leisure at one of the many turn-of-the-century seaside resorts dotting the Massachusetts coast, which appear repeatedly in Prendergast's oeuvre. Thanks to the railroad and the steamer, travel to such destinations was not beyond the means of many New Englanders, and representatives from all classes could find themselves parading through the public spaces of these modern vacation sites. Urban dwellers flocked to such seaside locales, eager to breathe in the salubrious ocean breezes and to promenade in their finest dress at the edge of the sea.[6]

The market for Prendergast's work expanded considerably in the last decade of his life, and collectors such as Duncan Phillips (1886–1968), Lillie P. Bliss (1864–1931), and Albert C. Barnes (1872–1951) eagerly purchased paintings for their burgeoning collections. Ferdinand Howald (1856–1934), a Columbus, Ohio, collector who purchased his first Prendergast in 1915, bought at least fifteen works, including *Massachusetts Shore*.[7]

JHR

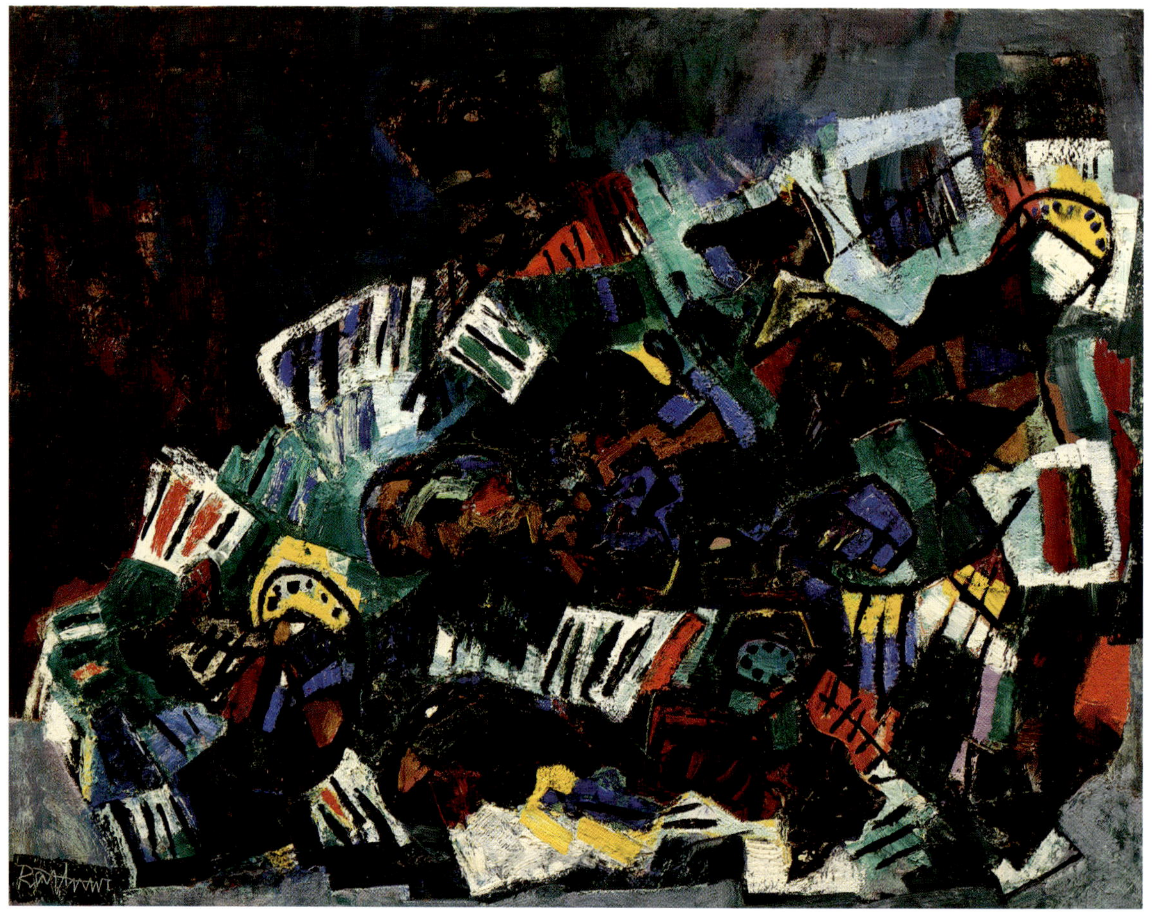

Old Shoe Arrangement No. V,
1954, oil on canvas,
25 3/4 x 32 inches

Abraham Rattner (1893–1978)

Abraham Rattner was born in 1893 in Poughkeepsie, New York, to Russian immigrant parents who had fled the anti-Semitism of their homeland in search of better opportunities in America.[1] After graduating from high school, Rattner initially pursued the study of architecture at George Washington University but soon enrolled at the Corcoran School of Art. In 1917, the young artist transferred to the Pennsylvania Academy of the Fine Arts and after only a year was called to serve his country as a camouflage specialist in World War I. Injured at the second Battle of the Marne, Rattner returned to the Academy in 1919 just long enough to secure a travel fellowship to Europe. Rattner would spend the next twenty years living an impoverished existence in Paris, studying for a time at the Ecole des Beaux-Arts, and exhibiting at such prominent venues as the Salon d'Automne and the Salon des Indépendants.

During these formative years in Paris, Rattner eagerly drank in the lessons of cubism and futurism, although ultimately his aesthetic proclivities led him in the direction of expressionism. The artist's first solo exhibitions would not happen until 1935, the year in which his work was spotlighted in both Paris and New York galleries. In 1940, fleeing the Nazi menace, Rattner returned to this country, abandoning twenty years of work that was never recovered. Disenchanted and very nearly ready to give up the artistic life, Rattner embarked on a tour of the United States with his friend and fellow expatriate, the novelist Henry Miller (1891–1980), and soon after discovering his own country, his country would discover him.[2]

Rattner went on to establish himself as a leading "American Expressionist," building a career on the gestural and philosophical vitality of his richly colored and passionately painted works, many of which drew added strength from their religious subject matter.[3] *Old Shoe Arrangement No. V*, an oil from 1954, demonstrates that Rattner did not need images of prophets and sacred events to embolden his art but could create powerful visual statements through the most humble of objects. The artist once indicated in his notebooks his intention "to make a statement so old—so everyday—of the thing of the backyard, the ordinary well known commonly experienced thing—nothing particular about it except my own experience of it, but not an ordinary thing after that—no now it is more alive than before existing more freshly discovered—intense as it is now inclusive of my own personal meaning."[4] One of several still lifes featuring shoes painted by the artist in the 1950s, the work calls on the great tradition of Byzantine mosaics, or perhaps stained glass windows, with its faceted, brilliantly colored forms held together by an emphatic linear armature.[5] As one scholar has so beautifully observed, "these shoes have taken the imprint of the human foot in its daily journeys; they are therefore sacred and they are painted thus, almost like relics in the old religions. We recall the shoes of Vincent Van Gogh and of the little tramp of Charlie Chaplin. We recall the endless tiring footsteps that compose a life."[6]

JHR

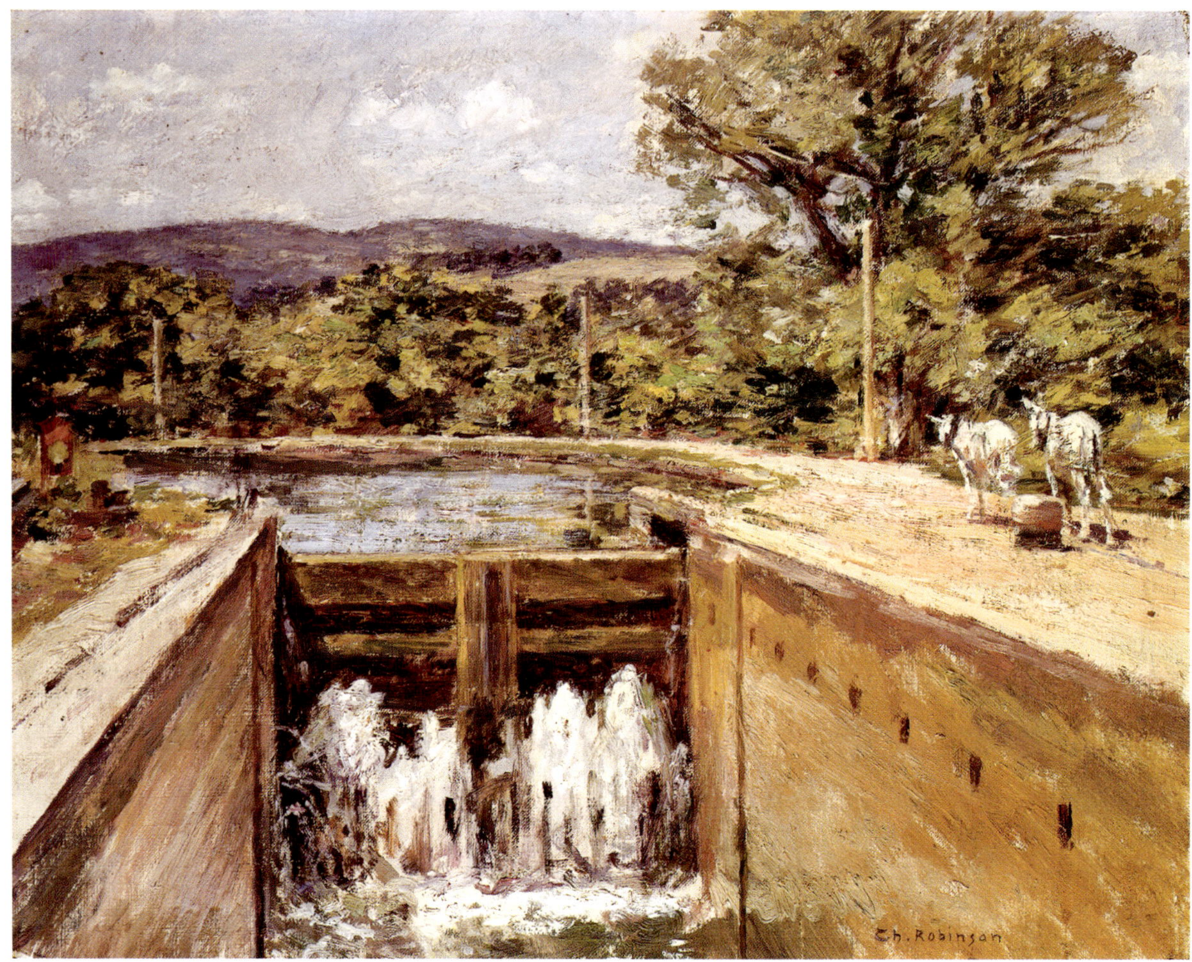

The Lock,
1893, oil on canvas,
18 x 22 inches

Theodore Robinson (1852–1896)

Theodore Robinson was but one of many American artists who flocked to Giverny, France, in the mid-1880s in search of quaint and picturesque vistas. The famed, yet reclusive impressionist painter Claude Monet (1840–1926) had moved to the Norman village in 1883, and his presence there no doubt inspired the would-be landscape painters, many of whom found themselves experimenting with brightened palettes and broken brushwork. Like many of these young expatriates, Robinson had spent considerable time in academic ateliers in Paris in the 1870s and studied with two eminently popular teachers, Charles-Auguste-Emile Duran (1837–1917), known as Carolus-Duran, and Jean-Léon Gérôme (1824–1904). Their approaches could not have been more different—the former an advocate of the importance of the painterly sketch, the latter a firm believer in the necessity of solid draftsmanship—and Robinson would struggle with this antinomy throughout his short career.[1]

Although Monet was never his teacher, Robinson lived next door to the elder statesman of the avant-garde from 1888 to 1892, and the two were close friends and colleagues. During his years in Giverny, Robinson experimented with the subjects and techniques of impressionism and on occasion followed Monet's lead in working serially; that is, painting the same motif in different atmospheric conditions.[2] Robinson returned to the States in 1892 and accepted a job the following summer teaching in Napanoch, New York, a small town situated along the Delaware and Hudson Canal. According to a contemporary newspaper account, Robinson often took his students—all female art students from New York—on plein-air excursions along the canal. "The Delaware and Hudson Canal runs through the village, and the towpath bristles with white umbrellas all day like a field with mushrooms after a fog. Parties board the boats and are towed from one lock to another. The canal men are kindly interested in the progress of art and aid it when they can pointing out 'the fresh greens' and 'tender purples' within sight." The bemused reporter noted further that this "artistic vernacular has become so common that the very drivers stop their horses to point out 'pretty bits' to the aspirants for artistic glory."[3]

Once his two-month teaching stint was completed, Robinson remained in Napanoch until late October, long enough to finish a series of canvases of the working canal.[4] *The Lock* is one of at least three views of this particular subject painted by the artist. In the version in the Snowiss collection, the lock is filling with water as two horses at the canal's edge wait patiently to continue pulling their load along the waterway. According to his diary accounts at the time, Robinson was eager to find appropriate *American* subjects for his impressionist canvases, noting that even Napanoch's unremarkable vernacular architecture should be considered a potential motif. "One or two of my canal things are in a good direction it seems to me," he remarked the day before he left town, "and still more courage, emancipation from old formulae and ideas of what is interesting or beautiful, from the European standpoint, will work wonders." Intrigued by a notably *un*-picturesque motif, Robinson successfully demonstrates in *The Lock* that local subject matter could lead to "new beauties, new oddities, [and] new points of interest."[5] The painting confirms, too, that "impressionist" canvases, however muted and tied to the solidity of form, could be found on—indeed could be inspired by—American soil.

JHR

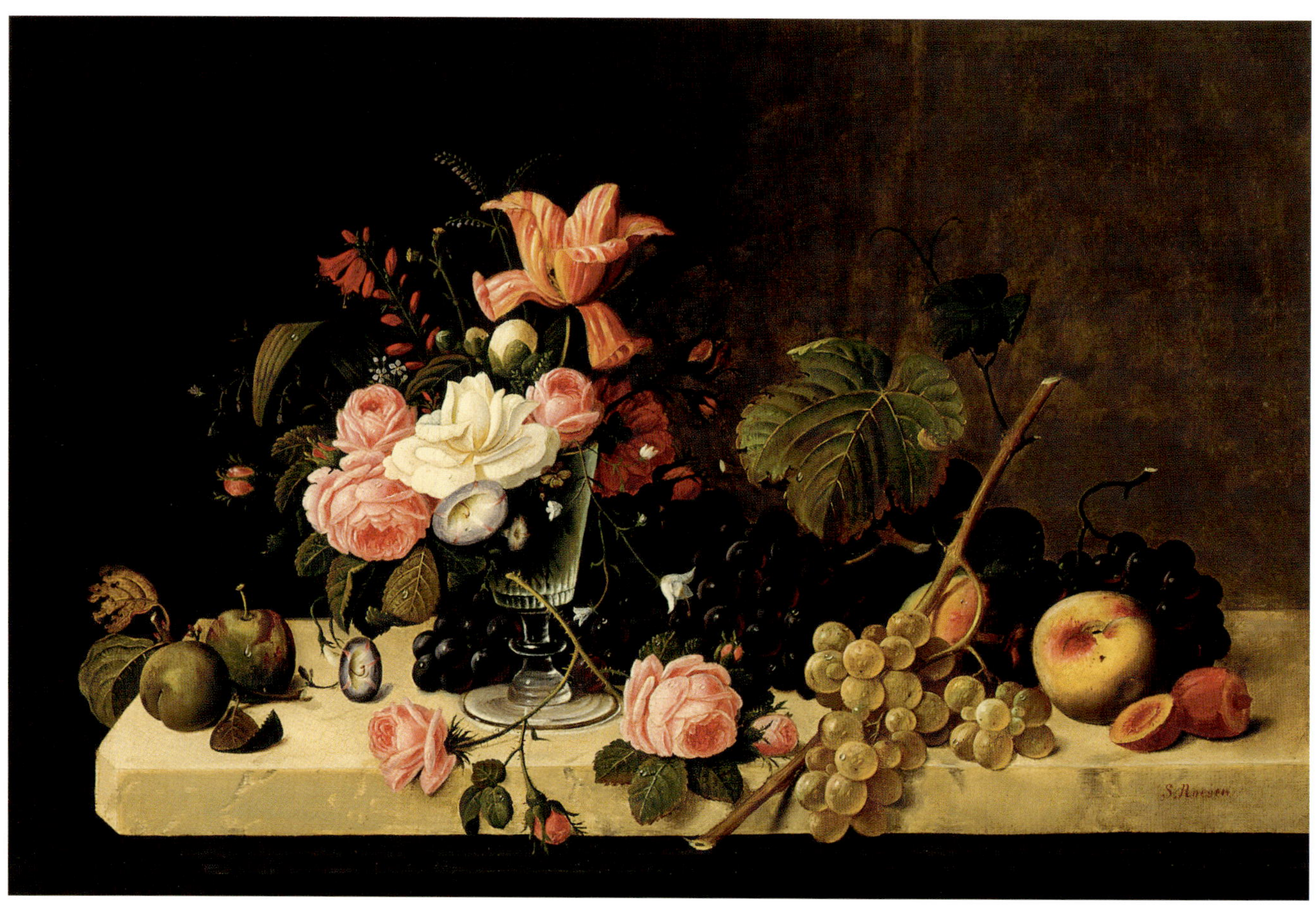

Still Life,
after 1860, oil on canvas,
23 1/2 x 32 inches

Severin Roesen (1815/16–1872 or later)

Unlike his meticulously detailed still lifes, the historical narrative of Severin Roesen's life remains hazy on a number of important counts.[1] Born in Germany and possibly having apprenticed as a decorative porcelain painter, Roesen immigrated to the United States in 1848 and set up shop as an already accomplished artist in New York City. For reasons that are not clear but possibly linked to the economic woes besieging the city, Roesen left New York—and his wife, whom he had married in this country, and their three children—in 1857 or early 1858, in search seemingly of better opportunities. After traveling through Philadelphia, Harrisburg, and Huntingdon, Pennsylvania, Roesen settled in 1860 in Williamsport, then a booming lumber town and home to a significant settlement of German immigrants. Roesen soon found eager clients and for more than a decade produced his signature lush still lifes—some of which he apparently traded for room and board, clothing, or drink—for the impressive homes and businesses of the town's *nouveaux riches*.

According to Judith O'Toole, the still life in the Snowiss collection is typical of the artist's late work, "when his style took on a clarity exaggerated by a heightened attention to detail, a greater intensity in the geometry of the elements and their placement in the composition, and a precise rendering of each piece."[2] The white stone ledge, a feature introduced in the early years in Williamsport, contrasts markedly with the dark background against which the vivid coloration of the still-life elements is brilliantly articulated. Somewhat unusually, the artist devoted equal time, as it were, to the fruit and floral components of the canvas, allowing neither to dominate. The diagonally placed grapevine, a device utilized in numerous Roesen still lifes, beautifully echoes the sweep of lush blossoms made up of pink and white cabbage roses, blue morning glories, and crowned by an exquisite variegated tulip. Clearly indebted to the seventeenth-century Dutch tradition, Roesen's flower and fruit still lifes celebrate the infinite bounty of nature and visually testify, to borrow O'Toole's apt phrasing, "to the plentiful natural resources found in the United States and the euphoria they inspired in its citizens regarding their good fortune."

JHR

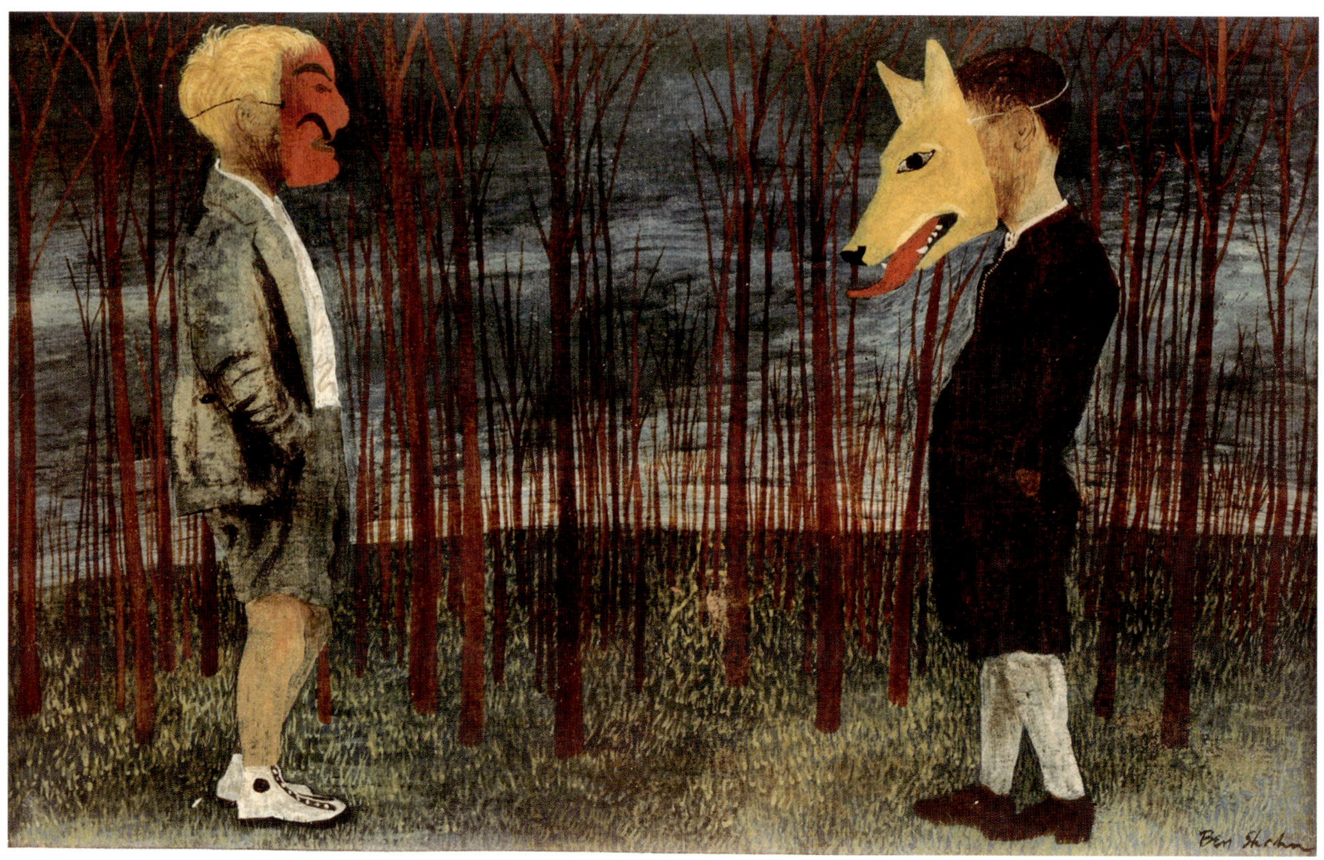

Peter and the Wolf,
1943, tempera on board,
6 1/4 x 10 1/4 inches

Ben Shahn (1898–1969)

In the introduction to his essay "The Biography of a Painting," Ben Shahn declared, "I have the right to believe freely. To be a slave to no man's authority." Whether addressing social concerns and injustice in his prints, murals, and photographs, or refusing to alter a small detail of a commissioned work, Shahn made it clear to his audience that "no man can command my conscience."[1]

Shahn was introduced to political controversy as a child. In his native Lithuania, Shahn's father, a craftsman who taught his son to draw at an early age, was branded a revolutionary and exiled to Siberia when the future artist was just 4 years old. The family regrouped in New York City in 1906, and by age 14 Shahn was apprenticed to a lithography shop in Manhattan. In the late teens, while working professionally as a journeyman lithographer, Shahn attended classes at a number of institutions and eventually enrolled at the National Academy of Design in 1921.[2]

Although Shahn first produced landscapes after his return from a trip to Europe in 1925, he soon turned his attention to social and political subject matter. His breakthrough series concerning the controversial trial, conviction, and execution of the Italian anarchists Sacco and Vanzetti was but one of many works he produced to address societal ills. The bleak years of the Great Depression funneled Shahn and many other artists into jobs created through government work programs. Employed by the Resettlement Administration and the Farm Security Administration during the years 1935 to 1938, he produced thousands of photographs documenting the abject poverty suffered by millions.[3] Shahn's subsequent work for the government included murals for the Social Security Building in Washington, D.C., and posters produced during World War II for the Office of War Information.

During the 1940s, Shahn began to accept commissions from such magazines as *Fortune* and *Time* and also produced promotional materials for the Chrysler Corporation, among others. In 1943, the Capehart Corporation commissioned an advertisement slated to promote a sound recording of Sergei Prokofiev's (1891–1953) folktale *Peter and the Wolf*.[4] The resulting tempera painting, at once whimsical and edgy, features two masked boys who confront each other in a barren woodland. The piece was created at a time when, as the artist later attested, his art was moving from social realism "into a sort of personal realism." For Shahn, the subject of wolves conjured up deep-seated emotions. "To me the wolf whether symbolic or real, is perhaps the most paralyzingly dreadful of beasts. Is my fear some instinctive strain out of my Russian background? I don't know. Is it merely the product of some of my mother's colorful tales about being pursued by wolves when she was with a wedding party, or again when she went alone from her village to another one nearby? … Whatever its source, my sense of panic concerning the wolf is real."[5] Despite the fact that James Thrall Soby described *Peter and the Wolf* as one of the artist's "most charming small paintings," an ominous sense of foreboding permeates the bleak landscape, linking it to other allegorical narratives produced by Shahn beginning in the early 1940s.[6]

When Capehart asked that minor changes be made to the sneakers worn by "Peter," Shahn balked at the request and refused to alter the work. He retained the painting and ultimately sold it to Aline Loucheim (1914–1972), the noted art critic and future wife of Finnish architect Eero Saarinen (1910–1961).[7] Indeed, whether documenting social and political strife or fashioning advertisements, Shahn remained steadfast in his vision: "To go against conscience is neither right nor safe. I cannot—I will not—recant."[8]

JD/JHR

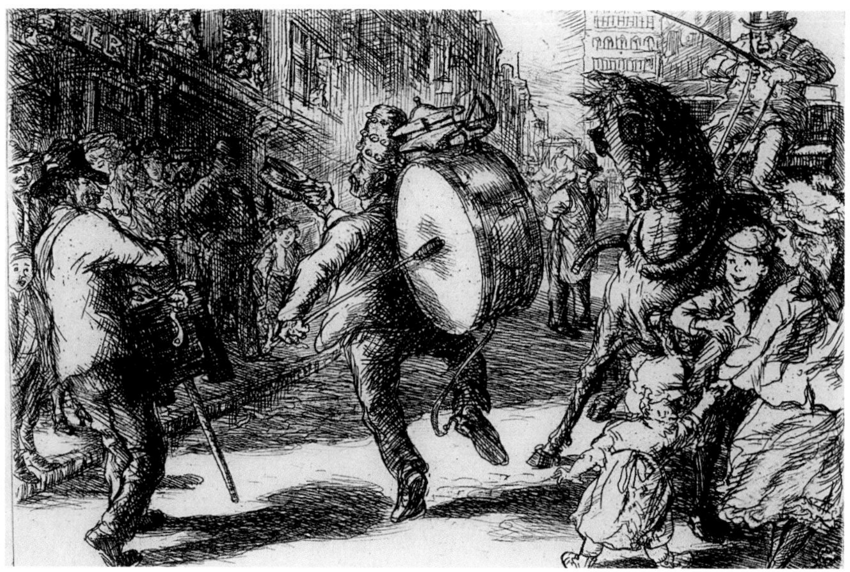

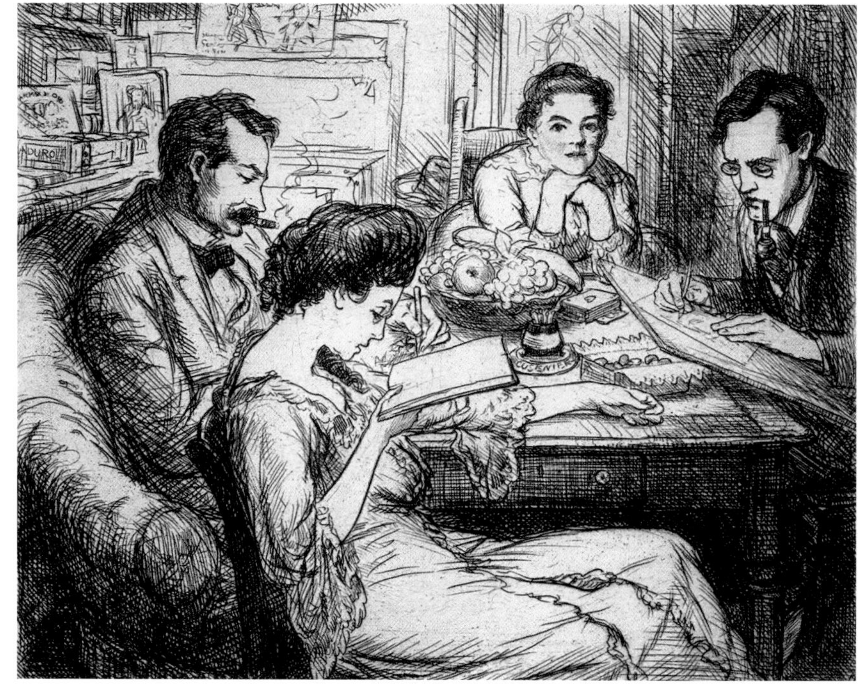

Man Monkey,
1905, etching,
5 x 7 inches (plate)

Memory,
1906, etching,
7 1/2 x 9 inches (plate)

John Sloan (1871–1951)

John Sloan once characterized himself as a "spectator of life," and indeed he devoted much of his career to capturing the variety and vitality of the world around him in both his prints and paintings. Sloan was born in the central Pennsylvania town of Lock Haven but moved to Philadelphia with his family as a boy. There he attended Central High School, but just months before he was to have graduated, Sloan was forced to withdraw to help support his family. A job as an assistant cashier at the book and print dealers Porter & Coates afforded the young Sloan the opportunity to read classic novels and to study fine art prints firsthand. Sloan taught himself to etch and was soon designing calendars and cards for a "fancy goods" store. In 1892, Sloan was hired as a newspaper illustrator in the art department of the *Philadelphia Inquirer*, a job he held until he left for a similar position at the *Philadelphia Press* in 1895. By this time Sloan was deeply immersed in the circle of artist-reporters who frequently found themselves congregating in the Walnut Street studio of their mentor, the painter Robert Henri (1865–1929). Sloan once commented that "Henri could make anyone want to be an artist," and it would not be too many years before he and his newspaper colleagues would find themselves in New York City, eager to try their hands at becoming full-time artists and turning their reporter's eyes onto the boisterous life of the city.[1]

The streets of New York provided Sloan with a seemingly endless spectacle of urban sights and activities. Not long after settling in the city in the spring of 1904, he began work on a set of etchings aptly titled "New York City Life." *Man Monkey*, one of ten prints from the original series, depicts a pair of street performers whose antics the artist witnessed not far from his apartment/studio on West 23rd Street.[2] "In the side streets of the Chelsea and Greenwich Village districts, the one man band with hand organ accompanist furnished free entertainment to those who dropped no pennies," Sloan later noted. "He worried the horse-drawn traffic of the time, but before many years the automobile and motor truck cleared him from the streets."[3] Like many of Sloan's prints, *Man Monkey* contains a great deal of "human interest" reportage translated visually with a sketch-like fluency of line. When Sloan submitted the series for exhibition with the American Water Color Society in New York, four of the prints—not including *Man Monkey*—were rejected for being "vulgar" and "indecent." Similar charges would be directed at the urban genre paintings of Sloan and comrades at the exhibition of The Eight a few short years later.

That Sloan was more than a witty observer of everyday life is evident in the etching *Memory*, a group portrait of Sloan and Henri with their wives.[4] The four had become close friends during their time together in New York and often spent quiet evenings together reading, sketching, and enjoying one another's company. The print, which gave the artist great difficulty, was made as a memorial to these intimate evenings soon after Linda Henri's death in December 1905. In the print, Linda is shown reading to the group seated at a table in the Henri home. "Henri was always amazed that I had remembered her gesture: her hand rolling her fingers as she read aloud. It was made purely from memory."[5] Both Sloan and Henri, who are shown intently sketching in the print, advocated working from memory. "Train yourself to use memory and imagination," Sloan once remarked, "or your drawing will show that the model and not your spirit dominated the idea."[6] Henri was reportedly pleased with the print, sensing in its tender characterizations, no doubt, the gentle spirit of the artist as well as the bittersweet memory of his departed wife.

JHR

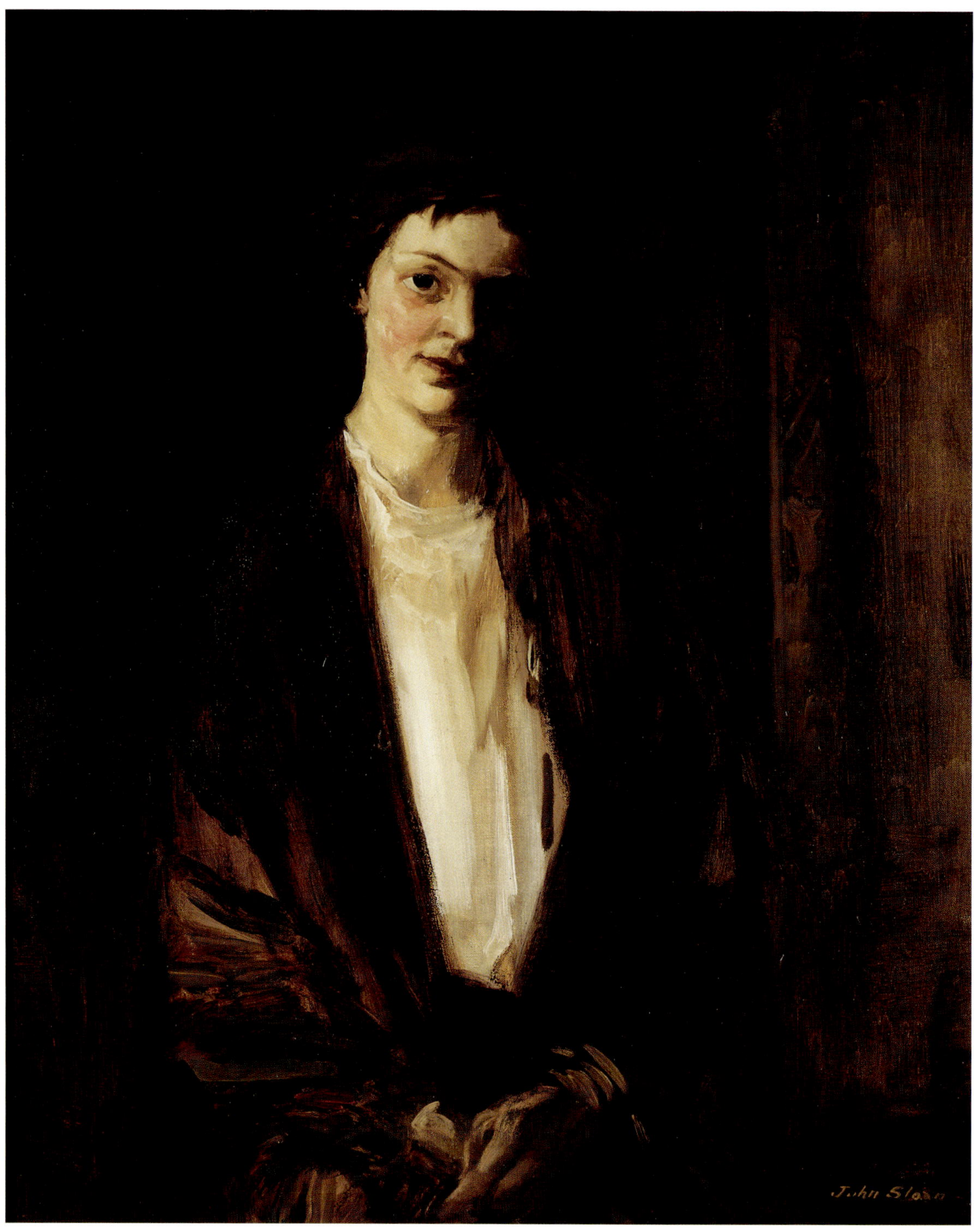

The Purple Shawl (Yolande),
1909, oil on canvas,
31 x 25 1/2 inches

John Sloan (1871–1951)

John Sloan likely would have concurred with his mentor Robert Henri (1865–1929) that "the first condition of a portrait" is finding "an interest in the subject."[1] According to Sloan's diary, Yolande Bugbee first sat for him on November 10, 1909. "Miss 'Yolande' posed for me this afternoon," he recorded. "A very bright nervous bird-like young lady of seventeen years. She was interesting, and I think that I have a good start on her portrait." At a time in his life when hiring models was an "expensive luxury," Sloan nonetheless delighted in his young sitter's "elfin personality" and "lovely fire and spirit" and apparently extended her initial engagement of one week. "She has a bright, fanciful mind and has been a great incentive to work," he commented. Four portraits of Yolande resulted from her time with the artist in late November, including *The Purple Shawl (Yolande)*, which Sloan began on the fifteenth of that month, the day after finishing *Yolande in Gray Tippet*.[2] "Worked on Miss Bugbee and I think I have another good one started." Two days later, the artist noted that he "went on with the Yolande Bugbee second picture, with shawl, and it's going all right." After another day's work on the hands, the painting was complete.[3]

With its dark tonalities and vigorous handling of paint, particularly in the hands and lower segments of the drape, *The Purple Shawl (Yolande)* clearly follows in the Henri painterly tradition. Sloan was greatly influenced by the animated brushwork of his friend and colleague, who maintained that a certain fluency of execution was crucial to capturing the spirit of a subject. Like Henri, Sloan enjoyed engaging the spirit of everyday people, and he characterized this particular portrait of Yolande as a "thing with a certain amount of tenderness, but not sentimental," the latter adjective linked in the artist's mind with stilted society portraits at the turn of the century.[4] Yolande would sit for Sloan in 1910 and again the following year. Apparently she was pleased with the results, for many years later, she contacted the artist hoping to purchase "'Blue' or 'Yolande with a Black Eye' or 'Yolande Weeping into her Tea Cup' or 'Yolande Anything' so long as Sloan painted it."[5]

JHR

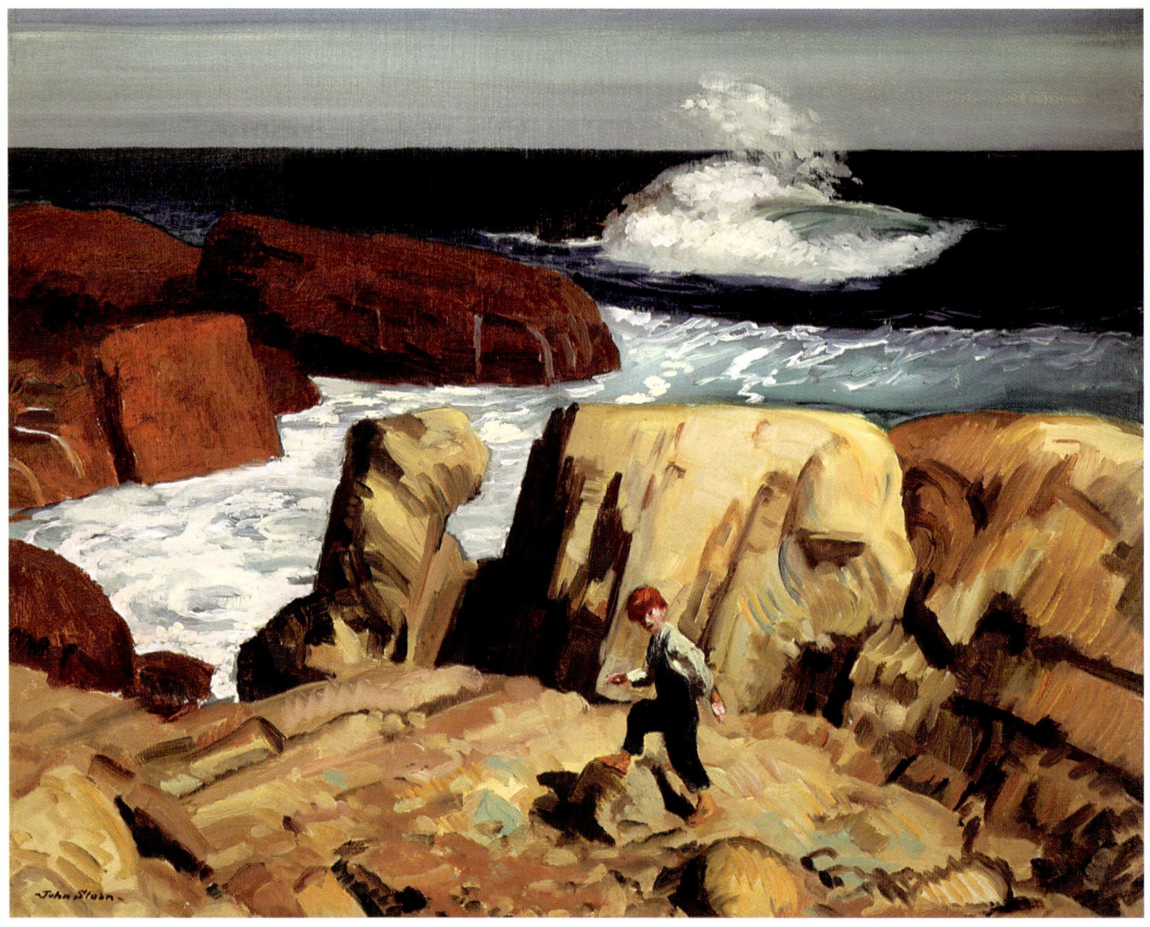

Reddy on the Rocks,
1917, oil on canvas,
26 x 32 inches

John Sloan (1871–1951)

Although the name of John Sloan typically conjures up images of bustling city streets, the artist was also a committed landscape painter. Sloan and his first wife, Dolly, spent their first summer in Gloucester, Massachusetts—which he called "one of the odd corners of America"—in 1914.[1] The trip was inspired by a desire on the artist's part to escape the harried professional life of the city in search of new artistic motivation. "I had been dependent on waiting for the inspiration to paint a picture because I had so little leisure time to work for myself," Sloan later recalled. "So I decided to save up enough money to take off a few months, go to the country and work from nature, to get fresh ideas about plastic design and color rhythms."[2] Sloan's choice of Gloucester for his summer retreat placed him in good company, for the quaint fishing town had played and would continue to play host to innumerable American artists, including Winslow Homer (1836–1910), Childe Hassam (1859–1935), Edward Hopper (1882–1967), and Stuart Davis (1894–1964). Among the most compelling features of the area was the cape's rocky coastline, and Sloan, like many other "fair-weather Gloucestermen," found a rich source of pictorial material in the town's varied geography.[3]

Sloan's first trip to Gloucester came fairly soon after his introduction to recent developments in modern art on display at the infamous Armory Show of 1913, and his work there over the next five summers reveals an artist coming to terms with the emphatic gestural brushwork and heightened palette of the European modernists. Because of its distance from the hallowed tradition of figure painting, Sloan viewed landscape as a freer mode for exploring the lessons of the post-impressionists. "There is no better subject matter to free one of color habits," Sloan noted. "The variety in nature offers new color combinations, new ideas. You also feel more free to take liberties with colors in nature than when painting from the figure."[4] Several years earlier, Sloan had been introduced to the color system of Hardesty Maratta (1864–1924), which offered artists a regular schema for determining appropriate color combinations and harmonies. Although preparation of the palette required a fairly significant amount of time, the Maratta system greatly facilitated Sloan's rapid production of Gloucester landscapes, most of which were painted directly from nature and finished on the spot. During his five summers in the New England town, Sloan produced nearly 300 paintings, more than he had produced in the previous twenty years and nearly one-fourth of his entire oeuvre in painting.[5]

The brilliant coloration of *Reddy on the Rocks*, while perhaps heightened by an awareness of European modernism and codified by the Maratta system, seems to have been derived from the site itself.[6] Sloan recalled the area's "red granite rocks" and the "great blue wall" of sea, and also remarked on his "distinct memory of that long, straight edge of the ocean at the horizon." Reddy, whom the artist described as a "friendly, likable, little fellow" with a "sun-pink face and carrotty hair," also contributed his part to the painting's vivid palette.[7] The weightiness of form and emphatic brushwork evident in the Snowiss picture also confirm that Sloan was coming to terms with the inherent expressivity of the formal language of art in his Gloucester landscapes. These formal elements provided Sloan with the perfect tools for conveying the site's powerful presence, for after all, a landscape is, as he once noted, "the portrait of a place."[8]

JHR

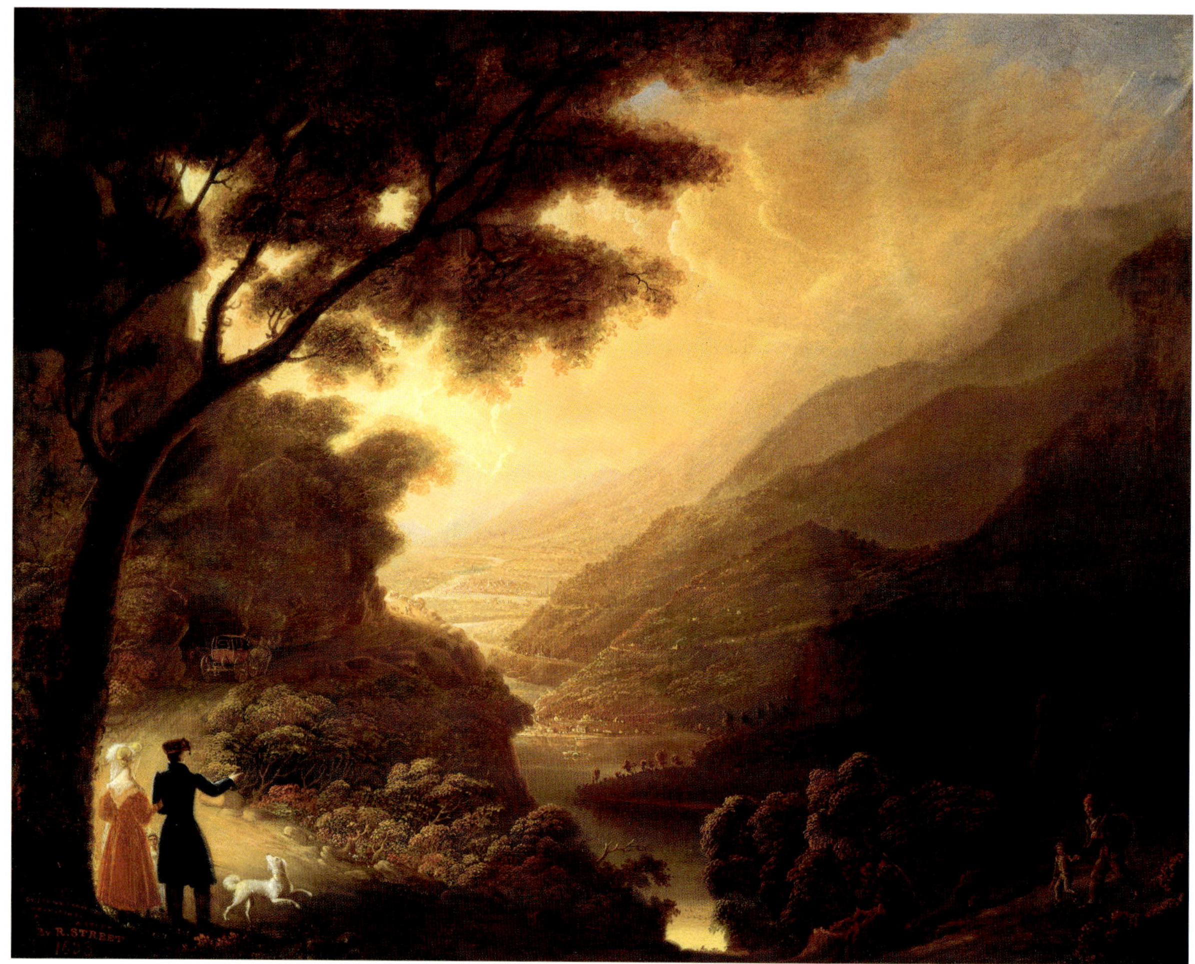

Descent from the Mountains,
1833, oil on canvas,
25 x 30 inches

Robert Street (1796–1865)

One does not frequently come across Robert Street's name in modern histories of American art. The Philadelphia-based painter, however, won acclaim in his lifetime as a portraitist and also made significant forays into landscape, still life, and history painting. He first gained renown, early in his career, for his portrait of the war hero and soon-to-be president Andrew Jackson.[1] From 1816 through 1861, the artist was included in several dozen exhibitions at the Pennsylvania Academy of the Fine Arts, and his works entered the collections of some of the most eminent Philadelphians.[2] As a testament to his rising celebrity, more than 200 of his works were featured in a one-man exhibition at the Artists' Fund Hall in Philadelphia in 1840.[3]

Over the years, the present picture has been called both *Descent from the Mountains, Hudson River Landscape* and *Descent from the Mountains, Pennsylvania.*[4] Whether the painting represents New York, Pennsylvania, or perhaps some other locale, it certainly matches the burgeoning taste for landscape painting and the growing favor of romanticized American scenery. In order to make their work desirable to exhibiting institutions and to appease patrons, nineteenth-century painters directed landscape imagery toward diverse and often disparate purposes. We can nonetheless isolate three common types of work in this genre. In the first category, natural wonders dominate and offset any human presence. Thomas Cole (1801–1848), Alvan Fisher (1792–1863), and other artists working in this mode used linear, precise styles to celebrate the grandeur of nature, as if preserving in paint a wilderness increasingly threatened by the industrial revolution. In contemporary history paintings, popular prints, and illustrated books, we find a second popular landscape type, one in which signs of civilization overshadow natural wonders, the blunt ruthlessness of industry suppressing the majesty of flora and fauna.

Descent from the Mountains, however, characterizes a third category of landscape representation increasingly found in nineteenth-century America, a reconciliation of the two above models. Street's painting celebrates nature insofar as it presents bucolic hinterlands bathed in a golden orange haze, emphasizing the richness and variety of fecund greenery. Yet, with the foreground figures, the road and buggy, and perhaps most significantly, the tree stump just right of center in the foreground, the picture also emblematizes the onward march of civilization.[5] Harmonizing modern industrial and pre-existing natural components so that they mesh in the picture plane, this third model is also found in such paintings as Cole's *View from Mount Holyoke, Northampton, Massachusetts, after a Thunderstorm (The Oxbow)* (1836, The Metropolitan Museum of Art) and George Inness' (1825–1894) *The Lackawanna Valley* (c. 1855, National Gallery of Art). An early example of the third type, Street's picture foreshadows some seventy-five years of landscape painting.

The manner in which Street grafted European artistic styles onto American scenery in *Descent from the Mountains* is equally innovative. Although an early biographer reported that Street owned paintings by Peter Paul Rubens (1577–1640), Annibale Carracci (1560–1609), and other artists, it is more likely that he had copies of their works.[6] What is certain, however, is that his own paintings demonstrate a veneration for the "old masters." With the figures in the close foreground and the river leading through a picturesque vista, Street signals his awareness of "ideal" landscape painting, particularly that of Carracci, who was also one of the first artists to use the device of the compositionally stabilizing tree we see at left in Street's painting. Because of its frequent appearance in the paintings of Claude Lorrain (1604–1682), this motif came to be called the "Claudean tree." Also Claudean in *Descent from the Mountains* is the creation of atmospheric perspective through hazy light and seemingly dissolving forms in the background. Street also honored Claude on a more personal level. Like Charles Willson Peale (1741–1827) before him, Street named his children after artists he admired, in the hopes that they would follow in his profession. The artist's son Claude Lorrain Street (1834–?) indeed became a professional portrait painter.[7]

LGM

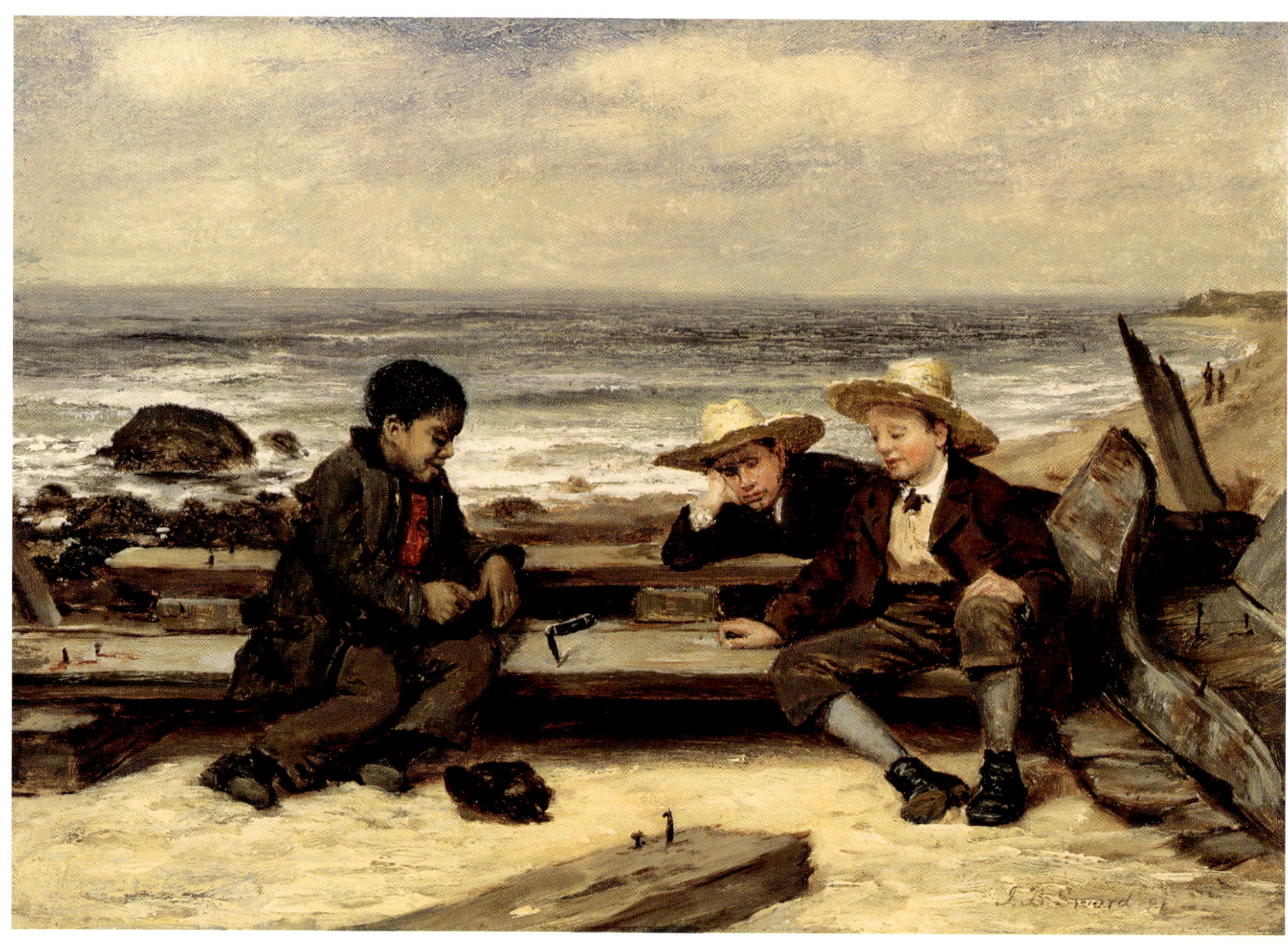

Mumbley Peg,
1881, oil on board,
10 x 14 inches

James Brade Sword (1839–1915)

Although he was born in Philadelphia and ultimately became identified as an artist of that city, James Brade Sword spent the first decade of his life in China, where his father worked in the tea and silk business. Educated in public schools after the family's return to Philadelphia, Sword pursued careers in civil engineering and the production of silverplated wares before settling into the life of the professional artist in the early 1870s.[1] By turns a landscape, portrait, and genre painter, Sword exhibited widely and was soon a prominent figure in several of Philadelphia's art organizations.

Mumbley Peg, a painting formerly in the collection of Mrs. Norman B. Woolworth, depicts a child's game, a theme highly favored by nineteenth-century American genre painters.[2] "Mumble-the-peg," variously known as "mumblety-peg," "mumbly peg," or, as in this case, "mumbley peg," was a popular and, from all appearances, dangerous game involving a pocketknife and a succession of varied throwing positions. The name derives from the game's stipulation that the losing player root out a peg driven into the ground by the victor. The choice of a seaside setting for the picture may have resulted from Sword's visit in 1881 to Conanicut Island, Rhode Island; the artist built a house there two years later and regularly spent his summers painting on the island's shores. Exhibited at the National Academy of Design the year it was painted, *Mumbley Peg* depicts three children of approximately the same age, two of whom are actively engaged in the knife-throwing segment of the game. The young black child's tattered and disheveled clothes suggest a different socioeconomic status than that of his white companions. Although the children are separated compositionally by a potent gap, their joining together in this seemingly innocent pastime represents a rather unusual document of harmonious race relations in post-Reconstruction America.

A handwritten note on the back of the painting indicates that *Mumbley Peg* was painted at 1520 Chestnut Street, an address in the "art-centre" of Philadelphia at the time. Like many prominent Philadelphia artists, Sword maintained a studio in the Baker Building, which, according to one contemporary account, was "the first structure erected in the city especially for the accommodation of artists."[3] Along with George Cochran Lambdin (1830–1896) and a host of other painters less familiar to us today, Sword welcomed the public to monthly studio receptions at the Baker Building, located at 1520 Chestnut Street. Although one critic found this monthly schedule too ambitious, he nonetheless conceded that the receptions "have been well attended, and have undoubtedly aided in promoting public interest in art matters and attracting attention to the painters and their current work."[4]

JHR

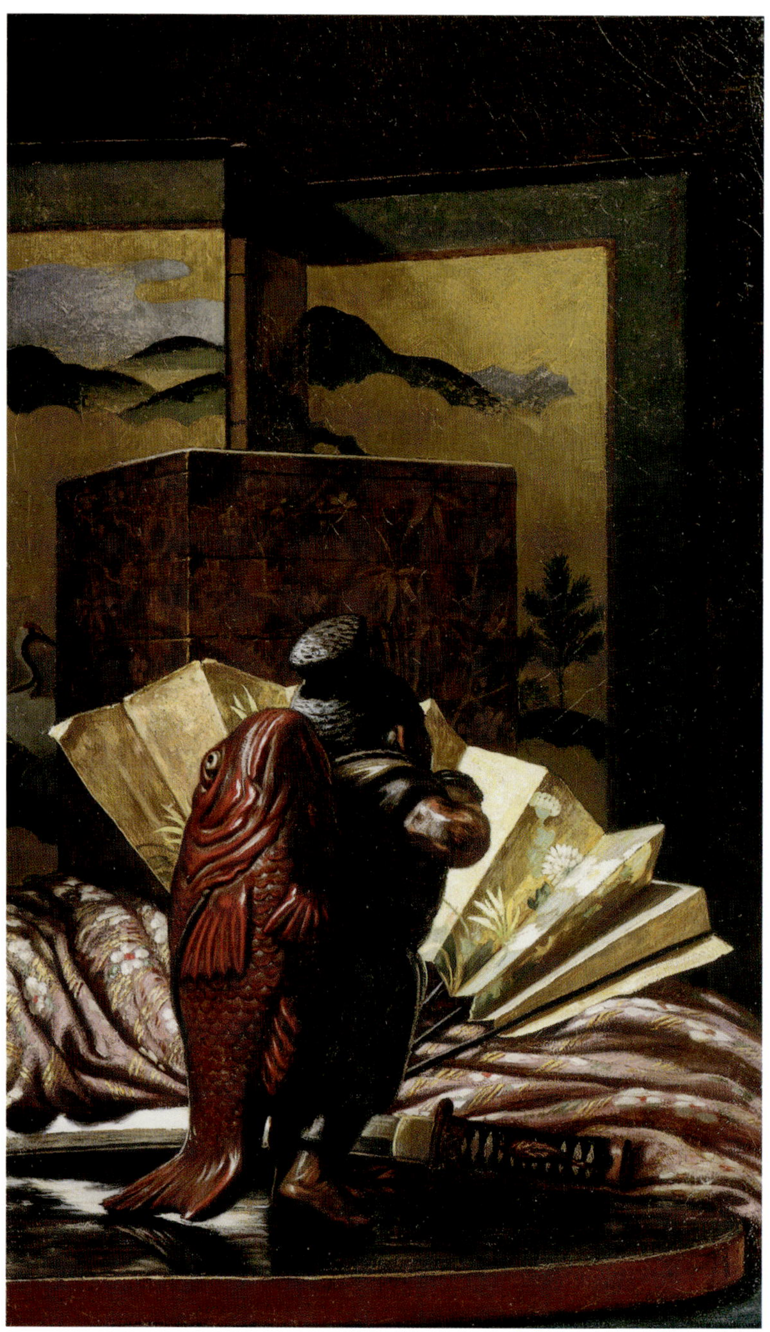

Japanese Still Life,
1892, oil on canvas,
28 x 16 inches

Elihu Vedder (1836–1923)

Elihu Vedder is typically regarded as a prescient symbolist artist, although his work remains less well known than that of his fellow "visionaries," Ralph Albert Blakelock (1847–1919) and Albert Pinkham Ryder (1847–1917). Vedder was raised in the disparate locales of Schenectady, New York, and Cuba, and educated in New York City boarding schools. At the age of 20, Vedder left for Paris, where he spent a few months drawing from classical casts in the academic studio of François Edouard Picot (1786–1868). By 1860, Vedder had made his way to Florence, Italy, and although he studied with an academician there, he also associated with a group of artists known as the "Macchiaioli" or "spot-painters," whose luminous landscapes were inspired by the direct observation of nature. Vedder soon returned to New York and began producing the literary, symbolic landscapes that would establish his reputation. Although the members of the National Academy of Design elected him a full academician in 1865, the following year Vedder moved to Rome, where, except for brief trips, he remained the rest of his life.[1]

Like most intellectuals of his day, Vedder was curious about a wide range of topics. In his biography, *The Digressions of V.*, he amusingly noted that his life was but a "succession of fads," particularly beginning with his "Roman period," during which "the fads became more serious and absorbing." Included in Vedder's list of intellectual diversions was "the canoe craze," "mycology" (the study of fungi), "a very serious flirt with stained glass," "aviation," and "Japanese objects and prints."[2] Vedder, who characterized himself as an "abject admirer of all things in Japanese Art," probably received his first introduction to the art of Japan in Boston in the company of his friend John La Farge (1835–1910).[3] La Farge's wife was a grand-niece of Commodore Matthew Perry (1794–1858), who in 1854 opened Japan to international trade with the West, and the artist apparently encountered Japanese prints as early as 1856 in Paris.[4] Unlike La Farge, who visited Japan in 1886, Vedder never traveled to the Far East, preferring instead to experience the country's artistic splendors from afar.

Japanese Still Life is indicative both of Vedder's versatility as an artist and of the general craze for "things Japanese" that swept America in the years following the 1876 Centennial Exposition in Philadelphia. Japan's pavilions at the exposition housed a rich array of decorative objects, including ceramics, bronzes, lacquer ware, and silk fabrics, affording audiences a view of "an exotic but artistic people whose ornamentation and aesthetic fantasies fit well the eclectic taste of Victorian America."[5] Vedder did not visit the Centennial exhibition, but he did maintain his own display of Japanese bric-a-brac, having received "three trunks full of beautiful Japanese objects" after the death of his brother, a naval surgeon stationed in Japan, in 1871.[6] Although signed 1892, *Japanese Still Life* is quite similar in feel to a work of the same title painted by the artist in 1879 and now in the permanent collection of the Los Angeles County Museum of Art. Like the work in the Snowiss collection, the earlier *Japanese Still Life* is a visual catalogue of Far Eastern "collectibles," from a large ceramic vase and a beautiful screen depicting herons in a landscape to brocaded cloths that cascade across the picture plane.[7] In the later picture, Vedder creates a sumptuous and, at the same time, hermetic environment comprised of exquisite Japanese *objets d'art*. Although better known ultimately for his visionary pictures of sphinxes and mermaids, Vedder offers us in this rarefied still life an "exotic" vision of decorative beauty as seen through the inquisitive eyes and acquisitive mindset of the West.

JHR

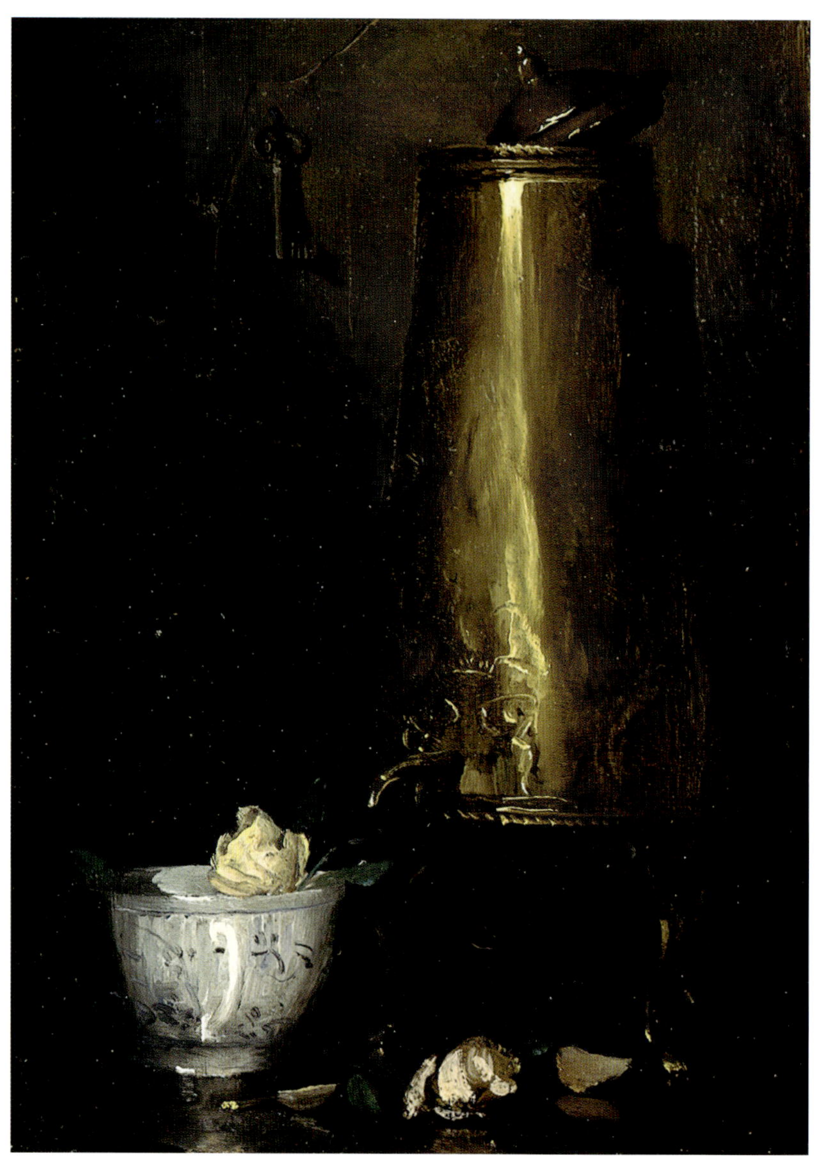

A Bit of Blue,
c. 1885–1889, oil on panel,
7 1/2 x 5 1/8 inches

J. Alden Weir (1852–1919)

Although J. Alden Weir is best known today as one of the leading practitioners of American Impressionism and an affiliate of the dissident group The Ten, his early work reveals an artist grounded in the fundamentals of academic training. His father, Robert W. Weir (1803–1889), was a drawing instructor at the U.S. Military Academy at West Point as well as an accomplished landscape and portrait painter, who instilled in his son a deep appreciation of the old masters. The elder Weir no doubt supported his youngest son's tenure of study at the National Academy of Design beginning in 1867, having already witnessed the matriculation of another son, John Ferguson Weir (1841–1926), and having himself been made an academician in 1829. By 1873, J. Alden Weir had embarked for Paris, where he would spend the next four years pursuing further education in the studio of Jean-Léon Gérôme (1824–1904) at the Ecole des Beaux-Arts.

Like many pupils in what was then the world's greatest artistic capital, Weir grew to be an accomplished artist with a solid grounding as a draftsman, but found himself increasingly attracted to the painterly brushwork of such artists as Franz Hals (1580–1666) and Frank Duveneck (1848–1919). Weir's initial response to the art of the French impressionists, whose work he characterized as "worse than a Chamber of Horrors" at their third exhibition in 1877, was vocally negative; however, he would soon echo their independent spirit as a founding member of the Society of American Artists that same year.[1] Although it would be well over a decade before he would fully embrace the technique and palette of the impressionists, his work of the 1880s reveals an ongoing dialogue with French art—both past and present.

Weir established himself as a professional artist in New York City upon his return from Europe in 1877, and still life would help to establish his reputation as a painter over the next several years.[2] Weir's first exhibition pieces in the genre were ambitious, large-scale works featuring floral arrangements and decorative objects. Around 1884, Weir returned to the modest kitchen subjects he had briefly experimented with in Paris and produced intimately scaled still lifes that were rarely exhibited and often painted for friends well into the late 1880s. One such work, *A Bit of Blue*, vividly betrays the influence of two French artists, namely the eighteenth-century master Jean-Baptiste-Siméon Chardin (1699–1779) and the contemporary renegade Edouard Manet (1832–1883). Chardin's reputation as an exquisite delineator of the most humble objects had risen considerably in the wake of the rise of Naturalism in France in the 1860s, and the metal urn featured in the Snowiss painting is an obvious homage to one of the most revered of that country's still-life painters. Weir had the opportunity to meet a modern, yet equally brilliant practitioner of still life when he met Manet in Paris in 1881, and his influence reveals itself in the fluid brushwork that so emphatically describes the delicate porcelain cup and fragile flowers in the foreground. One of the most diminutive still lifes painted by the artist, *A Bit of Blue* is a quiet gem of a picture and confirms what Duncan Phillips (1886–1968), a longtime supporter of Weir, once noted: "these things possess so delicious and unctuous a pigment, so charmingly rendering their subjects with especial regard to richness of tone and texture, that they would make Weir sure of a reputation as a painter's painter even if he had not gone on to greater achievements."[3]

JHR

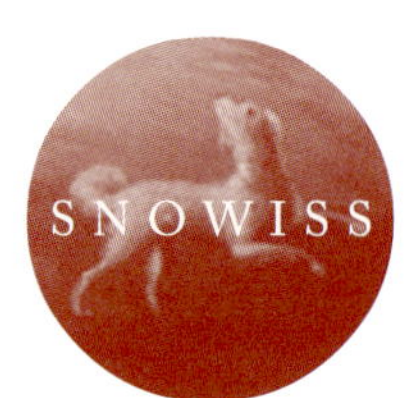
SNOWISS

ENDNOTES

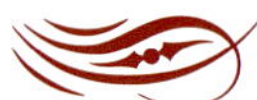

ENDNOTES

Panoramic Sensibilities in Nineteenth- and Twentieth-Century American Painting

[1] Charles Burchfield, journal entry, October 29, 1952; in *Burchfield's Seasons* (New York: Kennedy Galleries, 1982), n.p.

[2] *Oxford English Dictionary*, 2nd ed.

[3] For a history of the European panorama, see Oliver Grau, "Into the Belly of the Image: Historical Aspects of Virtual Reality," *Leonardo* 32 (1999): 365–71; and Stephan Oettermann, *The Panorama: History of a Mass Medium*, trans. Deborah Lucas Schneider (New York: Zone Books, 1997).

[4] See Oettermann, 314–15, 317.

[5] Banvard's panorama is thoughtfully examined in Angela Miller, "Space as Destiny: The Panorama Vogue in Mid-Nineteenth-Century America," in Irving Lavin, ed., *World Art: Themes of Unity in Diversity* (University Park, Pa.: The Pennsylvania State University Press, 1986), 739–42. See also Oetterman, 327–33.

[6] Miller, 741.

[7] *Oxford English Dictionary*, see entries for "panorama" and "panoramic."

[8] William Cullen Bryant, "Monument Mountain" (1824), lines 1, 10–12, as quoted in Albert Boime, *The Magisterial Gaze: Manifest Destiny and American Landscape Painting c. 1830–1865* (Washington, D.C.: Smithsonian Institution Press, 1991), 13.

[9] For two especially clear, critically informed introductions to Hudson River School landscape painting, see Angela Miller, *The Empire of the Eye: Landscape Representation and American Cultural Politics, 1825–1875* (Ithaca: Cornell University Press, 1993); and William H. Truettner and Alan Wallach, *Thomas Cole: Landscape into History* (Washington, D.C.: National Museum of American Art, 1994).

[10] For similar contemporary landscape paintings depicting a well-dressed couple pointing to the middle ground and distance, see Charles Fraser, *Trenton Falls*, c. 1830, oil on canvas (collection of Victor D. Spark), and Thomas Davies, *Chaudière Falls near Quebec, Canada*, 1792, watercolor and gouache over pencil on paper (Public Archives Canada, Ottawa); reproduced in Edward J. Nygren with Bruce Robertson, *Views and Visions: American Landscape before 1830* (Washington, D.C.: The Corcoran Gallery of Art, 1986), 57, 251, respectively.

[11] Literally "like a picture," *picturesque* has two time-honored but contested meanings. Some travelers deemed the picturesque to inhere physically within a landscape, a pleasing condition generated by the admixture of various terrains and natural features. Others thought that the picturesque existed not in the land but in one's mind, where beholders arranged the landscape before them in an edifying tableau.

[12] Alan Wallach, "Making a Picture of the View from Mt. Holyoke," in David C. Miller, ed., *American Iconology: New Approaches to Nineteenth-Century Art and Literature* (New Haven: Yale University Press, 1993), especially 83–84, 90–91.

[13] See for example Alfred B. Street, *Woods and Waters; or, The Saranacs and Racket* (New York: M. Doolady, 1860), 330–34.

[14] I am indebted here to Ernst Bloch's concept of "anticipatory illumination," which a painterly or literary passage elicits when it suggests a temporal or spatial realm beyond itself. Such illumination fills in the gaps of banal existence with that which has yet to happen, what Bloch calls "not-yet-conscious" and the "not-yet-become." See Jack Zipes, "Toward a Realization of Anticipatory Illumination," in Bloch, *The Utopian Function of Art and Literature: Selected Essays*, trans. Zipes and Frank Mecklenberg (Cambridge, Mass.: The MIT Press, 1988), xi–xliii.

[15] Clarence E. Dutton, "The Panorama from Point Sublime," in Dutton, *Tertiary History of the Grand Cañon District*, with *Atlas*, Monographs of the U.S. Geological Survey (Washington, D.C.: Government Printing Office, 1882); as quoted in Henry Sayre, "Surveying the Vast Profound: The Panoramic Landscape in American Consciousness," *Massachusetts Review* 24 (Winter 1983): 733.

[16] Typifying this philosophy, Bricher's contemporary, the landscape painter George Inness, noted "you must suggest to me reality, you can never show me reality." "Mr. Inness on Art Matters," *The Art Journal* [London] n.s. 5 (1879): 377.

[17] Patricia Junker, "Expressions of Art and Life in *The Artist's Studio in an Afternoon Fog*," in Philip C. Beam et al., *Winslow Homer in the 1890s: Prout's Neck Observed* (New York: Hudson Hills Press, 1990), especially 34, 36.

[18] See Franklin Kelly, "Time and Narrative Erased," in Nicolai Cikovsky Jr. and Franklin Kelly, *Winslow Homer* (Washington, D.C.: National Gallery of Art, 1995), 303.

[19] Wallach, 80–91, is probably the most insightful investigation of this dynamic.

[20] See Boime and Sayre, 733.

[21] Samuel Isham, *History of American Painting* (New York: Macmillan, 1905), 355; William Howe Downes, *The Life and Works of Winslow Homer* (Boston: Houghton Mifflin Company, 1911), 10; both authors are quoted in David Tatham, "Winslow Homer and the Sea," in Beam et al., *Winslow Homer in the 1890s*, 67.

[22] On the Sloan-Homer relationship, see Bruce Robertson, *Reckoning with Winslow Homer: His Late Paintings and Their Influence* (Cleveland: The Cleveland Museum of Art, 1990), 141–45.

[23] Leo Marx, *The Machine in the Garden: Technology and Pastoral Ideal in America* (New York: Oxford University Press, 1964).

[24] See Daniel Joseph Singal, "Towards a Definition of American Modernism," *American Quarterly* 39 (Spring 1987): 7–26.

[25] Thomas Jefferson, "Query XIX: Manufactures," from *Notes on the State of Virginia* (1787), in David A. Hollinger and Charles Capper, eds., *The American Intellectual Tradition: A Sourcebook. Volume 1: 1620–1865* (New York: Oxford University Press, 1989), 158.

[26] In his insightful recounting of American advertising, historian Jackson Lears observes that by the twentieth century "a reified notion of 'the machine' would replace the nurturant earth as the cornucopia." Lears, *Fables of Abundance: A Cultural History of Advertising* (New York: BasicBooks, 1994), 38.

Ivan Albright

[1] Courtney Graham Donnell et al., *Ivan Albright* (New York: Hudson Hills Press, 1997), 178.

[2] Phylis Floyd, *Ivan Albright—The Late Self-Portraits* (Hanover, N.H.: Hood Museum of Art, 1986), 9.

[3] Donnell, 74.

[4] Donnell, 50.

[5] Michael Croydon, *Ivan Albright* (New York: Abbeville Press, 1978), 272.

Albert Bierstadt

[1] J. Williams and N. Heller, "Albert Bierstadt: The American Wilderness," *American Artist* 40 (January 1976): 52.

[2] Nancy K. Anderson and Linda S. Ferber, *Albert Bierstadt: Art and Enterprise* (New York: Hudson Hills Press, 1991), 23.

[3] Williams and Heller, 53.

[4] Matthew Baigell, *Albert Bierstadt* (New York: Watson-Guptill Publications, 1981), 10.

[5] By the late nineteenth century, the meticulous German aesthetic Bierstadt favored had lost its appeal due in large part to the influence of Barbizon and impressionist painting, leaving the once wealthy artist at the mercy of creditors.

[6] Deidre Stein Greben, "Blazing a Trail into the Sunset," *Art News* 99 (October 2000): 152.

[7] *New York Tribune*, May 11, 1867.

[8] Fitz Hugh Ludlow, "Seven Weeks in the Great Yo-Semite," *Atlantic Monthly* 13 (June 1864): 745.

Alfred Thompson Bricher

[1] Jeffrey R. Brown, *Alfred Thompson Bricher, 1837–1908* (Indianapolis: Indianapolis Museum of Art, 1973), 15.

[2] Katharine Morrison McClinton, *The Chromolithographs of Louis Prang* (New York: Clarkson N. Potter, Inc., 1973), 172.

[3] Brown, 18.

[4] "American Painters—Alfred T. Bricher," *Art Journal* 38 (November 1875): 341.

Charles Burchfield

A Flash of Lightning at Night

[1] John I. H. Baur, "Introduction," in *Charles Burchfield at Kennedy Galleries: The Early Years, 1915–1929* (New York: Kennedy Galleries, 1977), n.p.

[2] *Charles Burchfield: Catalogue of Paintings in Public and Private Collections* (Utica, N.Y.: Munson-Williams-Proctor Institute, 1970), cat. no. 177, "Flash of Lightning at Night."

[3] Journal entry, September 7, 1916, as quoted in J. Benjamin Townsend, ed., *Charles Burchfield's Journals: The Poetry of Place* (Albany: State University of New York Press, 1993), 267.

[4] William H. Robinson, "Native Sons: Burchfield and the Cleveland School of Art," in Nannette V. Maciejunes and Michael D. Hall, *The Paintings of Charles Burchfield: North by Midwest* (Columbus, Ohio: Columbus Museum of Art), 62–72.

[5] For a reproduction of this sketch, see John I. H. Baur, *The Inlander: Life and Work of Charles Burchfield, 1893–1967* (Newark: University of Delaware Press, 1982), 79.

Country Road in December

[1] John I. H. Baur, *Charles Burchfield* (New York: Whitney Museum of American Art, 1956), 11–12.

[2] Nannette V. Maciejunes, *Trees as Seen Through the Eyes of John Marin and Charles Burchfield* (New York: Kennedy Galleries, 1991), n.p., cat. no. 34.

[3] Manuscript, "1955–1965," dated January 13, 1966, as quoted in J. Benjamin Townsend, ed., *Charles Burchfield's Journals: The Poetry of Place* (Albany: State University of New York Press, 1993), 434.

[4] John I. H. Baur, "Introduction," in *Charles E. Burchfield: The Middle Years, 1929 to 1950* (New York: Kennedy Galleries, 1978), n.p.

[5] Journal entry, October 29, 1952, as quoted in John I. H. Baur, *Burchfield's Seasons* (New York: Kennedy Galleries, 1982), n.p.

[6] As quoted in Baur, Burchfield's Seasons, n.p.

Samuel Colman

[1] Wayne Craven, "Samuel Colman (1832–1920): Rediscovered Painter of Far-Away Places," *American Art Journal* 8 (May 1976): 16. Craven's account remains the standard reference on the artist. See also *Samuel Colman: East and West from Portland* (Portland, Maine: Barridoff Galleries, 1981); *The Romantic Landscapes of Samuel Colman* (New York: Kennedy Galleries, 1983); and *The Poetic Landscapes of Samuel Colman (1832–1920)* (New York: Kennedy Galleries, 1999).

[2] Henry T. Tuckerman, *Book of the Artists, American Artist Life …* (New York: James F. Carr, 1867), 559.

[3] Kevin Avery, "Samuel Colman," in Barbara Novak and Annette Blaugrund, eds., *Next to Nature: Landscape Paintings from the National Academy of Design* (New York: National Academy of Design, 1980), 69. Avery notes that at the time of his death, Colman's private collection included two paintings by Inness, one of which had inscribed on the reverse: "I saw this picture in Inness' studio in 1854."

[4] See Abigail Booth Gerdts, *An American Collection: Paintings and Sculpture from the National Academy of Design* (New York: National Academy of Design, 1989), 46–47.

[5] Tuckerman, 560.

John Singleton Copley

[1] Copley to [Benjamin West or Captain R. G. Bruce], 1767(?), in *Letters & Papers of John Singleton Copley and Henry Pelham, 1739–1776* (Boston: Massachusetts Historical Society, 1914), 65–66; as quoted in Susan Rather, "Carpenter, Tailor, Shoemaker, Artist: Copley and Portrait Painting around 1770," *Art Bulletin* 79 (June 1997): 269.

[2] See T. H. Breen, "The Meaning of 'Likeness': Portrait Painting in an Eighteenth-Century Consumer Society," *Word & Image* 6 (October-December 1990): 325–50.

[3] François Nivelon, *Book of Genteel Behaviour* (1738); as quoted and discussed in Arline Meyer, "Re-dressing Classical Statuary: The Eighteenth-Century 'Hand-in-Waistcoat' Portrait," *Art Bulletin* 77 (March 1995): 53. For other depictions of the gesture by Copley see Carrie Rebora, *John Singleton Copley in America* (New York: The Metropolitan Museum of Art, 1995), 310, 311.

[4] Sir Joshua Reynolds, *Discourses on Art*, ed. Robert R. Wark (New Haven: Yale University Press, 1981), 158; as quoted in Margaretta Lovell, "Mrs. Sargent, Mr. Copley, and the Empirical Eye," *Winterthur Portfolio* 33 (Spring 1998): 15.

Arthur B. Davies

[1] The basic sources for Davies' life and career are Joseph S. Czestochowski, *The Works of Arthur B. Davies* (Chicago: The University of Chicago Press, 1979); and Bennard B. Perlman, *The Lives, Loves, and Art of Arthur B. Davies* (Albany: State University of New York Press), 1998.

[2] Dwight Williams, "Arthur B. Davies: A Biographical Sketch," in *Arthur B. Davies: Essays on the Man and His Art* (Washington, D.C.: Phillips Memorial Gallery, 1924), 29.

[3] Czestochowski, 10.

Stuart Davis

[1] Stuart Davis, "Autobiography," originally published in *Stuart Davis* (New York: American Artists Group, Inc., 1945), as excerpted in *Stuart Davis Scapes* (New York: Salander-O'Reilly Galleries, 1990), 18.

[2] Letter to cousin Hazel, August 5, 1915, as reprinted in Karen Wilkin, *Stuart Davis in Gloucester* (West Stockbridge, Mass.: Hard Press, Inc., 1999), 104.

[3] *Coast Town Landscape Study* will be included in the forthcoming Stuart Davis catalogue raisonné, eds. Ani Boyajian and Mark Rutkoski.

[4] See Lowery Stokes Sims, *Stuart Davis: American Painter* (New York: The Metropolitan Museum of Art, 1991), 175–76.

[5] The other two works, *Art Space No. 1*, 1940, oil on canvas (Collection of Mr. and Mrs. Perry J. Lewis), and *Triatic*, 1941/51, oil on canvas (private collection), are reproduced in Sims, 254.

[6] Wilkin, 56–58.

[7] Davis, "Autobiography," 18.

Charles Demuth

[1] On the Cézanne-Demuth relationship, see Barbara Haskell, *Charles Demuth* (New York: Whitney Museum of American Art, 1987), 125. Demuth's use of sloping roofs as framing devices, through which sinuous trees are seen, strongly recalls Cézanne's similarly titled graphite drawing, *Trees and Roof* (1882–1883, Museum Boymans-van Beuningen, Rotterdam), reproduced in Françoise Cachin et al., *Cézanne* (Philadelphia: Philadelphia Museum of Art, 1996), 250.

[2] For a genealogy of the usage of these terms, see Gail Stavitsky, "Reordering Reality: Precisionist Directions in American Art, 1915–1941," in *Precisionism in America, 1915–1941: Reordering Reality* (Montclair, N.J.: Montclair Art Museum, 1994), 15.

[3] Quoted in Michael Jacobs, *The Good and Simple Life: Artist Colonies in Europe and America* (Oxford: Phaidon Press, 1985), 173. For the Provincetown art colony and the Cape Cod School of Art, see Jacobs, 171–79.

[4] Helen Henderson, "Art and Artists Pass in Review," *Philadelphia Inquirer* (December 1, 1918), as quoted in Bruce Kellner, ed., *Letters of Charles Demuth, American Artist, 1883–1935* (Philadelphia: Temple University Press, 2000), 149.

Arthur Dove

[1] Alfred Stieglitz, as quoted in Dorothy Norman, "Writings and Conversations of Alfred Stieglitz," *Twice a Year* 1 (Fall-Winter 1938): 79.

[2] Dove as quoted in Melanie Kirschner, *Arthur Dove: Watercolors and Pastels* (New York: George Braziller, 1998), 37. See Kirschner for an in-depth discussion of Dove's work in watercolor.

[3] Duncan Phillips, "Retrospective Exhibition of Works in Various Media by Arthur G. Dove," (Washington, D.C.: Phillips Memorial Gallery, 1937), as quoted in Kirschner, 44.

[4] See Elizabeth Hutton Turner, "Going Home: Geneva, 1933–1938," in Debra Bricker Balken et al., *Arthur Dove: A Retrospective* (Andover, Mass.: Addison Gallery of American Art, 1997), 95–113.

[5] Dove to Stieglitz, June 29, 1937. Reprinted in Ann Lee Morgan, ed., *Dear Stieglitz, Dear Dove* (Newark: University of Delaware Press, 1988), 384–85.

[6] Lewis Mumford, "The Art Galleries: Surprise Party—Wit and Watercolors," *New Yorker* 10 (May 5, 1934): 56; as quoted in Turner, 101.

Thomas Eakins

[1] Lloyd Goodrich, *Thomas Eakins, His Life and Work* (New York: Whitney Museum of American Art, 1933), cat. no. 281.

[2] Kathleen A. Foster, *Thomas Eakins Rediscovered: Charles Bregler's Thomas Eakins Collection at the Pennsylvania Academy of the Fine Arts* (New Haven: Yale University Press, 1997), 32.

[3] Kathleen A. Foster, "Eakins and the Academy," in Darrell Sewell et al., *Thomas Eakins* (Philadelphia: Philadelphia Museum of Art, 2001), 99.

[4] *The Philadelphia Evening Item*, February 15, 1886.

[5] Elizabeth Johns, preface to *Thomas Eakins: The Heroism of Modern Life* (Princeton: Princeton University Press, 1983), xix.

[6] *The Pennsylvania Museum Bulletin* 25 (March 1930): 3–35.

[7] Johns, 146.

[8] *The Philadelphia Evening Item*, December 22, 1895.

[9] William C. Brownell, "The Art Schools of Philadelphia," *Scribner's Magazine* 18 (September 1879): 740.

[10] *The Philadelphia Evening Item*, December 22, 1895.

[11] There is an intermediate sketch for the portrait of Riter Fitzgerald, also executed in oil, which was formerly in the collection of Fitzgerald's niece, Mrs. J. K. Spare of Moylan, Pennsylvania.

Francis William Edmonds

[1] John Caldwell and Oswaldo Rodriguez Roque, *American Paintings in the Metropolitan Museum of Art*, vol. 1 (New York: The Metropolitan Museum of Art, 1994), 503.

[2] Maybelle Mann, *Francis William Edmonds* (Washington, D.C.: International Exhibits Foundation, 1975), 7.

[3] H. Nichols B. Clark, *Francis W. Edmonds: American Master in the Dutch Tradition* (Washington, D.C.: Smithsonian Institution Press, 1988), 39.

[4] Mann, 9.

[5] Clark, 54.

[6] Clark, 134.

De Scott Evans

[1] The essential details of the artist's career can be found in Nancy Troy, "From the Peanut Gallery: The Rediscovery of De Scott Evans," Yale University Art Gallery *Bulletin* 36 (Spring 1977): 36–43; and Nannette V. Maciejunes, *A New Variety, Try One: De Scott Evans or S. S. David* (Columbus, Ohio: Columbus Museum of Art, 1985).

[2] William H. Gerdts and Russell Burke, *American Still-Life Painting* (New York: Praeger, 1971), 167–68. See also Gerdts, *Painters of the Humble Truth: Masterpieces of American Still Life 1801–1939* (Tulsa, Okla.: Philbrook Art Center, 1981), 200–203.

[3] In 1985 Nannette V. Maciejunes brought together more than thirty paintings, including eleven trompe l'oeil pictures, by Evans (some signed David) in the exhibition *A New Variety, Try One: De Scott Evans or S. S. David.* The exhibition, organized by the Columbus Museum of Art, afforded the occasion for Maciejunes to undertake a detailed study of the works alongside conservators, art historians, and a handwriting expert. Their research at that time yielded no conclusive evidence regarding the attribution. Nearly twenty years later, Maciejunes remains skeptical about the attribution of so many trompe l'oeil paintings to Evans and is continuing her search for the artist S. S. David.

[4] Letter from Maciejunes to Martha Fleischman, Kennedy Galleries, July 12, 1991.

Henry F. Farny

[1] The essential details of Farny's life and career can be found in Denny Carter, *Henry Farny* (Cincinnati: Cincinnati Art Museum, 1978).

[2] Carolyn M. Appleton and Natasha S. Bartalini, "Henry Farny, 1847–1916," in *Henry Farny, 1847–1916* (Austin, Tex.: Archer M. Huntington Art Gallery, The University of Texas at Austin, 1983), 12.

[3] "Studio Studies," *Cincinnati Commercial*, December 1, 1881, as quoted in Carter, 21.

[4] A. W. Drake, Art Superintendent, *Century Magazine*, letter to Farny, July 13, 1882, Archives of American Art (microfilm 1233, frames 248–250), as quoted in Appleton and Bartalini, 13.

John F. Francis

[1] David W. Dunn, *A Suitable Likeness: The Paintings of John F. Francis, 1832–1879* (Lewisburg, Pa.: The Packwood House Museum, 1986), 4.

[2] *Selected American Master Paintings, 1764–1964* (New York: Kennedy Galleries, 1995), n.p.

[3] George L. Hersey, introduction to *A Catalogue of Paintings by John F. Francis* (Lewisburg, Pa.: Bucknell University, 1958), 7.

[4] Alfred Frankenstein, "J. F. Francis," *Antiques* 59 (May 1951): 376.

[5] Hersey, 8.

[6] Dunn, 5.

[7] William H. Gerdts, *Painters of the Humble Truth: Masterpieces of American Still Life 1801–1939* (Tulsa, Okla.: Philbrook Art Center, 1981), 90.

[8] William H. Gerdts and Russell Burke, *American Still-Life Painting* (New York: Praeger, 1971), 60.

William Glackens

Four Fruits

[1] For the Barnes-Glackens relationship see William H. Gerdts, *William Glackens* (New York: Abbeville Press, 1996), 96–97.

[2] Gerdts, 149.

[3] Albert C. Barnes, *The Art in Painting*, 3rd ed. (New York: Harcourt, Brace and Company, 1937), 96.

Study for The Soda Fountain

[1] William H. Gerdts, *William Glackens* (New York: Abbeville Press, 1996), 153.

[2] Anne Cooper Funderburg, *Sundae Best: A History of Soda Fountains* (Bowling Green, Ohio: Bowling Green State University Press, 2002), 101, 127, 124.

[3] Funderburg, *Sundae Best*, 132.

[4] See Ellen Wiley Todd, *The "New Woman" Revised: Painting and Gender Politics on Fourteenth Street* (Berkeley: University of California Press, 1994).

Richard La Barre Goodwin

[1] Not much has been written about Goodwin. Basic biographical information can be found in Alfred Frankenstein, *After the Hunt: William Michael Harnett and Other American Still Life Painters, 1870–1900*, rev. ed. (Berkeley: University of California Press, 1969), 132–35; and *Richard La Barre Goodwin, 1840–1910* (New York: Graham Gallery, 1963).

[2] A. A. Vantine & Co. (New York), Trade Catalog, c. 1880, as quoted in William Hosley, *The Japan Idea: Art and Life in Victorian America* (Hartford, Conn.: Wadsworth Atheneum, 1990), 44.

William Michael Harnett

[1] Nicolai Cikovsky Jr., "'Sordid Mechanics' and 'Monkey Talents': The Illusionistic Tradition," in Doreen Bolger, Marc Simpson, and John Wilmerding, eds., *William M. Harnett* (Fort Worth: Amon Carter Museum, 1992), 20–23.

[2] Nannette V. Maciejunes and Norine Hendricks, "William Michael Harnett," in Stephan Koja, ed., *America: The New World in 19th-Century Painting* (Vienna: Österreichische Galerie Belvedere, 1999), 260–61.

[3] Alfred Frankenstein, *After the Hunt: William Michael Harnett and Other American Still Life Painters, 1870–1900*, rev. ed. (Berkeley: University of California Press, 1969), cat. no. 55. The painting is catalogued as 1879; however, the date on the painting, the last digit of which is somewhat faded, appears to be 1878.

[4] Frankenstein, 42–43.

[5] Undated clipping [1889 or 1890] of an interview in the New York *News*, quoted in Frankenstein, 29.

[6] Doreen Bolger, "The Patrons of the Artist: Emblems of Commerce and Culture," in Bolger et al., *William M. Harnett*, 78–79.

[7] See Laura A. Coyle, "'The Best Index of American Life': Newspapers in the Artist's Work," in Bolger et al., *William M. Harnett*, 223–31.

[8] Barbara S. Groseclose, "Vanity and the Artist: Some Still-Life Paintings by William Michael Harnett," *American Art Journal* 19 (1987): 56–57.

Marsden Hartley

[1] Barbara Haskell, *Marsden Hartley* (New York: Whitney Museum of American Art, 1980), 71.

[2] Marsden Hartley, "Somehow a Past: Prologue to Imaginative Living," in Susan Elizabeth Ryan, ed., *Somehow a Past: The Autobiography of Marsden Hartley* (Cambridge, Mass.: The MIT Press, 1997), 136.

[3] Marsden Hartley, "Art—and the Personal Life," *Creative Art* (June 1928): 31–34; reprinted in Gail R. Scott, ed., *On Art by Marsden Hartley* (New York: Horizon Press, 1982), 70–73.

[4] Townsend Ludington, *Seeking the Spiritual: The Paintings of Marsden Hartley* (Ithaca: Cornell University Press, 1998), 46.

Childe Hassam

[1] The essential details of Hassam's life and career can be found in Ulrich W. Hiesinger, *Childe Hassam: American Impressionist* (New York: Jordan-Volpe Gallery, 1994); and Warren Adelson, Jay E. Cantor, and William H. Gerdts, *Childe Hassam, Impressionist* (New York: Abbeville Press, 1999).

[2] Hiesinger, 128.

Martin Johnson Heade

[1] Theodore E. Stebbins Jr. et al., "Introduction," in *Martin Johnson Heade* (Boston: Museum of Fine Arts, Boston, 1999), 4.

[2] Theodore E. Stebbins Jr., *The Life and Work of Martin Johnson Heade: A Critical Analysis and Catalogue Raisonné* (New Haven: Yale University Press, 2000), cat. no. 582.

[3] John I. H. Baur, "Introduction," in *Commemorative Exhibition: Paintings by Martin J. Heade and Fitz Hugh Lane from the Private Collection of Maxim Karolik and the M. & M. Karolik Collection of American Paintings from the Museum of Fine Arts, Boston* (New York: M. Knoedler, 1954), n.p.; and William H. Gerdts, *Painters of the Humble Truth: Masterpieces of American Still Life 1801–1939* (Tulsa, Okla.: Philbrook Art Center, 1981), 130.

[4] Stebbins, *Life and Work*, 162; cat. nos. 581, 582, 587, 588, 590, and 632.

[5] Heade's method was to make quick oil sketches of flowers directly from nature; these sketches in turn provided the basic vocabulary for the magnolia pictures. A group of these sketches now resides in the collection of the St. Augustine Historical Society. See Timothy A. Eaton, *Martin Johnson Heade: The Floral and Hummingbird Studies from the St. Augustine Historical Society* (Boca Raton: Boca Raton Museum of Art, 1992). According to Stebbins, the location of the oil sketch for the left-facing magnolia, which appears in so many of the still lifes, is unknown.

Winslow Homer

[1] Philip C. Beam, *Winslow Homer at Prout's Neck* (Boston: Little, Brown and Company, 1966), 31.

[2] Lois Homer Graham, "The Homers and Prout's Neck," in Philip C. Beam et al., *Winslow Homer in the 1890s: Prout's Neck Observed* (New York: Hudson Hills Press, 1990), 29.

[3] Philip C. Beam, "Exhibition Checklist of Paintings and Drawings," in *Winslow Homer in the 1890s*, 120.

[4] Lloyd Goodrich, "Winslow Homer," *Perspectives USA* 14 (1956): 51.

Edward Hopper

[1] The essential details of the artist's life can be found in Gail Levin, *Edward Hopper: An Intimate Biography* (New York: Alfred A. Knopf, 1995).

[2] Gail Levin, *Edward Hopper: A Catalogue Raisonné*, vol. 1 (New York: Whitney Museum of American Art, 1995), cat. no. O–13.

[3] Levin, *Edward Hopper: A Catalogue Raisonné*, 41–42.

[4] As quoted in Levin, *Edward Hopper: A Catalogue Raisonné*, 41.

John O'Brien Inman

[1] See Richard J. Koke et al., "John O'Brien Inman," in *A Catalog of the Collection, Including Historical, Narrative, and Marine Art* (New York: The New-York Historical Society, 1982), 221; and Carolyn B. Wilkinson, "John O'Brien Inman," *Antiques* 154 (November 1998): 722–27.

[2] William H. Gerdts and Russell Burke, *American Still-Life Painting* (New York: Praeger, 1971), 69.

[3] William H. Gerdts, "The Bric-a-Brac Still Life," *Antiques* 100 (November 1971): 744.

David Johnson

[1] John I. H. Baur, "' … the exact brushwork of Mr. David Johnson,' An American Landscape Painter, 1827–1908," *American Art Journal* 12 (Autumn 1980): 32–65.

[2] Gwendolyn Owens, *Nature Transcribed: The Landscapes and Still Lifes of David Johnson (1827–1908)* (Ithaca: Herbert F. Johnson Museum of Art, 1988), 14.

[3] Owens, 13.

[4] Paul Schneider, *The Adirondacks: A History of America's First Wilderness* (New York: Henry Holt and Company, 1998), 54.

[5] See Owens, 36–39.

[6] Owens, 39.

Eastman Johnson

[1] I am borrowing these terms from Michael Fried's well-known study of the manner in which viewers conceptually approach—and in which subjects appear in—eighteenth-century French painting, *Absorption and Theatricality: Painting and Beholder in the Age of Diderot* (Chicago: The University of Chicago Press, 1980).

[2] On "interiority" in American art after the Civil War, see Susan Sidlauskas, *Body, Place, and Self in Nineteenth-Century Painting* (New York: Cambridge University Press, 2000), 61–90.

[3] Patricia Hills, "Painting Race: Eastman Johnson's Pictures of Slaves, Ex-Slaves, and Freedmen," in Teresa A. Carbone and Patricia Hills, *Eastman Johnson: Painting America* (Brooklyn: Brooklyn Museum of Art, 1999), 133, 136.

[4] César Daly, Heinrich Wölfflin, and Hippolyte Taine are among those who advanced such theories; see Sidlauskas, 10–11.

Walt Kuhn

[1] Frank Getlein, *Walt Kuhn, 1877–1949* (New York: Kennedy Galleries, 1967), n.p.

[2] Fridolf Johnson, "Walt Kuhn, American Master," *American Artist* 31 (December 1967): 57.

[3] Getlein, 3.

[4] Efram Laurent Burk, *Walt Kuhn, 1877–1949* (Orono, Me.: University of Maine Museum of Art, 1989), 7.

[5] Philip Rhys Adams, *Walt Kuhn, Painter: His Life and Work* (Columbus, Ohio: Ohio State University Press, 1978), 171.

[6] "Back Stage with Walt Kuhn," *Newsweek* 18 (December 8, 1941): 79.

[7] Adams, cat. no. 505. Adams erroneously provides an alternate title, *The White Rider,* for *Rider with Blue Sash. The White Rider,* which is illustrated in *Walt Kuhn, 1877–1949* (New York: Kennedy Galleries, 1967), no. 38, is a separate portrait of the same sitter.

[8] Adams, 214.

John La Farge

[1] Kathleen A. Foster, "John La Farge and the American Watercolor Movement: Art for the 'Decorative Age,'" in Henry Adams et al., *John La Farge* (Washington, D.C.: National Museum of American Art, 1987), 125.

[2] John La Farge, preface, *Mostly Records of Travel 1886 and 1890–91* (1895), as quoted in James L. Yarnall, *Recreation and Idleness: The Pacific Travels of John La Farge* (New York: Vance Jordan Fine Art, 1998), 2. Yarnall has written extensively on La Farge's life and on the South Seas trip in particular. See also Yarnall, "John La Farge and Henry Adams in the South Seas," *American Art Journal* 20 (1988): 51–109; and Yarnall, "Nature and Art in the Painting of John La Farge," in Adams et al., *John La Farge,* 79–121. Earlier articles on the subject include Henry La Farge, "John La Farge and the South Sea Idyll," *Journal of the Warburg and Courtauld Institutes* 7 (1944): 34–39; and Louis Auchincloss, "In Search of Innocence," *American Heritage* 21 (June 1970): 28–33.

[3] See Marilyn S. Kushner, *The Lure of Tahiti: Gauguin, His Predecessors and Followers* (New Brunswick, N.J.: The Jane Voorhees Zimmerli Art Museum, 1988).

[4] Yarnall, *Recreation and Idleness,* 97. John La Farge, "Passages from a Diary in the Pacific: Tahiti," *Scribner's Magazine* 30 (July 1901): 69–83. See also John La Farge, *Reminiscences of the South Seas* (Garden City, N.Y.: Doubleday, Page and Co., 1912).

[5] *Women Bathing in Papara River* appears to have been exhibited at both the Boston (Doll & Richards Gallery) and New York (Durand-Ruel Galleries) venues of *Records of Travel.*

George Cochran Lambdin

[1] The standard reference on the artist is Ruth Irwin Weidner, *George Cochran Lambdin 1830–1896* (Chadds Ford, Pa.: Brandywine River Museum, 1986).

[2] Weidner, 27.

[3] George Cochran Lambdin, "The Charm of the Rose," *Art Union Magazine* 1 (June-July 1884): 137.

[4] See Weidner, 27–32.

[5] Natalie Spassky, *American Paintings in the Metropolitan Museum of Art*, vol. 2 (New York: The Metropolitan Museum of Art, 1985), 318.

John Marin

Weehawken Railroad Yards and Grain Elevators

[1] Sheldon Reich, *John Marin: A Stylistic Analysis and Catalogue Raisonné* (Tucson: University of Arizona Press, 1970), cat. no. 10.89.

[2] Ruth E. Fine, *John Marin* (Washington, D.C.: National Gallery of Art, 1990), 112.

[3] John I. H. Baur, "Introduction," in *John Marin's New York* (New York: Kennedy Galleries, 1981), n.p.

Street Movement, New York

[1] John Marin Jr., statement in *John Marin's New York* (New York: Kennedy Galleries, 1981), n.p.

[2] *Street Movement, New York* is not catalogued in Sheldon Reich, *John Marin: A Stylistic Analysis and Catalogue Raisonné* (Tucson: University of Arizona Press, 1970). *Manhattan Movement* is listed as cat. no. 32.20; however, the dimensions listed are reversed.

[3] Meredith Ward, *Movement: Marin* (New York: Richard York Gallery, 2001), 7.

[4] Ruth E. Fine, *John Marin* (Washington, D.C.: National Gallery of Art, 1990), 148.

Sailboat and Sea, Maine

[1] Letter from Marin to Stieglitz, August 18, 1935, in Dorothy Norman, ed., *The Selected Writings of John Marin* (New York: Pellegrini and Cudahy, 1949), 167.

[2] As quoted in Klaus Kertess, *Marin in Oil* (Southampton, N.Y.: The Parrish Art Museum, 1987), 43.

[3] See John I. H. Baur, *John Marin and the Sea* (New York: Kennedy Galleries, 1982); and Kertess.

[4] Ruth E. Fine, *John Marin* (Washington, D.C.: National Gallery of Art, 1990), 229.

[5] Letter from Marin to Stieglitz, September 10, 1936, in Norman, 171.

[6] MacKinley Helm, *John Marin* (Boston: Institute of Contemporary Art, 1948), 72.

[7] Sheldon Reich, *John Marin: A Stylistic Analysis and Catalogue Raisonné* (Tucson: University of Arizona Press, 1970), cat. no. 38.27. A stamp on the back of the painting indicates that the work was exhibited at Stieglitz's last gallery, An American Place.

[8] Marin, as quoted in Helm, 80.

John Harrison Mills

[1] All biographical information here is from Mills' autobiography, reprinted in Robert Taft, *Artists and Illustrators of the Old West: 1850–1900* (Princeton: Princeton University Press, 1982; reprint), 345–47.

[2] See for example Mills' comments in Victor Fischer and Michael B. Frank, eds., *Mark Twain's Letters* (Berkeley: University of California Press, 1992), vol. 3, 296, n. 2. See also vol. 3, 360, n. 2, in which Twain expresses his dissatisfaction with Mills' inability to produce illustrations for his *Buffalo Express* article "The Last Words of Great Men."

[3] Twain continued, "Indeed, upon second thought, I will not even use it then, for it is unchristian, inelegant and degrading—though to speak truly I do not see how house-rent and taxes are going to be discussed worth a cent without it." Twain, "Salutatory," *Buffalo Express* (August 21, 1869); reprinted in Joseph B. McCullough and Janice McIntire-Strasburg, eds., *Mark Twain at the* Buffalo Express: *Articles and Sketches by America's Favorite Humorist* (DeKalb, Ill.: Northern Illinois University Press, 1999), 6.

[4] By 1865, the government imposed a 5% tax on incomes between $600 and $5,000, and 10% on incomes over $5,000. See William L. Barney, *Battleground for the Union: The Era of the Civil War and Reconstruction, 1848–1877* (Englewood Cliffs, N.J.: Prentice Hall, 1990), 164; and W. Elliot Brownlee, *Federal Taxation in America: A Short History* (New York: Cambridge University Press, 1996), 26–28.

[5] *Artist Painting a Satirical Painting* also bears stylistic and thematic affinity with *Self-Portrait in the Tenth Street Studio* (oil on canvas, n.d., The New-York Historical Society), by Mills' teacher/mentor, William Holbrook Beard. I am grateful to Sarah Burns for bringing this painting to my attention.

Louis Moeller

[1] The standard reference on the artist is William H. Gerdts, *Louis Moeller, N.A. (1855–1930): A Victorian Man's World* (New York: Grand Central Art Galleries, 1984).

[2] Gerdts, 4.

[3] F. Wellington Ruckstuhl, "A Sculptor's Opinion of a Painter," *The Quarterly Illustrator* 2 (October, November, and December 1894): 349.

Walter Murch

[1] Barry Schwabsky, "Is there Still Life in Still Life?," *Arts Magazine* 59 (November 1984): 132.

[2] Arlene Jacobowitz, interview with Walter Murch, December 1967, as quoted in Judy Kay Collischan Van Wagner, *Walter Murch* (catalogue raisonné), 3 vols. (Ph.D. diss., The University of Iowa, 1972), 46.

[3] Ernest W. Watson, "Walter Murch: Painter of the Impossible," *American Artist* 19 (October 1955): 24.

[4] Van Wagner, *Walter Murch*, cat. no. 349, "Study for Sounds [sic] of Silver," 1965, watercolor on paper, 17 1/4 x 18 3/4 inches, estate of the artist. The finished painting is listed in Van Wagner as "Sound of Silver," 1965, oil on canvas, 32 1/2 x 46 1/2 inches, collection of Mr. and Mrs. Lee A. Ault, New York. The present location of the painting is unknown.

[5] *Vogue* magazine, November 1, 1963, 172–75.

[6] Watson, 23.

Georgia O'Keeffe

[1] As quoted in Katherine Kuh, *The Artist's Voice: Talks with Seventeen Artists* (New York: Harper & Row, 1962), 190, and Elizabeth Hutton Turner, *Georgia O'Keeffe: The Poetry of Things* (New Haven: Yale University Press, 1999), 1.

[2]"I long ago came to the conclusion that even if I could put down accurately the thing that I saw and enjoyed, it would not give the observer the kind of feeling it gave me. I had to create an equivalent for what I felt about what I was looking at—not copy it." From Georgia O'Keeffe, *Georgia O'Keeffe* (New York, 1976), n.p., as quoted in Marjorie P. Balge-Crozier, "Still Life Redefined," in Turner, 69.

[3] Lisa Mintz Messinger, *Georgia O'Keeffe* (New York and London: Thames and Hudson, 2001), 140–41. See also Charles C. Eldredge, *Georgia O'Keeffe: American and Modern* (New Haven: Yale University Press, 1993), 27–28.

[4] Barbara Buhler Lynes, *Georgia O'Keeffe: Catalogue Raisonné*, vol. 2 (New Haven: Yale University Press, 1999), cat. no. 985, as *Patio No. II.* The second painting is titled *The Patio—No. I*, cat. no. 986.

[5] Sharyn Udall, *Carr, O'Keeffe, Kahlo: Places of Their Own* (New Haven: Yale University Press, 2000), 220.

Charles Willson Peale

[1] Charles Willson Peale, *Introduction to a Course of Lectures on Natural History*, as quoted in Brooke Hindle, "Charles Willson Peale's Science and Technology," in Edgar P. Richardson et al., *Charles Willson Peale and His World* (New York: Harry N. Abrams, 1983), 122.

[2] Brandon Brame Fortune, "Charles Willson Peale's Portrait Gallery: Persuasion and the Plain Style," *Word & Image* 6 (October-December 1990): 308.

[3] Lillian B. Miller, ed., *The Selected Papers of Charles Willson Peale and His Family*, vol. 1 (New Haven: Yale University Press, 1983), 33.

[4] Lillian B. Miller, "Biography of a Family," in Lillian B. Miller, ed., *The Peale Family: Creation of a Legacy, 1770–1870* (Washington, D.C.: National Portrait Gallery, 1996), 19.

[5] Charles Coleman Sellers, *Portraits and Miniatures by Charles Willson Peale* (Philadelphia: American Philosophical Society, 1952), cat. no. 517.

[6] Fortune, 315.

[7] Sellers, 136.

Rubens Peale

[1] Paul D. Schweizer, "Fruits of Perseverance: The Art of Rubens Peale, 1855–1865," in Lillian B. Miller, ed., *The Peale Family: Creation of a Legacy, 1770–1870* (Washington, D.C.: National Portrait Gallery, 1996), 172.

[2] For a reproduction of the work by Raphaelle Peale see Sotheby's *Important American Paintings, Drawings and Sculpture* (New York, December 3, 1987), lot 42.

[3] Charles Coleman Sellers, "Rubens Peale: A Painter's Decade," *Art Quarterly* 23 (Summer 1960): cat. no 125. "Still-Life. Plate of cake and wine. Com. June 7, 1865; fin. June 12, 1865." The work was painted for one of his wife's relatives, Mrs. Frederick Patterson. Its present title is an erroneous, modern addition.

[4] See Brandon Brame Fortune, "A Delicate Balance: Raphaelle Peale's Still-Life Paintings and the Ideal of Temperance," in Miller, ed., *The Peale Family*, 145–47, for a discussion of the possible symbolic meanings of cake and wine in the work of Raphaelle Peale.

John Frederick Peto

[1] See Alfred Frankenstein, "Harnett, True and False," *Art Bulletin* 31 (March 1949): 38–56; and Lloyd Goodrich, "Harnett and Peto: A Note on Style," *Art Bulletin* 31 (March 1949): 57–59.

[2] The primary sources for Peto's life are Alfred Frankenstein, *After the Hunt: William Michael Harnett and Other American Still Life Painters, 1870–1900*, rev. ed. (Berkeley: University of California Press, 1969); and John Wilmerding, *Important Information Inside: The Art of John F. Peto and the Idea of Still-Life Painting in Nineteenth-Century America* (Washington, D.C.: National Gallery of Art, 1983).

[3] See E. Jane Connell, "Vertical Still Lifes: Relief and Projection," in *More Than Meets the Eye: The Art of Trompe l'Oeil* (Columbus, Ohio: Columbus Museum of Art, 1985), 76–78.

[4] Bruce W. Chambers, *Old Money: American Trompe l'Oeil Images of Currency* (New York: Berry-Hill Galleries, 1988), 20.

[5] Wilmerding, 187.

[6] William H. Gerdts, *Painters of the Humble Truth: Masterpieces of American Still Life 1801–1939* (Tulsa, Okla.: Philbrook Art Center, 1981), 186.

Charles Prendergast

[1] The essential details of Charles Prendergast's life and career can be found in Nancy Mowll Mathews, "'Beauties … of a Quiet Kind': The Art of Charles Prendergast," in Mathews, *The Art of Charles Prendergast from the Collections of the Williams College Museum of Art and Mrs. Charles Prendergast* (Williamstown, Mass.: Williams College Museum of Art, 1993).

[2] Ross Anderson, "Charles Prendergast," in Carol Clark, Nancy Mowll Mathews, and Gwendolyn Owens, *Maurice Brazil Prendergast, Charles Prendergast: A Catalogue Raisonné* (Williamstown, Mass.: Williams College Museum of Art, 1990), 87.

[3] Marion M. Goethals, "'My Work is Done in Gesso the Old Italian Method … ,'" in Mathews, *The Art of Charles Prendergast*, 49.

[4] Hamilton Basso, "Profile: A Glimpse of Heaven, II," *The New Yorker*, August 3, 1946, 30–34.

[5] *Maurice Brazil Prendergast, Charles Prendergast: A Catalogue Raisonné*, cat. no. 2268.

[6] Goethals, 49.

Maurice Prendergast

[1] Nancy Mowll Mathews, *Maurice Prendergast* (Williamstown, Mass.: Williams College Museum of Art, 1990), 13.

[2] On Prendergast's early career see Richard J. Wattenmaker, *Maurice Prendergast* (New York: Harry N. Abrams, 1994).

[3] Prendergast to Mrs. Oliver E. Williams, October 10, 1907, as quoted in Wattenmaker, 87.

[4] Arthur Hoeber, "Art and Artists," *Globe and Commercial Advertiser*, February 5, 1908, 9, as quoted in Mathews, 26.

[5] Carol Clark, Nancy Mowll Mathews, and Gwendolyn Owens, *Maurice Brazil Prendergast, Charles Prendergast: A Catalogue Raisonné* (Williamstown, Mass.: Williams College Museum of Art, 1990), cat. no. 984.

[6] See Nancy Mowll Mathews, *The Art of Leisure: Maurice Prendergast in the Williams College Museum of Art* (Williamstown, Mass.: Williams College Museum of Art, 1999).

[7] Howald's collection was given to the Columbus Gallery of Fine Arts, now the Columbus Museum of Art, in 1931. *Massachusetts Shore* was deaccessioned in 1980. See Marcia Tucker, *American Paintings in the Ferdinand Howald Collection* (Columbus, Ohio: The Columbus Gallery of Fine Arts, 1969).

Abraham Rattner

[1] Rattner's birth year is typically listed as 1895; however, census reports and travel permits issued to the artist reveal that the year of birth is 1893. See Piri Halasz, "Abraham Rattner: Rebel with a Cause," *Archives of American Art Journal* 32 (1992): 23.

[2] Frank Getlein, *Abraham Rattner* (New York: Kennedy Galleries, 1969), 9.

[3] Lloyd Goodrich and John I. H. Baur, *Four American Expressionists: Doris Caesar, Chaim Gross, Karl Knaths, Abraham Rattner* (New York: Whitney Museum of American Art, 1959).

[4] As quoted in Baur, "Abraham Rattner," in Goodrich and Baur, 46.

[5] Baur, 46.

[6] Getlein, 12.

Theodore Robinson

[1] See Stephanie Mayer, *First Exposure: The Sketchbooks and Photographs of Theodore Robinson* (Giverny, France: Musée d'Art Américain Giverny, 2000) for a recent discussion of Robinson's early training and his years in Giverny.

[2] William H. Gerdts, *American Impressionism* (New York: Abbeville Press, 1984), 73–74.

[3] "Women and Their Interests," unidentified newspaper clipping, as quoted in Sona Johnston, *Theodore Robinson, 1852–1896* (Baltimore: The Baltimore Museum of Art, 1973), xxiii.

[4] See Johnston, cat. nos. 49–53.

[5] Diary entry, October 29, 1893, as quoted in John I. H. Baur, *Theodore Robinson, 1852–1896* (Brooklyn: The Brooklyn Museum, 1946), 37–38. See also Susan G. Larkin, "Light, Time, and Tide: Theodore Robinson at Cos Cob," *American Art Journal* 23 (1991): 77–80, for a discussion of the canal pictures.

Severin Roesen

[1] The standard reference on the artist is Judith Hansen O'Toole, *Severin Roesen* (London and Toronto: Associated University Presses, 1992).

[2] Judith Hansen O'Toole, "Severin Roesen, *Still Life*," documentation provided for The Schwarz Gallery, Philadelphia. The analysis of the painting put forward here is indebted to Dr. O'Toole's observations.

Ben Shahn

[1] Ben Shahn, *The Biography of a Painting* (New York: Paragraphic Books, 1966), n.p.

[2] For a biography of the artist see Howard Greenfeld, *Ben Shahn: An Artist's Life* (New York: Random House, 1998).

[3] Susan H. Edwards, *Ben Shahn and the Task of Photography in Thirties America* (New York: Hunter College, 1995), 5.

[4] James Thrall Soby, *Ben Shahn: Paintings* (New York: George Braziller, 1963), 20.

[5] Shahn, *The Biography of a Painting*, n.p. Although Shahn's comments about the wolf were made with regard to the beast imagery in his tempera painting *Allegory* (1948, Modern Art Museum of Fort Worth), the 1966 publication of the "biography" essay includes a sketch of the boy with the wolf mask alongside this text.

[6] Soby, 20. See Frances K. Pohl, "Allegory in the Work of Ben Shahn," in Susan Chevlowe et al., *Common Man, Mythic Vision: The Paintings of Ben Shahn* (New York: The Jewish Museum, 1998), 111–41.

[7] Greenfeld, 247.

[8] Shahn, n.p.

John Sloan

Man Monkey and *Memory*

[1] See John Loughery, *John Sloan: Painter and Rebel* (New York: Henry Holt and Company, 1995) for the details of Sloan's early years in Philadelphia.

[2] Peter Morse, *John Sloan's Prints: A Catalogue Raisonné of the Etchings, Lithographs, and Posters* (New Haven: Yale University Press, 1969), cat. no. 130.

[3] Comments made by the artist for the catalogue accompanying the exhibition "John Sloan: Paintings and Prints" (Dartmouth College, 1946), as quoted in Morse, 139.

[4] Morse, cat. no. 136.

[5] John Sloan, unpublished notes, as quoted in Morse, 146.

[6] John Sloan, *Gist of Art* (New York: American Artists Group, 1939), 99.

The Purple Shawl (Yolande)

[1] Robert Henri, "Letter to the Class, Art Students League, 1915," in *The Art Spirit* (New York: J. B. Lippincott, 1951), 5.

[2] Rowland Elzea, *John Sloan's Oil Paintings: A Catalogue Raisonné*, part one (Newark: University of Delaware Press, 1991), cat. no. 159 (*Yolande in Gray Tippet*); cat. no. 160 (*The Purple Shawl*); cat. no. 162 (*Iolanthe*); and cat. no. 163 (*Yolande Singing*).

[3] Excerpts from Sloan's diaries, the originals of which are housed at the Delaware Art Museum, can be found in Elzea, 101–2; and John Sloan, *Gist of Art* (New York: American Artists Group, 1939), 225. See also Bruce St. John, ed., *John Sloan's New York Scene* (New York: Harper & Row, 1965).

[4] "Character is just as much a motive for creating a work of art as it ever was. But it should not be the kind of sentimental, visual realism artists were trying for in the Nineties." Sloan, *Gist of Art*, 106.

[5] Yolande S. Van Reesema to Sloan, November 12, 1946, as quoted in Elzea, 110.

Reddy on the Rocks

[1] *New York Times*, February 22, 1925, as quoted in *John Sloan: The Gloucester Years* (Springfield, Mass.: Museum of Fine Arts, 1980), 12.

[2] As quoted in *John Sloan: The Gloucester Years* (New York: Kraushaar Galleries, 1994), n.p.

[3] See *Portrait of a Place: Some American Landscape Painters in Gloucester* (Gloucester, Mass.: Cape Ann Historical Association, 1973).

[4] As quoted in *John Sloan: The Gloucester Years* (New York: Kraushaar Galleries, 1994), n.p.

[5] Rowland Elzea, *John Sloan's Oil Paintings: A Catalogue Raisonné*, part one (Newark: University of Delaware Press, 1991), 22–25.

[6] Elzea, cat. no. 522. A color diagram dated September 24, 1917, and inscribed "Reddy and Wave breaking" is in the collection of the Delaware Art Museum.

[7] John Sloan, *Gist of Art* (New York: American Artists Group, 1939), 250–51.

[8] Sloan, *Gist of Art*, 146.

Robert Street

[1] *Who was Who in American Art, 1564–1975: 400 Years of Artists in America*, vol. 3 (Madison, Conn.: Sound View Press, 1999), 3202.

[2] Peter Hastings Falk, ed., *The Annual Exhibition Record of the Pennsylvania Academy of the Fine Arts* (Madison, Conn.: Sound View Press, 1988), 216.

[3] Kurt M. Semon, "Who Was Robert Street?" *American Collector* 14 (June 1945): 6.

[4] Object file, Kennedy Galleries, New York; *Nineteenth Century American Topographic Painters* (Miami: The Lowe Art Museum, University of Miami, 1974), 58.

[5] See Nicolai Cikovsky Jr., "'The Ravages of the Axe': The Meaning of the Tree Stump in Nineteenth-Century American Art," *Art Bulletin* 61 (December 1979): 611–26.

[6] Semon, 6.

[7] Semon, 7; *Who was Who in American Art*, 3202. Street also had children named after Andrea del Sarto (1486–1530) and Antonio Correggio (1486–1534).

James Brade Sword

[1] Biographical information provided by Robert D. Schwarz, The Schwarz Gallery, Philadelphia.

[2] *The American Painting Collection of Mrs. Norman B. Woolworth* (New York: Coe Kerr Gallery, Inc., 1970), essay by William H. Gerdts, reproduced, 62.

[3] *The American* (September 6, 1884): 349.

[4] *The American* (May 31, 1884): 125.

Elihu Vedder

[1] See Regina Soria, *Elihu Vedder: American Visionary Artist in Rome (1836–1923)* (Rutherford, N.J.: Fairleigh Dickinson University Press, 1970).

[2] Elihu Vedder, *The Digressions of V.* (Boston and New York: Houghton Mifflin Co., 1910), 316.

[3] Soria, 43.

[4] James L. Yarnall, *Recreation and Idleness: The Pacific Travels of John La Farge* (New York: Vance Jordan Fine Art, 1998), 10.

[5] Neil Harris, "All the World a Melting Pot? Japan at American Fairs, 1876–1904," in Akira Iriye, *Mutual Images: Essays in American-Japanese Relations* (Cambridge: Harvard University Press, 1975), 46.

[6] Vedder, *The Digressions of V.*, 471.

[7] William H. Gerdts, *Painters of the Humble Truth: Masterpieces of American Still Life 1801–1939* (Tulsa, Okla.: Philbrook Art Center, 1981), 148.

J. Alden Weir

[1] William H. Gerdts, *American Impressionism* (Seattle: The Henry Art Gallery, University of Washington, Seattle, 1980), 71–72.

[2] For an in-depth discussion of Weir's still-life painting, see Doreen Bolger Burke, *J. Alden Weir: An American Impressionist* (Newark: University of Delaware Press, 1983), 126–42.

[3] Duncan Phillips, "J. Alden Weir," *Art Bulletin* 2 (June 1920): 199, as quoted in William H. Gerdts, *Painters of the Humble Truth: Masterpieces of American Still Life 1801–1939* (Tulsa, Okla.: Philbrook Art Center, 1981), 221.

INDEX OF ARTISTS

ACKNOWLEDGMENTS

INDEX OF ARTISTS

ACKNOWLEDGMENTS

Many people facilitated the production of this catalogue. Special thanks go to Dick Ackley, Image Resource Center, Penn State, whose expertise and cheerful professionalism greatly eased the task of photographing much of the collection; and to Martha Fleischman, director, Kennedy Galleries, New York, and her staff for graciously responding to numerous inquiries, scholarly and otherwise. The following individuals generously gave of their time by answering a variety of queries: William Sargent, curator of Asian Export Art, Peabody Essex Museum, Salem, Massachusetts; Carole M. Pesner, director, Kraushaar Galleries, New York; Melissa Carr, The New-York Historical Society; Robert D. Schwarz, director, The Schwarz Gallery, Philadelphia; Don Sparacin, director, Owen Gallery, New York; John Driscoll, director, Babcock Galleries, New York; Janis Conner and Joel Rosenkranz, directors, Conner-Rosenkranz LLC, New York; Craig Zabel, head, Department of Art History, Penn State; Sarah Burns, Ruth N. Halls professor, Department of the History of Art, Indiana University, Bloomington; Rachael DeLue, assistant professor of Art History, University of Illinois; Erika Doss, professor of Art History, Fine Arts Department, University of Boulder, Colorado; Corinne Woodcock, director, Demuth Foundation and Charles Demuth Museum, Lancaster, Pennsylvania; Jorge Santis, curator of collections, Museum of Art, Fort Lauderdale; and Nannette V. Maciejunes, senior curator, Columbus Museum of Art, Columbus, Ohio. I would also like to thank several individuals for their assistance with photographic rights and reproductions: Eugenia Alonso, Rights and Reproductions Department, Museo Thyssen-Bornemisza, Madrid, Spain; Brad Nugent, associate director for

Imaging, and Nicole G. Finzer, Photographic Rights assistant, The Art Institute of Chicago; Rebecca Davis, registrar, The Butler Institute of American Art, Youngstown, Ohio; and the staff of the Rights and Reproductions Department, Pennsylvania Academy of the Fine Arts.

Several graduate assistants, particularly Jennifer Noonan, Julia Dolan, and Jan Abbott, contributed enormously to the preliminary research for the catalogue and worked tirelessly to help solve the ongoing, seemingly endless stream of questions that arose. More recently, Sarah Lippert, Vessela Anguelova, Beverlie Hartnett, and Johanna Neuberger helped with last-minute tasks. Special thanks go, too, to Betsy Warner, administrative assistant, and Barbara Weaver, staff assistant, and Amy Marshall, editor, College of Arts and Architecture, for their efficient and thorough editing and proofreading of the text; and to Jan Muhlert, director; Patrick McGrady, Charles V. Hallman curator; and Leo Mazow, curator of American art, for their collegiality and informed opinions on a wide range of topics pertaining to the collection. I am greatly indebted to Julia Dolan, who researched and wrote several entries, and to Dr. Mazow, who brought a truly "panoramic" knowledge of American art and culture to his compelling introductory essay. Finally, my sincere thanks to Jean and Alvin Snowiss, whose love and knowledge of American art have been exemplary. Work on this catalogue has been greatly sustained by their friendship and generosity.

JOYCE HENRI ROBINSON, *Curator*

PHOTO CREDITS

References are to page numbers.

Richard Ackley, Image Resource Center, The Pennsylvania State University
16, 20, 24, 28, 30A, 32A, 38A, 40, 42, 43, 44A, 48, 50, 52, 58, 62,
64, 68, 70, 74, 82, 84, 86, 88, 102, 104, 108, 110, 112, 116

©2002, The Art Institute of Chicago. All Rights Reserved. 32B

The Butler Institute of American Art, Youngstown, Ohio 27

Kennedy Galleries, Inc., New York
10, 12, 14, 18, 22A, 26, 30B, 34, 36, 46, 54, 56, 60, 66,
72, 75, 76, 78, 80, 90, 92, 94, 96, 98, 106, 114

©Museo Thyssen-Bornemisza, Madrid 22B

Palmer Museum of Art, University Park 59

Pennsylvania Academy of the Fine Arts, Philadelphia 44B

The Schwarz Gallery, Philadelphia 100

Overleaf:

DAVID JOHNSON
Rogers Slide,
Lake George, New York,
1870, oil on canvas,
13 1/2 x 21 3/8 inches

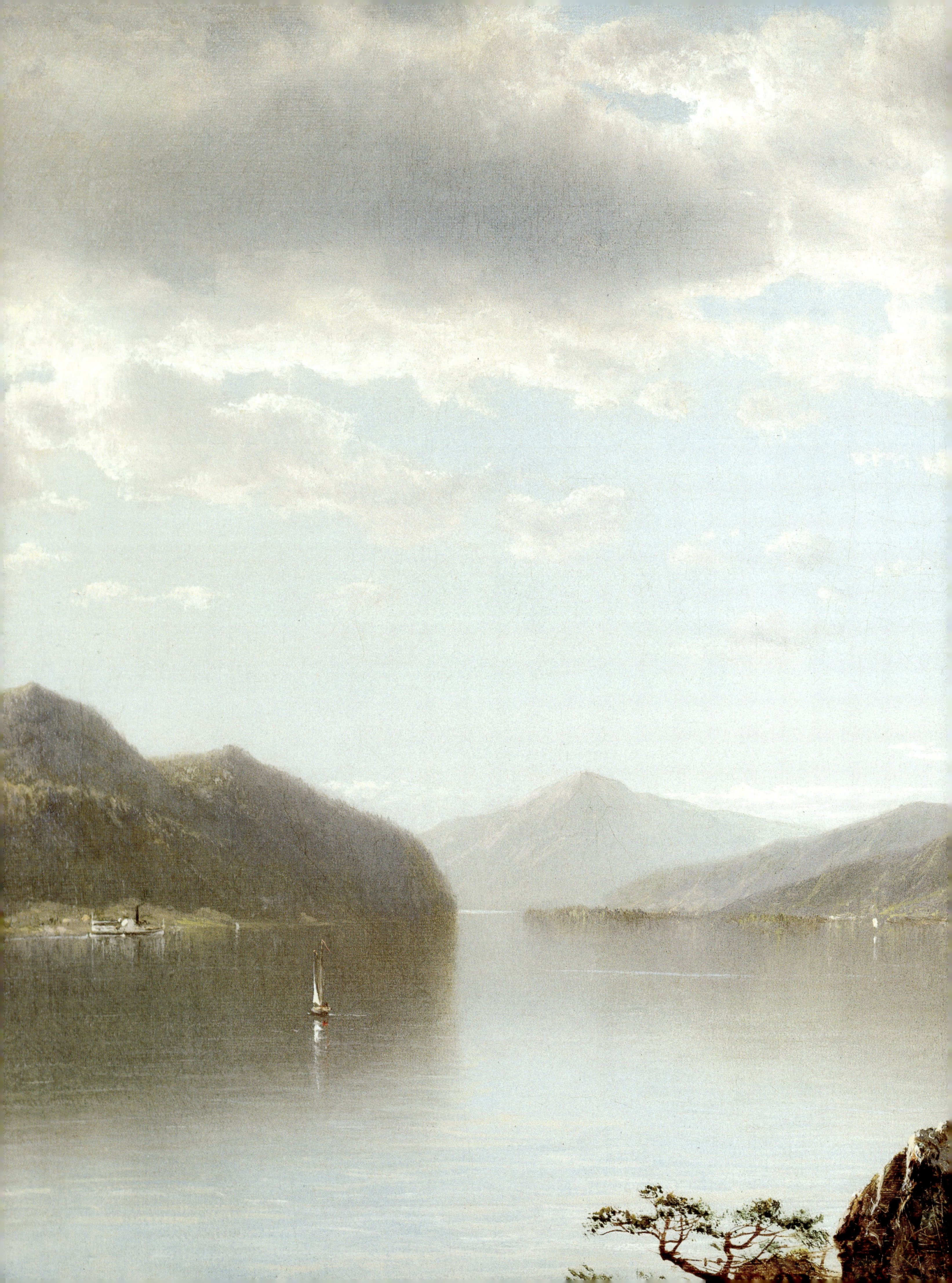

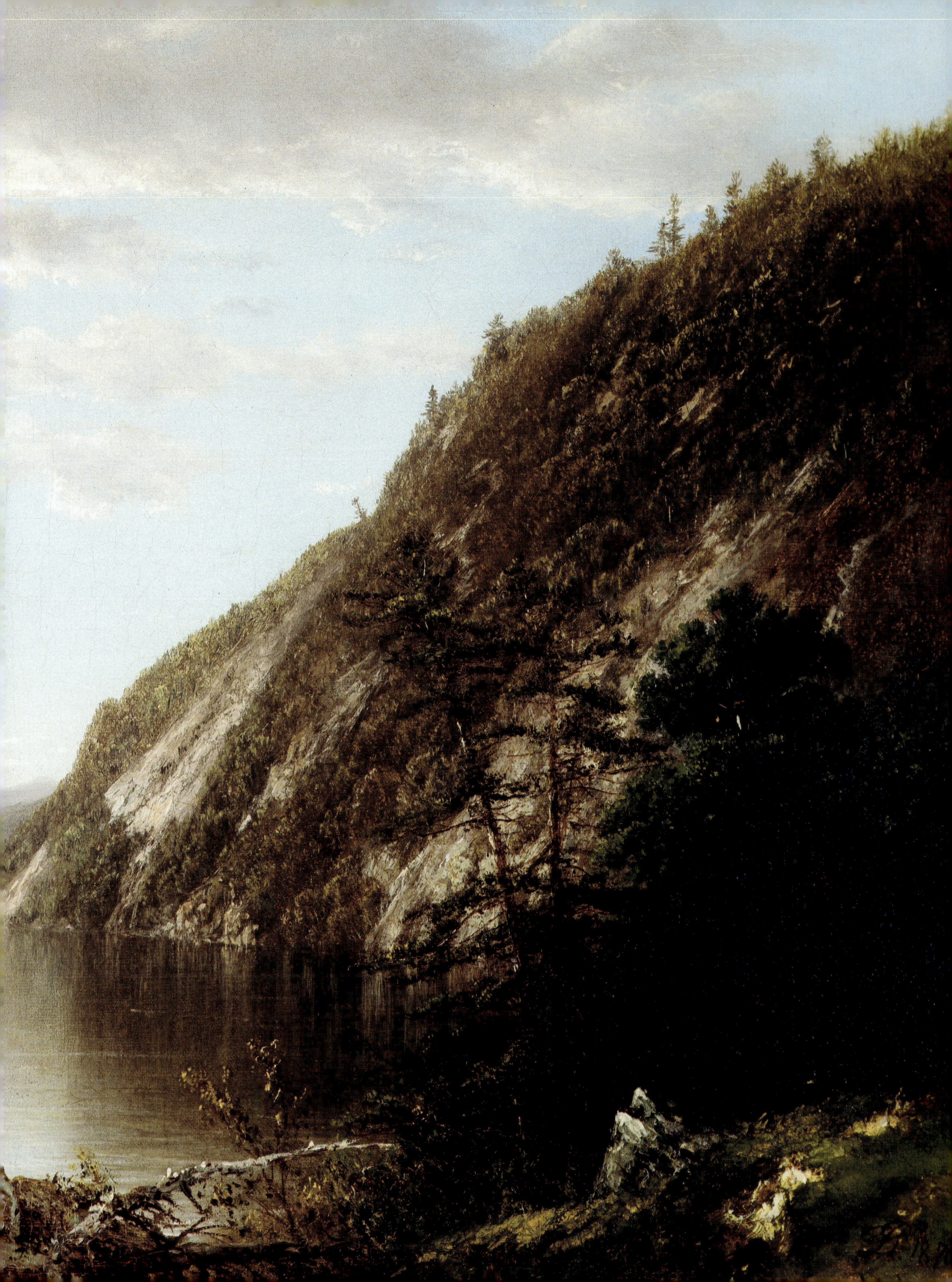

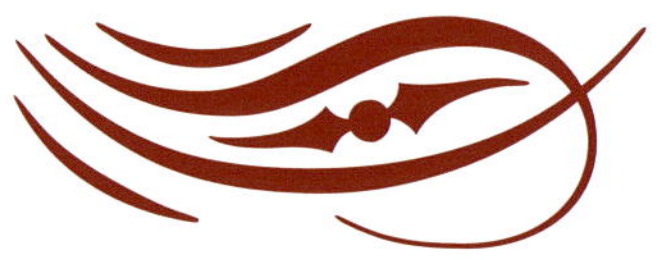